Climate Change: Climate Collapse

Science Exploration by Rolf A. F. Witzsche

Climate Change: Climate Collapse

The Red Square Nebula

This book contains the transcript with images of the exploration video with the above title:
see: http://www.ice-age-ahead-iaa.ca/

Lead in:

The exploration addresses seven basic critical facts in truthful climate science

Fact 1   The Earth is in a terminal phase of global cooling.
Fact 2   Global Warming did happen, was caused by the Sun, and has ended in the 1990s.
Fact 3   The Manmade Global Warming doctrine was impelled by political reasons.
Fact 4   The science of the Sun and solar dynamics was intentionally perverted.
Fact 5   Atmospheric CO2 is at a 600-million-years low. The biosphere is starving.
Fact 6   Manmade carbon gases are no bigger than a mouse, vs the World Trade towers.
Fact 7   The political driver is a long train of latent philosophical errors, amplified in 1790.

These facts reflect the result of numerous types of scientific physical measurements - not just one or two, but many types of measurements - that all tell us the same story, which is essentially one single story, a story of measured facts.

Some of the measurements were conducted in space, some on the ground, some in the atmosphere, and some were also obtained with numerous types of visual observations. The book addresses seven of these measured, mostly self-evident, but often obscured, facts.

Because the subject of Climate Change has four major facets, each of a different type, I have divided the exploration book into an introduction and four segments, and presented each one as a differently focused exploration.

Introduction and 4 segments

Segment 1 - Swamp of Latent Errors
Segment 2 - Global Cooling is Real
Segment 3 - Carbon, Climate, and the Sun
Segment 4 - To Create a New World

This book, like the original video series, is presented in honor and support of President Trump's considering, or launching, a Presidential Committee on Climate Science.

Table of Contents

Introduction: Re-open the closed box of Climate Science

Donald Trump

45th President of the United States of America

inaugurated, January 20, 2017

The President's intention to re-open the closed box of Climate Science, has unleashed a firestorm of protests in politics before the project was even announced.

The President is challenging the so-called Science of Manmade Global Warming, and is referring to it as 'fake.'

"How dare he!" - the politicians cry - "This science is settled!"

Seven basic critical facts

Seven basic critical facts in truthful climate science

Fact 1	The Earth is in a terminal phase of global cooling.
Fact 2	Global Warming did happen, was caused by the Sun, and has ended in the 1990s.
Fact 3	The Manmade Global Warming doctrine was impelled by political reasons.
Fact 4	The science of the Sun and solar dynamics was intentionally perverted.
Fact 5	Atmospheric CO2 is at a 600-million-years low. The biosphere is starving.
Fact 6	Manmade carbon gases are no bigger than a mouse, vs the World Trade towers.
Fact 7	The political driver is a long train of latent philosophical errors, amplified in 1790.

Seven basic critical facts in truthful climate science

Fact 1 The Earth is in a terminal phase of global cooling.

Fact 2 Global Warming did happen, was caused by the Sun, and has ended in the 1990s.

Fact 3 The Manmade Global Warming doctrine was impelled by political reasons.

Fact 4 The science of the Sun and solar dynamics was intentionally perverted.

Fact 5 Atmospheric CO2 is at a 600-million-years low. The biosphere is starving.

Fact 6 Manmade carbon gases are no bigger than a mouse, vs the World Trade towers.

Fact 7 The political driver is a long train of latent philosophical errors, amplified in 1790.

I am presenting in this video seven basic facts that are often hidden for political objectives, but are critical for everyone's living on the Earth. These facts reflect the result of numerous types of scientific physical measurements - not just one or two, but many types of measurements - that all tell us the same story, which is essentially one single story, a story of measured facts.

Some of the measurements were conducted in space, some on the ground, some in the atmosphere, and some were also obtained with numerous types of visual observations. The book addresses seven of these measured, mostly self-evident, but often obscured, facts.

Fact 1 - The Earth is in a terminal phase of global cooling that is increasing and has already begun to affect agriculture, which is the main source of our food supply. My concern is that if we don't respond to the known facts of the ongoing global cooling, entire nations will likely vanish in 5-15 years as the result of agricultural collapse that can still be avoided, caused by the climate collapse. The fact is, we are nearing the end of agriculture as we have come to know it.

Fact 2 - Global Warming! It did happen. We have enjoyed it for nearly 300 years, but it was not manmade. It was caused by the up-ramping of the Sun. However, the warming is now history. It ended in the 1990s. It will be fully reversed by the 2030s or 2040s. What we still enjoy of it, is presently collapsing 5-times faster than it had originally developed.

Fact 3 - The doctrine of Manmade Global Warming was not impelled by climate considerations, but by political objectives. The timing and the circumstances prove this rather well.

Fact 4 - The science of the Sun and solar dynamics has been intentionally perverted to effectively inhibit human development.

Fact 5 - Atmospheric CO_2 is not a danger, but is presently at a more than 600-million-years low. The biosphere is CO_2 starved. A massive CO_2 increase is required to prevent a potential crisis.

Fact 6 - All the manmade carbon gases in the world, added together, are no bigger as a greenhouse factor than a mouse in comparison with the historic World Trade towers of New York. Nor is the greenhouse effect increasing. It is dangerously collapsing under soar cosmic-ray effects.

Fact 7 - The political driver for the Manmade Global Warming doctrine is a long train of philosophical errors that became amplified in the 1790s when the U.S. Constitution was erected, and became escalated ever since.

Climate Change has four major facets

Segment 1 - Swamp of Latent Errors

Segment 2 - Global Cooling is Real

Segment 3 - Carbon, Climate, and the Sun

Segment 4 - To Create a New World

Segment 1 - Swamp of Latent Errors

Segment 2 - Global Cooling is Real

Segment 3 - Carbon, Climate, and the Sun

Segment 4 - To Create a New World

Because the subject of Climate Change has four major facets, each of a different type, I have divided the exploration book into four segments, and presented each one as a separate segment.

The great swamp of historic errors

Segment 1 - Swamp of Latent Errors
Segment 2 - Global Cooling is Real
Segment 3 - Carbon, Climate, and the Sun
Segment 4 - To Create a New World

The first segment deals with the great swamp of historic errors, which became overlaid with layers upon layers of modern errors, which altogether have shaped civilization and the policies of nations. The exploration of the swamp is important, because the Manmade Global Warming doctrine is a 'son' of that swamp, as is the system of empire that champions the swamp. Both are features of it from the beginning. Both are glaring errors in civilization that society has allowed to come upon it and still bows to. Evidently, the swamp is large.

Segment 1 - Swamp of Latent Errors

Segment 1 - Swamp of Latent Errors

Part 1	Is the current Climate Science "fake?"
Part 2	We have to offer up scary scenarios
Part 3	The Earth has Cancer, and this Cancer is man
Part 4	The Ortes / Aristotle / Malthus / Eugenics Axis of Errors
Part 5	'Son' of the Swamp
Part 6	Manmade Climate Change has no leg to stand on
Part 7	1974 - The Swamp is Going Global
Part 8	"In Lies We Trust!" The truth be damned
Part 9	A scientist without a background in physical science
Part 10	Opposition Movements in the Science Community
Part 11	Is the Earth getting colder everywhere?
Part 12	Climate Change IS happening, but is NOT manmade
Part 13	The breakout to REAL climate science is possible.

Segment 1 - Swamp of Latent Errors

Part 1 Is the current Climate Science "fake?"

Part 2 We have to offer up scary scenarios

Part 3 The Earth has Cancer, and this Cancer is man

Part 4 The Ortes / Aristotle / Malthus / Eugenics Axis of Errors

Part 5 'Son' of the Swamp

Part 6 Manmade Climate Change has no leg to stand on

Part 7 1974 - The Swamp is Going Global

Part 8 "In Lies We Trust!" The truth be damned

Part 9 A scientist without a background in physical science

Part 10 Opposition Movements in the Science Community

Part 11 Is the Earth getting colder everywhere?

Part 12 Climate Change IS happening, but is NOT manmade

Part 13 The breakout to REAL climate science is possible.

The vast scene of latent errors, and intentional errors, from which the doctrine of Manmade Climate Change is drawn, is being focused on in Segment 1.

A small feature of this segment is the wide scene of the Science Opposition movements that have opposed the Manmade Global Warming doctrine, and still do. The scene comprises upwards to 50,000 individual scientist, where the real science consensus is located on this issue.

Ironically, the vast opposition movement is itself stuck, in it own swamp of errors, as it remains blinded against the principles that actually do cause Climate Change. While some opposition groups come closer to the mark than others, they all fail on the critical core issue of what actually stands behind the climate dynamics.

A few scientists go as far as to acknowledge that the Earth is getting noticeably colder, which is actually hard to avoid as the process is already far advanced. They even counter the media's crying about global overheating, with proven reports of evermore cold and evermore snow, but they still fail to discern the underlying cause. This failure is tragic, as they thereby fail to recognize the necessary responses by society, to the climate cooling.

In this scene healing is needed. Being stuck in a swamp of errors is not the legitimate status of man. Freedom with the truth, alone, is legitimate.

Segment 2 - Global Cooling is Real

Segment 1 - Swamp of Latent Errors

Segment 2 - Global Cooling is Real

Segment 3 - Carbon, Climate, and the Sun

Segment 4 - To Create a New World

Segment 1 - Swamp of Latent Errors

Segment 2 - Global Cooling is Real

Segment 3 - Carbon, Climate, and the Sun

Segment 4 - To Create a New World

Segment 2 has a totally different focus. It deals with what is real; with what is really happening. It deals with the cooling of the Earth and its effect on agriculture.

Segment 2 - Global Cooling is Real

Segment 2 - Global Cooling is Real

Part 1	How do we know that global cooling is real?
Part 2	Agriculture in Danger of Collapsing
Part 3	Is the climate on Earth forced by the Sun?
Part 4	Solar Collapse, Measured by the Ulysses Spacecraft
Part 5	Proof of Solar Cosmic-Ray Flux
Part 6	Measurements that quantify solar activity collapse
Part 7	Climate Recovery NOT Possible anymore
Part 8	Building a Climate-Independent New World

Segment 2 - Global Cooling is Real

Part 1 How do we know that global cooling is real?

Part 2 Agriculture in Danger of Collapsing

Part 3 Is the climate on Earth forced by the Sun?

Part 4 Solar Collapse, Measured by the Ulysses Spacecraft

Part 5 Proof of Solar Cosmic-Ray Flux

Part 6 Measurements that quantify solar activity collapse

Part 7 Climate Recovery NOT Possible anymore

Part 8 Building a Climate-Independent New World

Segment 2 deals with aspects that no one wants to hear about, namely that the climate on Earth is forced by the Sun, by way of solar cosmic-ray interaction with the Earth's atmosphere that increases cloudiness, which in turn cools the Earth. Society is taught that all cosmic rays are galactic and do not change, so that all change on Earth is manmade.

The reality lies in the opposite. Our climate is affected almost exclusively by solar cosmic-ray flux. Solar activity cycles are expressed as climate cycles, by way of changing solar cosmic ray flux. I should add that the historically observed climate cycles are fast fading with the weakening solar dynamics. This means that our cooling climate is on a collapsing path from which a recovery is not possible anymore.

Segment 3 - Carbon, Climate, and the Sun

Segment 1 - Swamp of Latent Errors

Segment 2 - Global Cooling is Real

Segment 3 - Carbon, Climate, and the Sun

Segment 4 - To Create a New World

Segment 1 - Swamp of Latent Errors

Segment 2 - Global Cooling is Real

Segment 3 - Carbon, Climate, and the Sun

Segment 4 - To Create a New World

Segment 3 has a different focus again. It is focused to resolve a paradox. People are scared of manmade carbon gases that are said to be overheating the earth, but which isn't happening, or ever can happen, while they are taught to close their eyes to the real danger that threatens their very existence, which they deny.

Segment 3 counters tenacious false concepts

Segment 3 - Carbon, Climate, and the Sun

Part 1	The Towers and the Mouse (the real CO2 story)
Part 2	Who Speaks for the Biosphere?
Part 3	Ice Ages are Radical Events - like falling off a cliff
Part 4	Who Speaks for the Sun?
Part 5	Ice Ages are Digital Events
Part 6	Proof of the Hibernating Sun

Segment 3 - Carbon, Climate, and the Sun

Part 1 The Towers and the Mouse (the real CO2 story)

Part 2 Who Speaks for the Biosphere?

Part 3 Ice Ages are Radical Events - like falling off a cliff

Part 4 Who Speaks for the Sun?

Part 5 Ice Ages are Digital Events

Part 6 Proof of the Hibernating Sun

This denial of reality is prevalent in numerous different ways. Society denies the carbon reality that is not only climate harmless, but is life-giving. Society also denies the climate dynamics that science has measured and has observed collapsing. It even denies the Sun by defending the doctrine of a model that is physically impossible, which its historic timing suggests, was created intentionally to be false with the obvious consequences.

Segment 3 counters these types of tenacious false concepts, including that of the Sun, and presents what is actually real.

The symbol for this video series

The Red Square Nebula

Here, in Segment 3, is where the symbol for this video series is located. The symbol is the Red Square Nebula. In the nebula, all the complex principles are visible in the large, which presently enable our Sun to operate in its high-powered interglacial mode, and to operate as a variable star with effects that cause large climate changes on Earth.

The explicit features of the nebula have all been experimentally replicated and explored in laboratory settings, and have thereby been proven in principle. Thus the nebula illustrates in principle the dynamics that power our Sun.

Segment 4 - To Create a New World

Segment 1 - Swamp of Latent Errors

Segment 2 - Global Cooling is Real

Segment 3 - Carbon, Climate, and the Sun

Segment 4 - To Create a New World

Segment 1 - Swamp of Latent Errors

Segment 2 - Global Cooling is Real

Segment 3 - Carbon, Climate, and the Sun

Segment 4 - To Create a New World

Segment 4 has again a different focus. It explores the principles required for humanity to have a future. Climate Change means Climate Collapse. This means Agriculture ends as we know it, globally. The whole world is affected. But we have the power to create us a New World with a new platform for agriculture that is largely climate independent.

A technological New World

Segment 4 - To Create a New World

Segment 4 - To Create a New World

Part 1 Challenged to Create a New World

Part 2 Who Speaks for Draining the Swamp?

Part 3 Real History that we Cannot Step Away From

Part 4 World Development Project with Forgiveness

Part 5 Climate is Not a Factor in the unfolding history of love

Part 6 Who Speaks for Humanity?

Part 7 Speaking the Truth is Liberating

Segment 4 explores on what basis humanity is able to shed its divisions and social and national isolation, and join hands to build itself a technological New World for the realization of a common future.

This is a critical subject in the current age as the End of Agriculture is fast approaching.

We face a complex paradox here. The climate is collapsing, the universe warns us, mainstream science denies it, and society that is deeply affected is fast asleep.

Shakespeare understood this type of paradox and gave it a face in his play, Hamlet. He asks in the context of the play, Who speaks for humanity? In his play no one does. In the play, society, the tragic fool, perishes.

Building of a New World, unaffected by climate

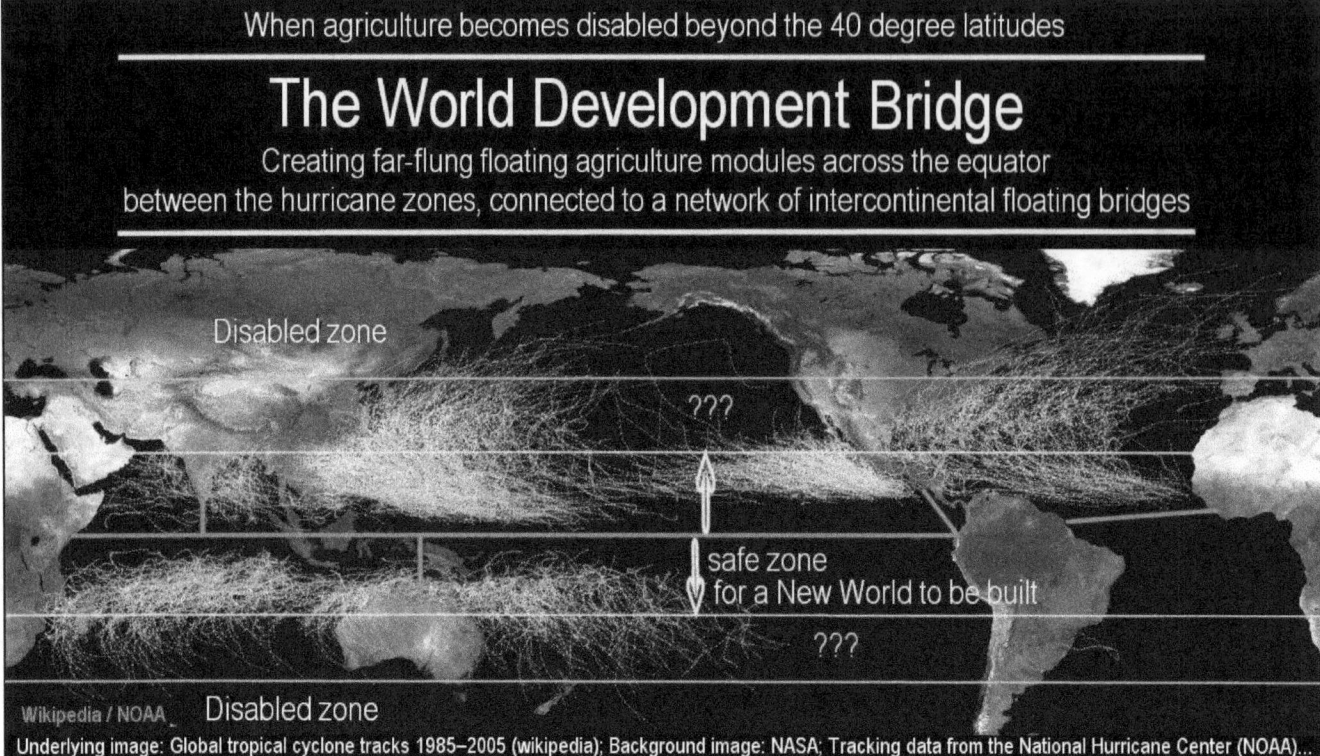

On today's stage the question needs to be, Who speaks for the building of a New World, unaffected by climate, in which agriculture may continue artificially, unhindered by the natural end of agriculture in the world at large? In other words, Who speaks for humanity?

Physically, the task to create a New World that the climate collapse cannot affect, appears overwhelmingly large. Physically it is so large that no individual, tribe, or nation can build the project alone. And that's where the problem begins. The core of the problem is that society has become conditioned not to see itself as one single humanity, but to see itself as divided, isolated, and poised against one another on a wide front, politically, socially, and also in the domain of science.

In the face of the global climate collapse that no one is exempted from, it becomes critical for society to break out of its numerous traps in order to assure its future existence on this planet.

While it is possible for society to achieve the necessary breakout from its traps, with the Principle of Universal Love to embrace our common humanity, the track record of society on this critical front where we must succeed without fail, is utterly dismal.

Our track record is in the arena of nuclear war

Annihilation is assured

500,000 times Hiroshima in one hour

Castle Bravo - the first U.S. test of a dry fuel thermonuclear hydrogen bomb - March 1, 1954 at Bikini Atoll, Marshall Islands

Just look at how dismal our track record is in the arena of nuclear war, all by itself. Humanity has built itself tens of thousands of nuclear bombs to threaten and exterminate one another with. This takes us as far away as one can get from being in love with our common humanity that we all share. If this contempt of humanity isn't the most dismal failure in civilization, what is? The failure doesn't render a nation great which wields these weapons of contempt, but renders it stupid.

The size of a nation's nuclear arsenal is far from being a measure of greatness. It is a measure of its utter stupidity. Humanity is presently in a race with each other to determine which nation is the most stupid in the world. But this isn't the worst of it, because the Manmade Global Warming doctrine falls into the same category of stupidity, except its effect is worse.

While it is physically possible to destroy all nuclear weapons in a week, with which humanity would free itself of its terror, the solar global Climate Collapse that the Manmade Global Warming doctrine hides, cannot be so easily overcome. This is the context in which the doctrine needs to be seen. It needs to be set aside, and the real climate issue, the Climate Collapse be addressed, which by its nature would reflect itself also onto the lesser issue of nuclear war and obsolete it.

The global climate is collapsing without a recovery

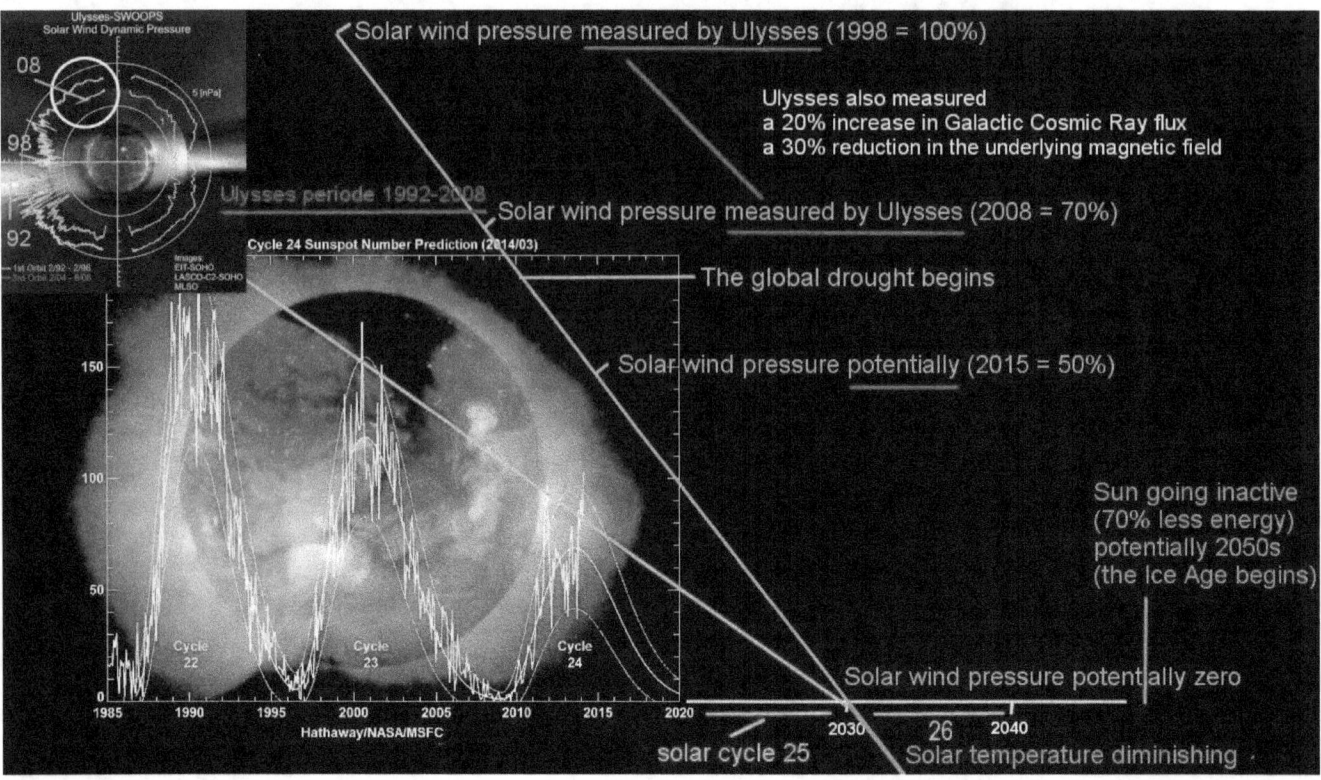

The global climate is collapsing without a recovery in sight. The astrophysical processes are in motion relentlessly, and are diminishing. We are in the boundary zone towards the astrophysical phase shift towards the next Ice Age in potentially the 2050s. This changes the global dynamics, socially, politically, and economically. It is futile to run against this 'movement.'

Numerous measurements point in the direction of the Ice Age phase shift occurring in the 2050s, which the Manmade Global Warming doctrine blocks the recognition of, and with it, blocks the building of the technological New World that we need for us to have a future. This means that the Manmade Global Warming doctrine must not be addressed as an academic issue, but be addressed in the larger context of the boundary zone to the next Ice Age that we are already in. Nor should the "Climate Change" issue, as the doctrine is now called, be swept aside as being "just weather," which hides the issue even more. It wasn't just "weather" that collapsed the Australian wheat production in 2018, by 40%. It was a systemic effect that caused this large loss.

Climate extremes and food production losses

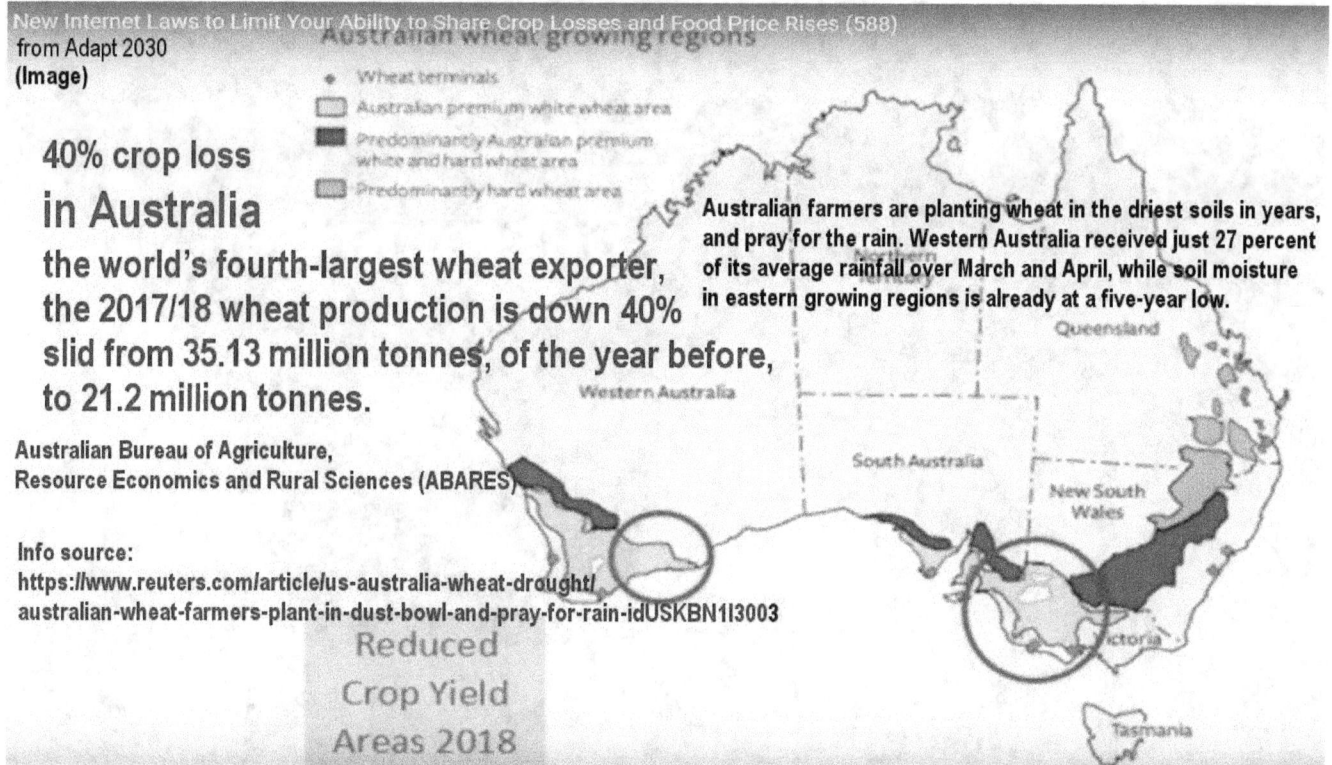

Australian wheat harvest down by 40% in the 2017/18 crop season.

While the Climate Collapse is real and is evident in numerous physical measurements and is experienced worldwide in ever-greater climate extremes and in food production losses, society is far from recognizing the already unfolding climate collapse to be actually real. People joke about it, or brush it off as just weather patterns. Nobody dreams that the climate collapse that is still only faintly evident, is a part of a larger long-term process towards the Ice Age phase shift that would terminate humanity's very existence if a New World was not created that assures the continuity of its agriculture that the world food supply depends on.

The greater challenge smallness in thinking

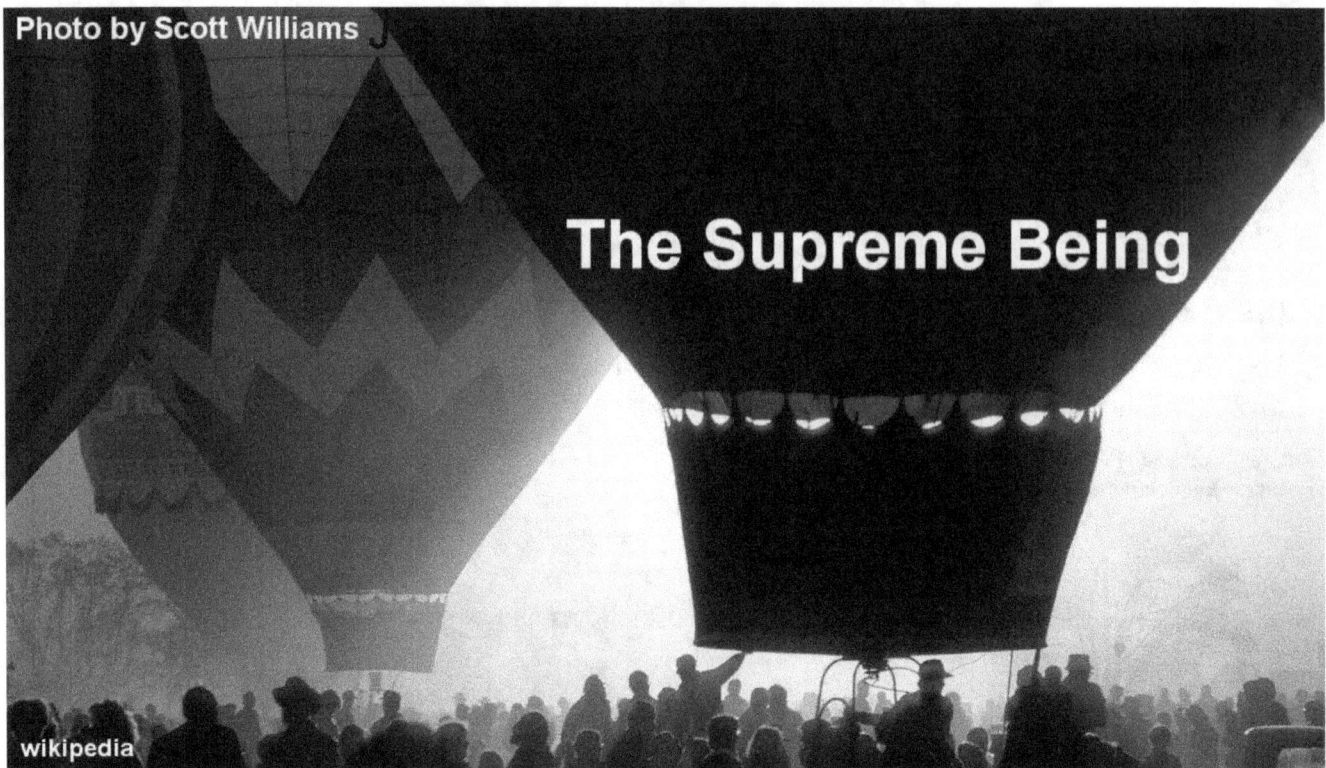

Photo by Scott Williams

The Supreme Being

wikipedia

This means that the greatest challenge for us to overcome, is not the physical challenge of the Climate Collapse itself. We can respond to the physical challenge, and will come out richer when we do. The greater challenge, which is much harder to overcome, is society's universal smallness in thinking.

Its smallness in thinking is a feature of society that resulted from it being tied to the vast swamp of latent errors that keep it tied to the ground. The swamp imposes on society its staunch denial of itself and of its power to fly above it. Fettered to a swamp of climate errors, society finds itself clinging tenaciously to crippling doctrines that it hails and defends on faith, such as the carbon-warming doctrine, and the impossible Sun-model doctrine, which are both intentionally false, instead of it unleashing its ability to flying above the swamp and gain higher-level views of reality.

So, how does one deal with that?

Four-part exploration production

How does one purge errors from the landscape?
How does one become free of imposed ignorance?
How does one overcome false assumptions?
How does one break away from intentional falsities?

How does one purge errors from the landscape?

How does one become free of imposed ignorance?

How does one overcome false assumptions?

How does one break away from intentional falsities?

Hopefully the following four-part exploration production will inspire some answers. The production is designed as a high-level overview of the four major focal points.

My videos on Climate Change

My numerous related exploration videos that I have created on the wide subject of Climate Change, furnish a resource for filling in the fine details. These videos are primarily focused on physical issues, scientific issues, and technological issues.

The human relationship issues

The human relationship issues, in turn, require deeper explorations, such as to gain freedom from division, isolation, domination, and so on, ranging from the social to the international level. The point is that for as long as humanity remains divided, isolated, and choked with domination, the physical, scientific, and technological solutions that would assure humanity a future, will remain unrealized. Nothing will be built to meet the needs of the future, near or far, for as long as humanity remains 'small' and divided.

An inner renaissance

The challenge to break out from this 'inner' trap with an inner renaissance, is the high-level focus of my 14 novels, of which 12 carry a single epic story focused on developing lateral relationships at the grass-roots level on the elusive platform of the Principle of Universal Love.

The Principle of Universal Love in 1648

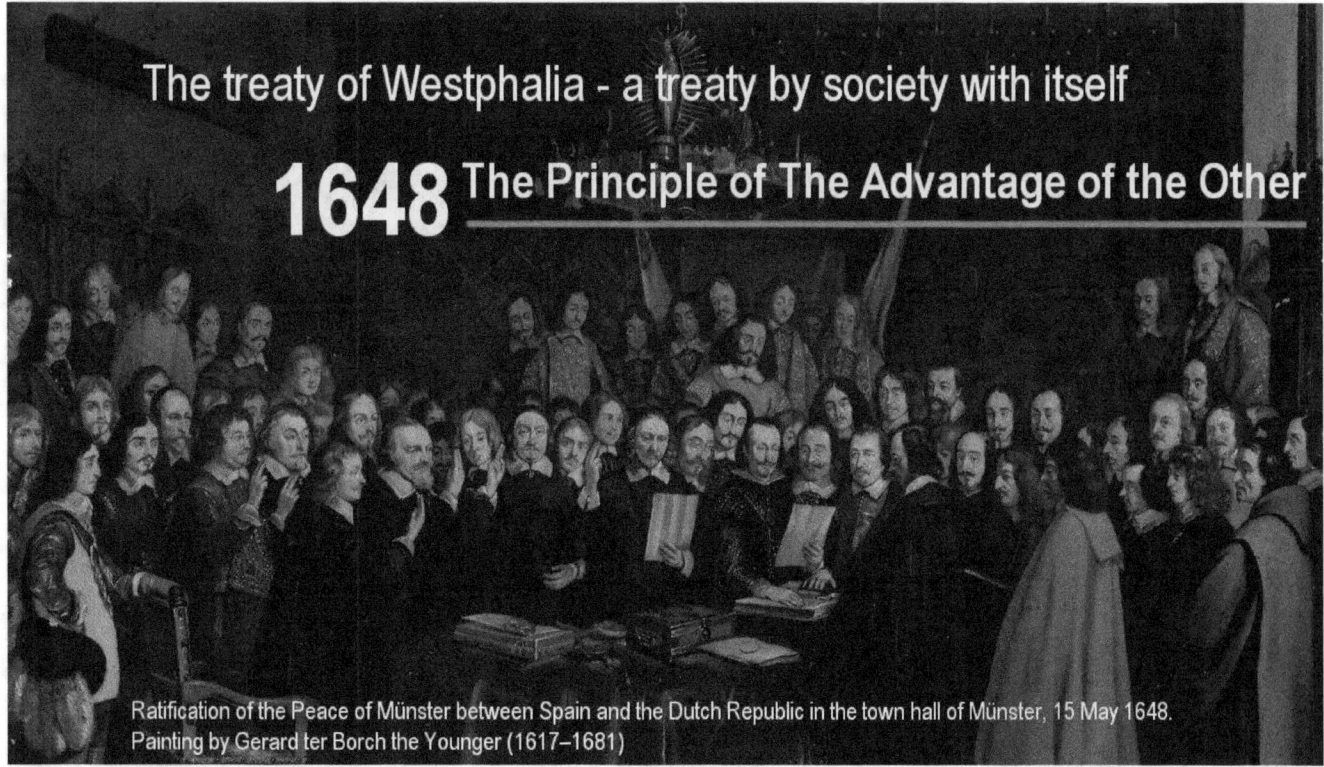

The treaty of Westphalia - a treaty by society with itself

1648 The Principle of The Advantage of the Other

Ratification of the Peace of Münster between Spain and the Dutch Republic in the town hall of Münster, 15 May 1648.
Painting by Gerard ter Borch the Younger (1617–1681)

The Principle of Universal Love was the principle that was once faintly applied politically back in 1648 with the Peace of Westphalia, the greatest peace treaty by society with itself, that had ended 100 years of clashes, war, and destruction, and had enabled Europe to live again.

A New World may yet be built

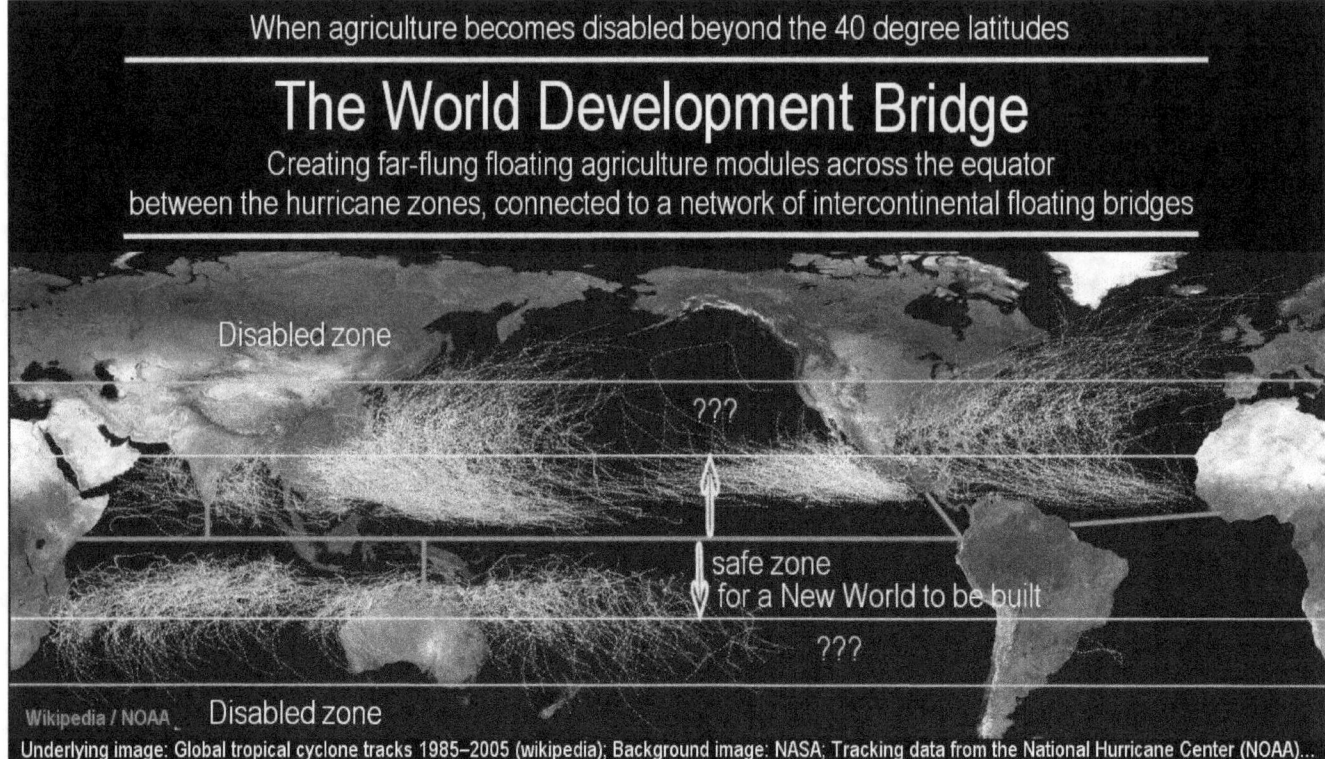

When agriculture becomes disabled beyond the 40 degree latitudes

The World Development Bridge

Creating far-flung floating agriculture modules across the equator
between the hurricane zones, connected to a network of intercontinental floating bridges

Disabled zone

???

safe zone
for a New World to be built

???

Wikipedia / NOAA   Disabled zone

Underlying image: Global tropical cyclone tracks 1985–2005 (wikipedia); Background image: NASA; Tracking data from the National Hurricane Center (NOAA)...

On this path, a New World may yet be built, and be build in our time, with all people of the world participating in the building of it for the fulfillment of the common aims of mankind to have a bright and livable future in which to grow and develop for evermore. For this to happen, the Principle of Universal Love may need to be projected deeper and uplift society from the grassroots level upwards which would enable it to reclaim its politics from the swamp.

Then war, even nuclear war, become obsolete on the higher-level platform as a matter of principle. That this is not likely possible on any lesser basis is evident by the fact that war and nuclear terror are still being promoted. Millions of prayers have likely reached high heaven, with hope for an end of the nuclear terror game, but with no end in sight after 70 years. The answer for this hoped for liberation lies evidently in the climate collapse for which society needs to dig deeper into its humanity, for which a New World needs to be built that becomes a challenge on the deeper level where a phase shift in humanity must happen that rouses it to uplift itself to match the scope of the climate challenge that cannot be evaded, but must be won. War falls by the wayside on this deeper path where the artificial isolation of humanity falls away.

This is not pie in the sky stuff

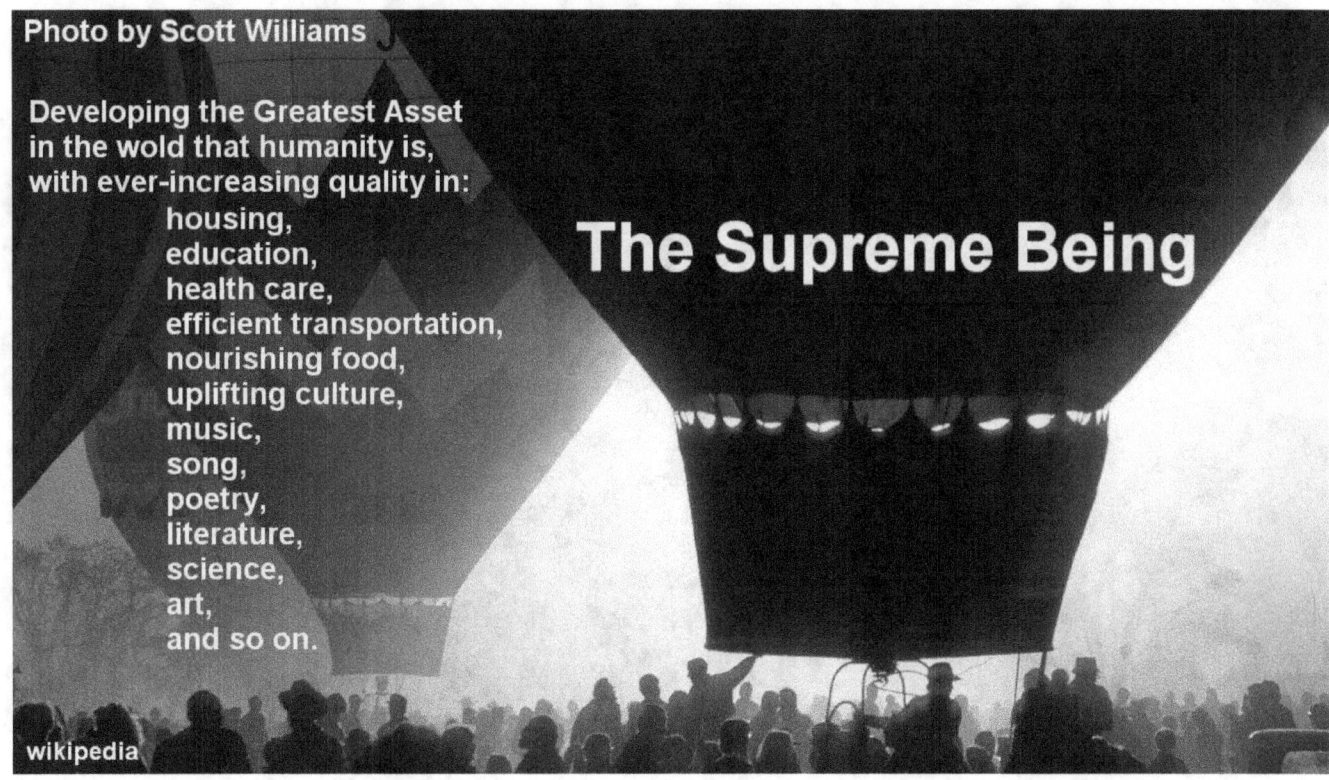

This is not pie in the sky stuff, as it might appear at first glance. Instead it is the natural next step in the progression of human civilization, which in the case at hand is prompted by the climate-collapse event.

It is, as if the universe is saying to us all, you better get out of your easy chair, fly high, and gear up for a renaissance wealth-festival that you need, in order to have a future, and which you are capable of.

When he put the space program onto the national plate

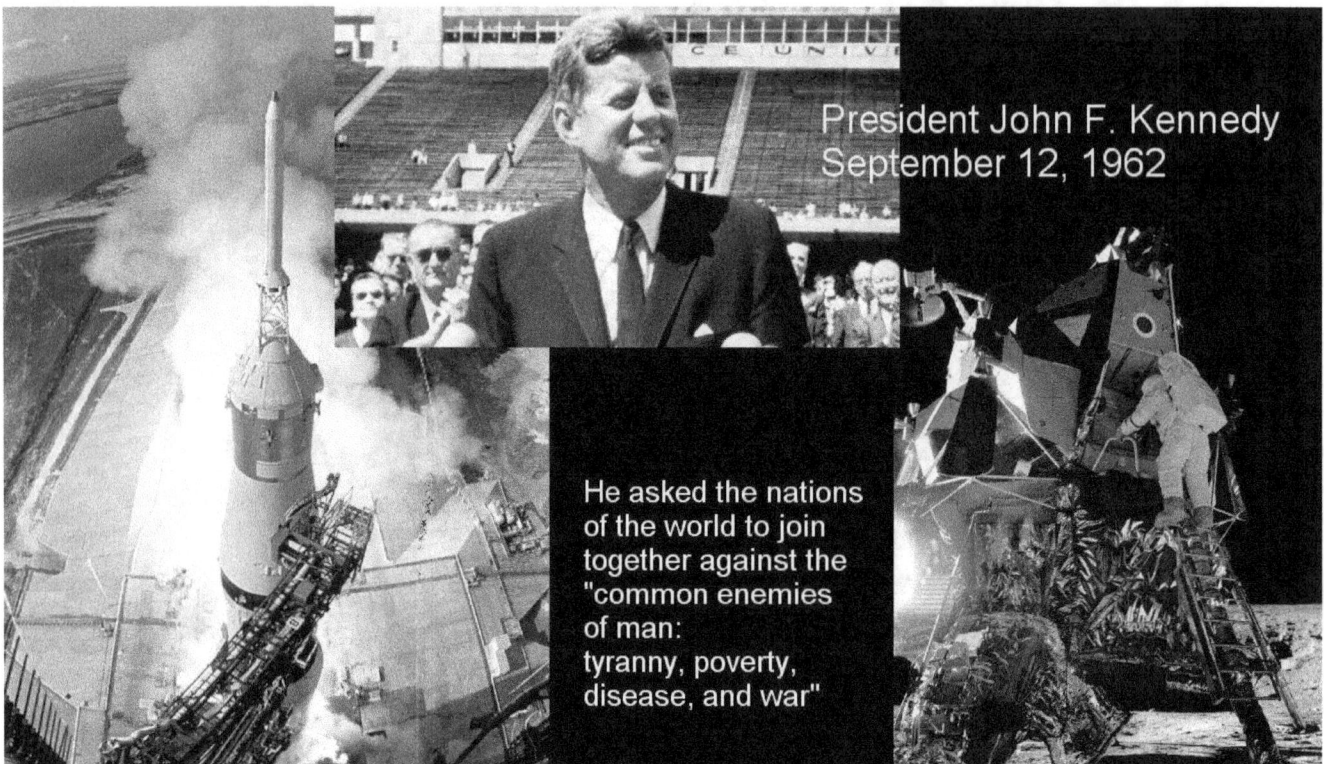

President John F. Kennedy
September 12, 1962

He asked the nations of the world to join together against the "common enemies of man: tyranny, poverty, disease, and war"

That's what President Kennedy had said in essence when he put the space program onto the national plate. He called on America to step out of its self-encumbering smallness and take hold of its inner potential that had laid largely dormant and underdeveloped for far too long.

To break out of its small-minded shell

It evidently wasn't the case that we desperately needed to stand on the moon as a physical necessity for survival. The great need was, for society to break out of its small-minded shell and become more fully human.

America needed a Creative-Wealth Festival

America needed a Creative-Wealth Festival

America needed a Creative-Wealth Festival

America needed a Wealth Festival that typically flows from the type of process with which great projects are accomplished. America became richer by it as a nation, even economically.

Fourteen-times in scientific and technological side benefits

NASA
wikipedia

For every dollar America spent on the path to open itself a window to space, it created itself fourteen-times the amount spent, in scientific and technological side benefits, and this in addition to the spiritual benefits of experiencing what a human being is capable of in stepping beyond assumed limits.

The World-Bridge infrastructure project

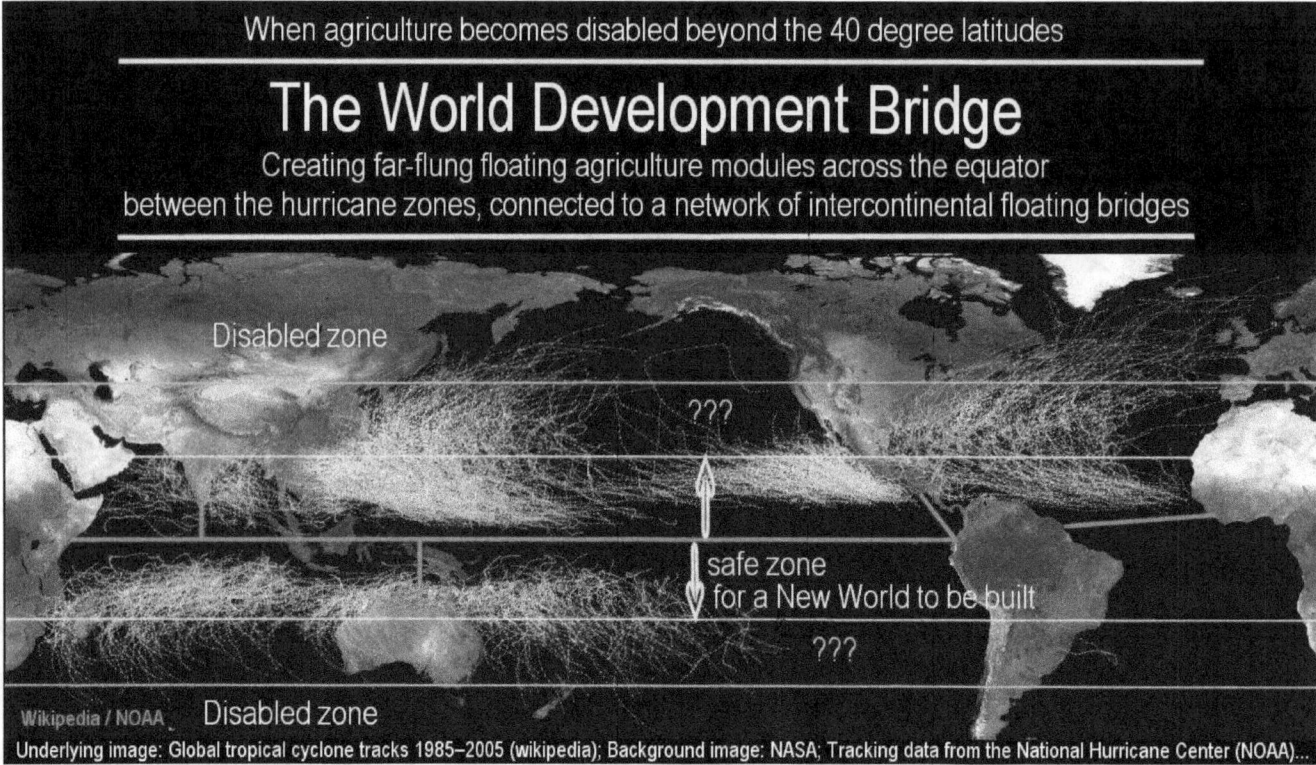

The World-Bridge infrastructure project, with which we create us a New World to match the Ice Age Challenge, should be seen in the same light. It should NOT be seen as a chore that is necessary for our common survival in the changing climate that is imposed on us. Instead it should be seen as a natural step forward in the development of civilization that must never stall or go stale. Nor should it be seen as merely another Apollo-type project that had uplifted America in its time.

It should be seen as a World Development Project

It should be seen as a World Development Project

a Creative Development Project that furnishes 100-fold gains

It should be seen as a World Development Project

a Creative Development Project that furnishes 100-fold gains

It should be seen as a World Project - a world-development project that portents to unleash a World Wealth Festival with the power to furnish us a 100-fold gain in benefits for society's investment in efforts to develop its potential.

Universal high-quality free housing

Just imagine living on a radically higher-level platform than we presently have. Imagine a world rich with universal high-quality free housing. It would end homelessness, poverty, slum living, rent slavery, and would replace these with expanded living conditions that are more productive for the inner development of the human potential, which is presently largely wasted in sub-human environments. Universal free housing, as an investment by society into itself, would all by itself spark a Wealth Festival revolution. In fact, the New World cannot be built on any lesser platform, like the monetarist platform that we presently have.

To produce 2 billion new homes

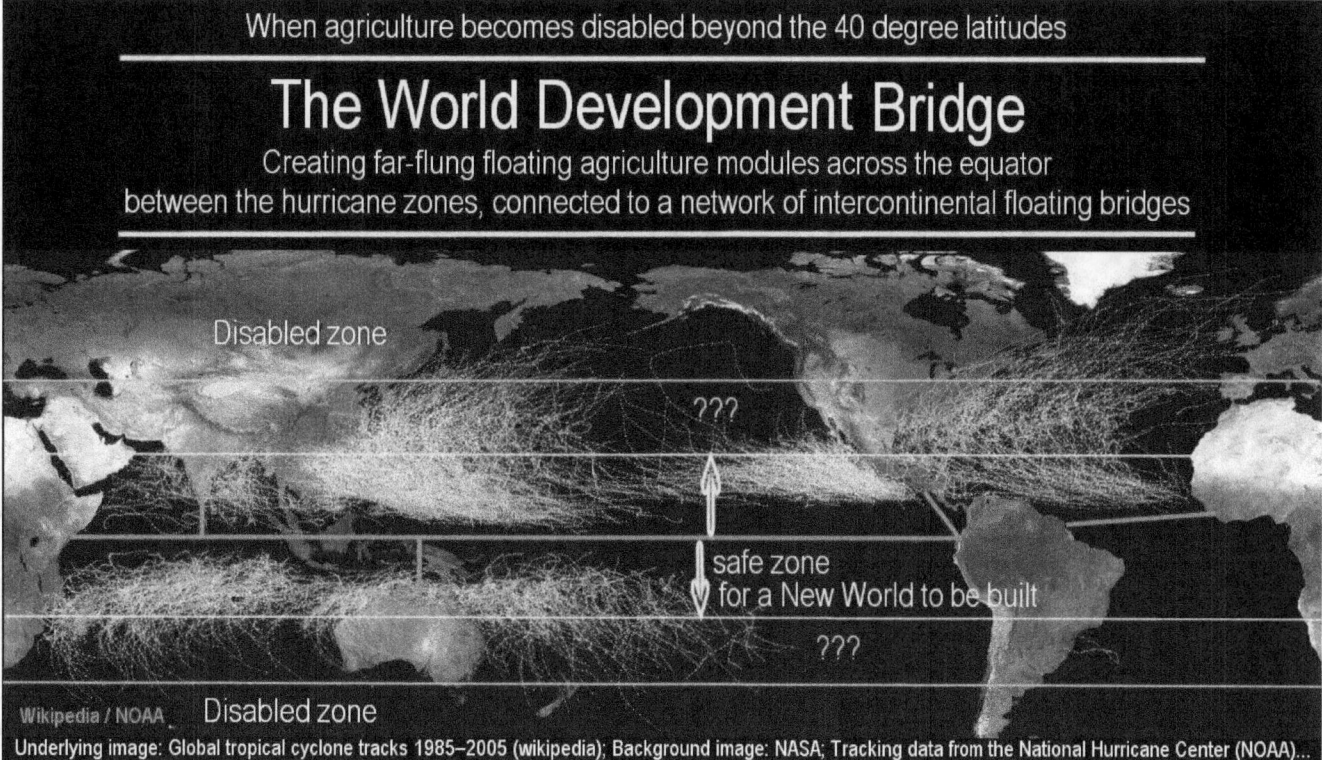

To meet the Climate Collapse Challenge that is already in its beginning stages, we need to produce 2 billion new homes afloat on the Equatorial seas, with floating agriculture attached to nourish 6 billion people, and we need to have these in place and operational when the present world agriculture begins to break down, which may happen between 5 and 15 years from now.

Not gold, property, privatization, and money estates

"Lord Mayor of London ; John Stuttard , Nov 2006" by Diliff - Own work. Licensed under CC BY 2.5 via Commons -

It is self-evident that the building of a vast project on a worldwide scale cannot be accomplished on the property-oriented basis of private monetarism and profiteering. The monetarist platform is an impotent platform. A phase shift is needed here towards a higher-level platform that does not yet exist.

A more powerful platform is needed, where the driver is not gold, property, privatization, and money estates, but is the human spirit.

Humanist Economics

Humanist Economics

The Principle of Economics is, to fulfill the obligation by society to meet its needs.

When Development Projects are completed, the debt (in obligations) is extinguished.

Humanist Development Credits are NOT a debt that society needs to repay to itself!

Credits are uttered by society to make its world and itself more efficiently productive.

When this is accomplished, the objective is met, the debt has been fulfilled. That's economics.

Development credits must NEVER be repaid - it would diminish the economic achievement.

Humanist Economics

The Principle of Economics is, to fulfill the obligation by society to meet its needs.

When Development Projects are completed, the debt (in obligations) is extinguished.

Humanist Development Credits are NOT a debt that society needs to repay to itself!

Credits are uttered by society to make its world and itself more efficiently productive.

When this is accomplished, the objective is met, the debt has been fulfilled. That's economics.

Development credits must NEVER be repaid - it would diminish the economic achievement.

A New World across the equatorial seas

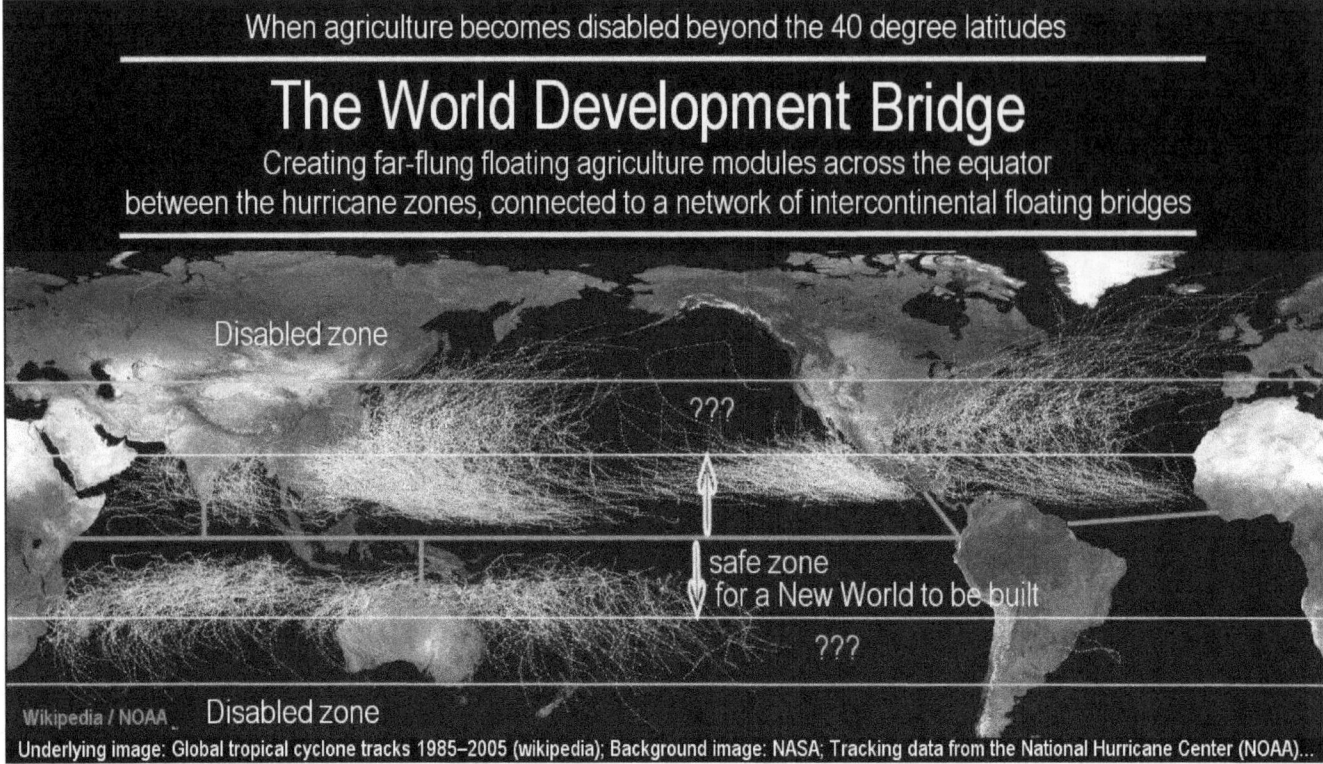

As a physical project, the giant project to build a New World across the equatorial seas, doesn't pose much of a challenge. The New World can be constructed with modules made of basalt, produced in automated large scale industrial processes powered by high-temperature nuclear energy systems. Little human labor would be involved. Once the process is automated, the main labor would be to supervise the operation of the automated processes. Even the production of the industries that produce the infrastructures could be largely automated.

Why should society waste itself on human labor? The greatest pearl of wealth that society has, is itself, which deserves the greatest care and devotion to develop it to the utmost, for it to shine.

With this focus established in the heart and soul, the building of the World-Bridge infrastructure for a New World might actually yield a thousand-fold gain in beneficial returns on the efforts to build it. And even the thousand-fold gain in potential benefits would be a gross underachievement in comparison with the standard of the universe.

An atom is 100,000-times larger than the sum of its parts

**atoms are electrically neutral plasma structures
that are 100,000 times larger than their parts
but are 'millions' times smaller
than their parts dispersed
in unbound plasma**

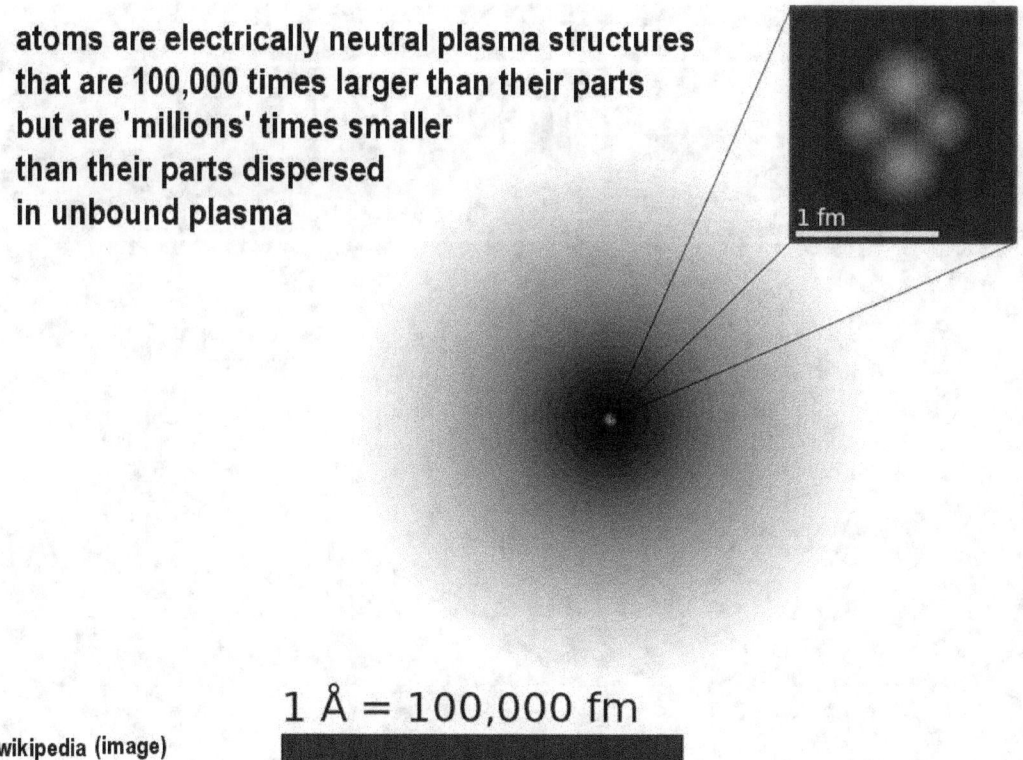

1 fm

wikipedia (image)

$$1\ \text{Å} = 100{,}000\ \text{fm}$$

When the universe constructs an atom, the result is 100,000-times larger than the sum of its parts. This means that we have a long way yet to go to match the creative standard of the universe.

Inversely, if the World-Bridge infrastructure would not be built, the loss incurred thereby would be infinite, because the loss incurred by the loss of civilization, would be immeasurably great. That's the scope of what is at stake.

Our reaching for a potential 1000-fold gain

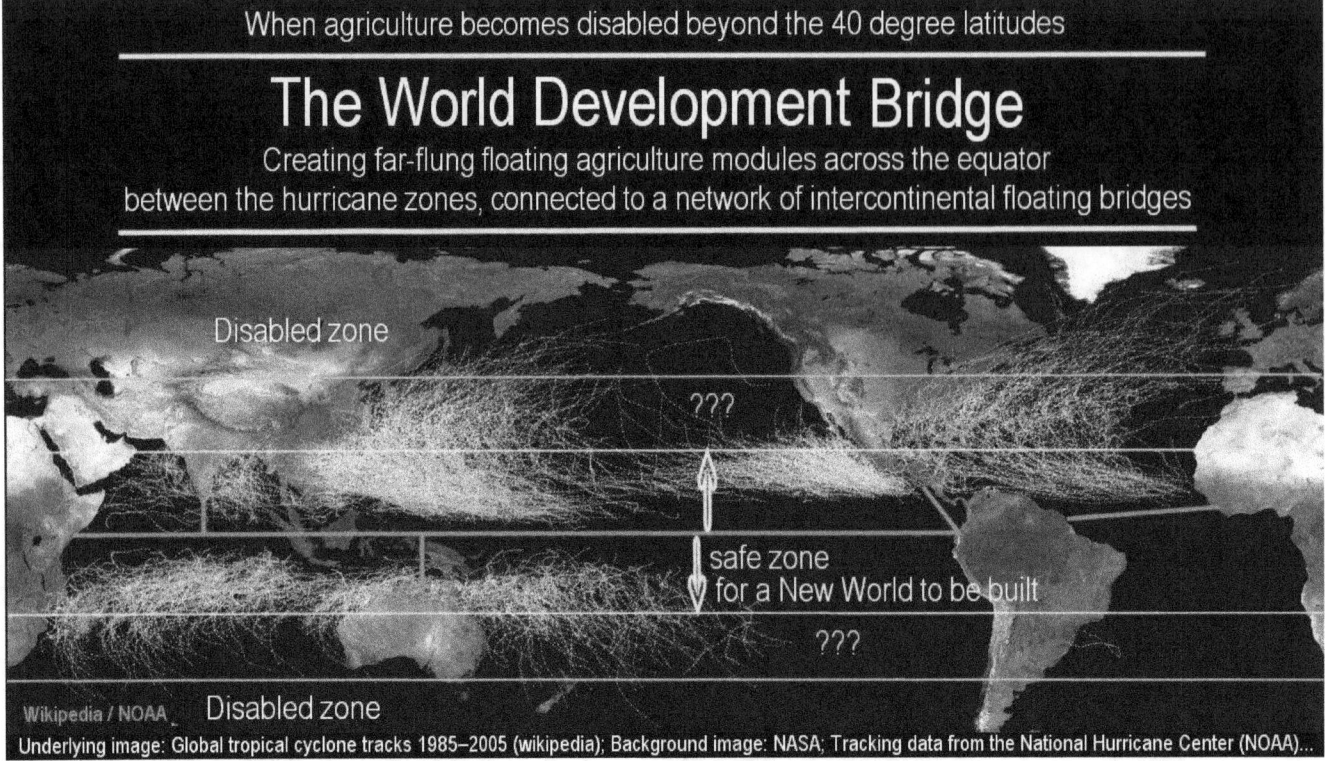

Our reaching for a potential 1000-fold gain, from building the World-Bridge infrastructure, appears to be fully realizable, even while the value of an up-lifted civilization is not actually quantifiable.

When the Ice Age phase shift occurs, potentially in the 2050s, with the World-Bridge infrastructure having been built, our present 7 billion world population, would not diminish, but would continue to grow instead, both in numbers and in the power of its living, and also in its power to enrich the planet. This world-enriching aspect is critical.

The Earth's biosphere is severely CO2-starved

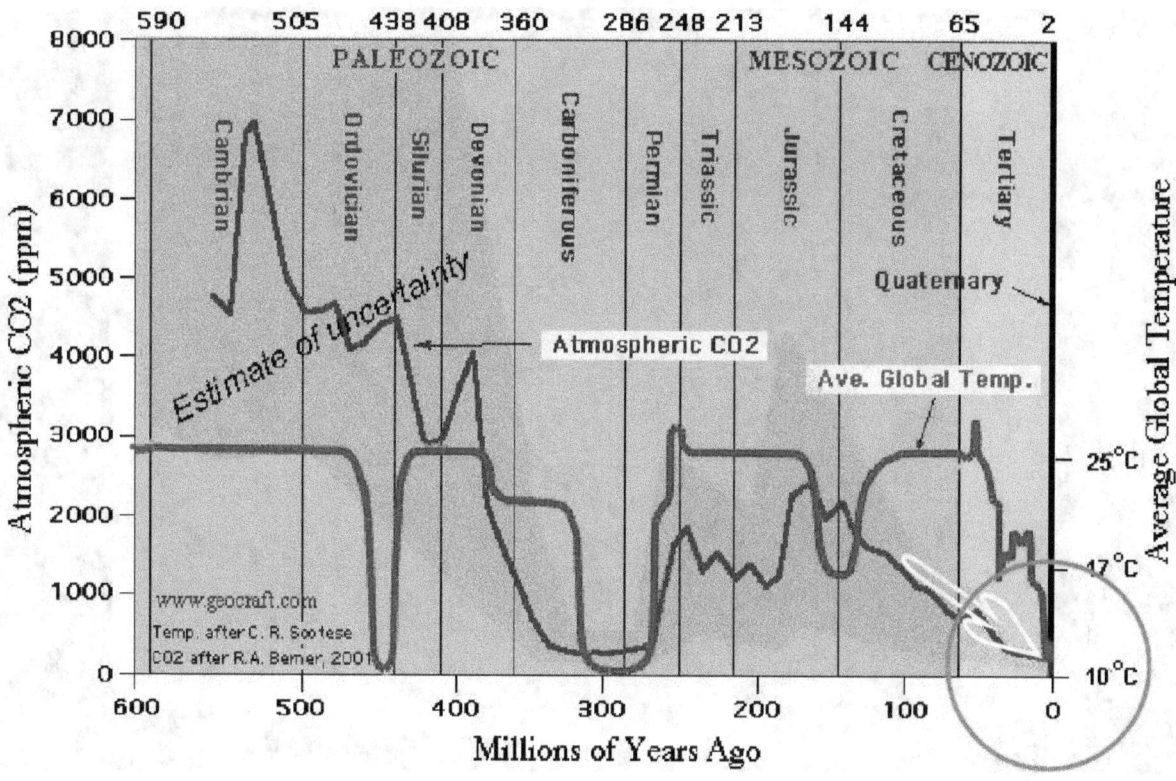

When humanity enters the new Ice Age in the 2050s as a highly developed industrial society, it would bring to the the planet the technological capability to up-lift the CO2 concentration in the atmosphere in large measures. The Earth's biosphere is presently severely CO2-starved. The CO2 concentration that is critical for all life, is presently the lowest it has been in more than 500 million years. If this would be increased 10-fold, the biosphere would be protected under Ice Age conditions, and would not suffer the enormous losses that normally occur during glacial periods when large volumes of CO2 are absorbed in the colder waters of the oceans.

In this context the human response to the climate collapse, would be of critical importance for all life on Earth. Fifty times as much CO2 is dissolved in the oceans, than is dispersed in the air. We can liberate some of that technologically to support the biosphere. Thus our role as the most advanced and most creative species of life on Earth is of critical importance to life itself. We can accomplish some things technologically, which the universe cannot and needs our help with.

We stand at the cross-roads today

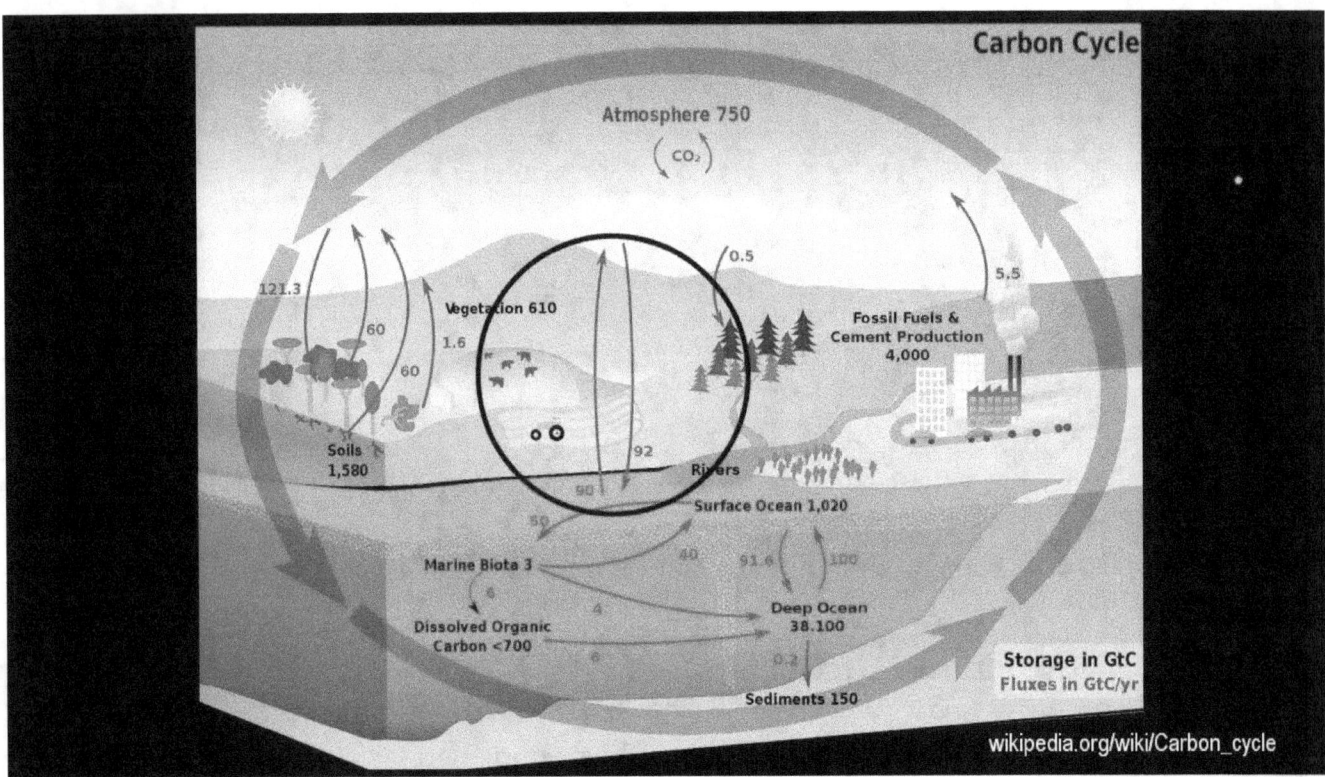

Thus we stand at the cross-roads today with the potential capability that we have at hand, to soften the impact of the next Ice Age on this planet. This capability has never existed before, but it exists now, and may be more needed than we can know. Our response to today's climate change issue is that far-reaching.

While society's present reaction to the Climate Challenge, and to our ability to master it, is a resounding "so what?" and society is more inclined to lay itself down to die, together with much of the biosphere, the option exists nevertheless for society to rouse itself and become more fully human, and thus to answer "yes" to the challenge, and fulfill the role that we have developed us to play for the benefit of all life on Earth that promises to be greater than we can yet imagine.

Could the stone age people have ever imagined

Could the stone age people have ever imagined that humanity would achieve the capability to fly to the moon, and to visit distant planets that appeared as but faint stars to them? Of course not.

Thus we, today, like them, cannot fully recognize

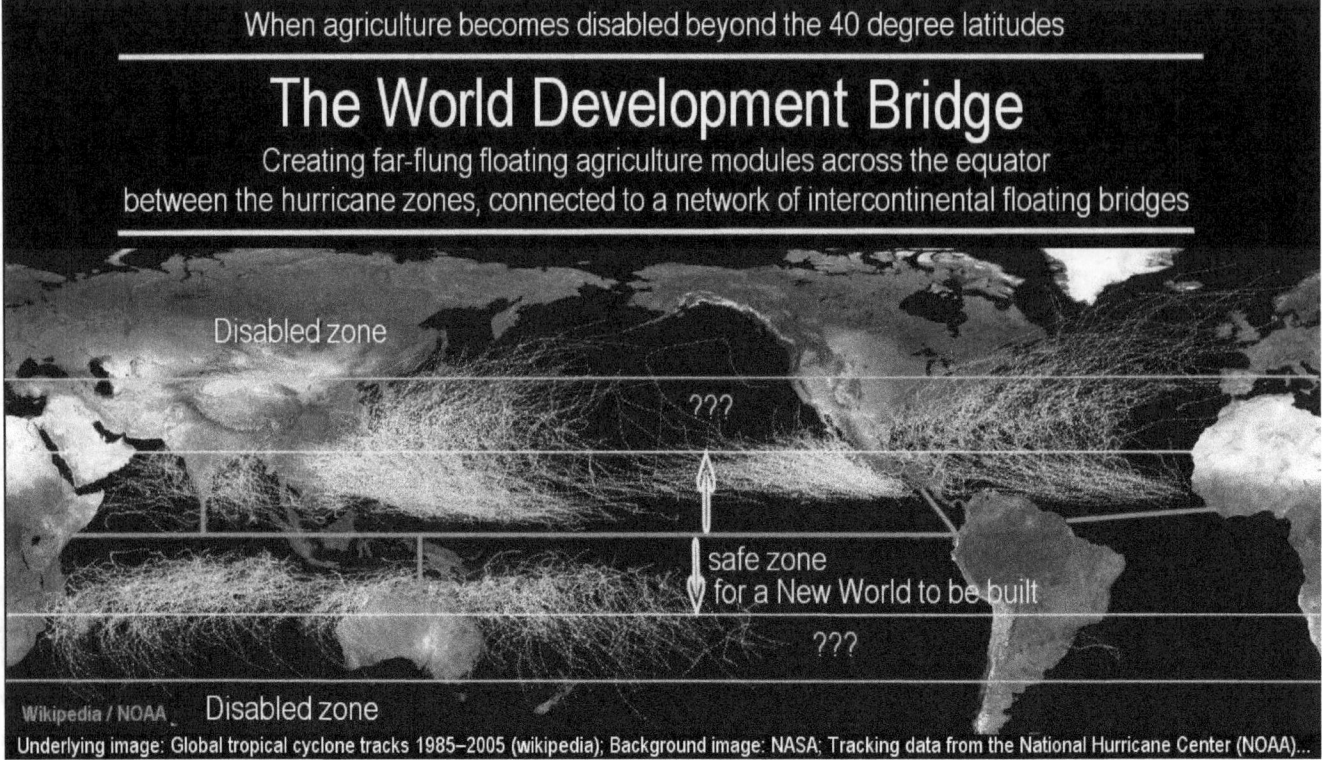

Thus we, today, like them, cannot fully recognize what wonders we may yet achieve far in the future, with potentials unimaginable.

With this in mind we can say to challenges of today, large as they may be, "can they change the principle of civilization?" Thus we face and master the challenges that we cannot avoid anyway without us denying ourselves.

With this potential on our side, why should we fail and not respond truthfully to the Global Cooling Ice Age Challenge and raise us out of the swamp of latent errors and be free. Why should we fail when such riches lay in our hands as we carry within by being human.

To experience these riches from within, and to experience them evermore-fully, is our native destiny and our joy.

Exploration series seen as stepping stones

Segment 1 - Swamp of Latent Errors

Segment 2 - Global Cooling is Real

Segment 3 - Carbon, Climate, and the Sun

Segment 4 - To Create a New World

Segment 1 - Swamp of Latent Errors;

Segment 2 - Global Cooling is Real;

Segment 3 - Carbon, Climate, and the Sun;

Segment 4 - To Create a New World.

The 4 main videos of this exploration series might be seen as stepping stones towards the wider realization of our potential joy.

Segment 1 - Swamp of Latent Errors

Segment 1 - Swamp of Latent Errors

Part 1	Is the current Climate Science "fake?"
Part 2	We have to offer up scary scenarios
Part 3	The Earth has Cancer, and this Cancer is man
Part 4	The Ortes / Aristotle / Malthus / Eugenics Axis of Errors
Part 5	'Son' of the Swamp
Part 6	Manmade Climate Change has no leg to stand on
Part 7	1974 - The Swamp is Going Global
Part 8	"In Lies We Trust!" The truth be damned
Part 9	A scientist without a background in physical science
Part 10	Opposition Movements in the Science Community
Part 11	Is the Earth getting colder everywhere?
Part 12	Climate Change IS happening, but is NOT manmade
Part 13	The breakout to REAL climate science is possible.

Segment 1 - Swamp of Latent Errors

Part 1 Is the current Climate Science 'fake?'

Part 2 We have to offer up scary scenarios

Part 3 The Earth has Cancer, and this Cancer is man

Part 4 The Ortes / Aristotle / Malthus / Eugenics Axis of Errors

Part 5 'Son' of the Swamp

Part 6 Manmade Climate Change has no leg to stand on

Part 7 1974 - The Swamp is Going Global

Part 8 'In Lies We Trust!' The truth be damned

Part 9 A scientist without a background in physical science

Part 10 Opposition Movements in the Science Community

Part 11 Is the Earth getting colder everywhere?

Part 12 Climate Change IS happening, but is NOT manmade

Part 13 The breakout to REAL climate science is possible.

Welcome to the Swamp of Latent Errors

Welcome to the Swamp of Latent Errors

Welcome to the Swamp of Latent Errors

Is the current Climate Science 'fake?'

> But is the current Climate Science "fake?"
> Is searching for the truth "dangerous?"

But is the current Climate Science 'fake?'

Is searching for the truth "dangerous?"

The term "fake" is a dangerous term. It implies an intention to deceive.

Searching for the truth is liberating. It needs to be hailed, because it unmasks whatever is erroneous. Unmasking the erroneous covers a wider field than "fake." Climate science is littered with erroneous concepts.

Some of the errors involved are latent errors from historic time that were perpetuated rather than healed, and them having been perpetuated over long periods, they gain somewhat the appearance of truth. They are often even defended as the truth, at times contrary to evidence and honest recognition.

We have to offer up scary scenarios

> "We have to offer up scary scenarios,
> make simplified, dramatic statements,
> and make little mention of any doubts we may have.
>
> "Each of us has to decide what is the right balance
> between being effective and being honest."

One of the original activist for the Manmade Global Warming doctrine, which he apparently found hard to justify, had put it this way:

"We have to offer up scary scenarios, make simplified, dramatic statements, and make little mention of any doubts we may have.

"Each of us has to decide what is the right balance between being effective and being honest."

'In lies we trust' - The truth be damned

> "In Lies We Trust!"
> The truth be damned

He was saying in essence:

'In lies we trust' - The truth be damned

The man's stated trust in lies makes him one of a multitude in modern time. The truth has been buried in may ways by many people, over long periods of time, especially in politics, that latent errors become defended with lies.

President Trump is proposing

Donald Trump

45th President of the United States of America
inaugurated, January 20, 2017

President Trump is proposing that we get back to being honest, to the truth, unearth it, open its coffin, resurrect it.

Yes, this will disturb the swamp of politics that goes back centuries to distant times when the truth had little meaning, when truth was 'adjusted' by objectives.

The Manmade Global Warming doctrine appears to have been born in this type of swamp of latent errors. The errors, of course, were magnified to serve the desired political purpose.

The Earth has Cancer, and this Cancer is man.

"The Earth has Cancer,
and this Cancer is man."
(Ideology promoted in the late 1960s)

"The Earth has Cancer, and this Cancer is man."

(Ideology promoted in the late 1960s)

It appears that the ideological war of empire against humanity became escalated in the late 1960s, during an epoch in history in which empire was fast loosing ground. A wave of worldwide cultural optimism had erupted that flowed out of NASA's moon landing missions. The masters of empire responded with a counter-ideology to defeat the rising light of humanity.

Who remembers the 60s, likely remembers the banners "The Earth has cancer, and that cancer is man."

Defeat the wave of cultural optimism

How else could the masters of empire defeat the wave of cultural optimism that raised the platform of man in a renaissance type environment that came out of the space program, from which flowed a sense of freedom, humanist power, and set up a new high-level horizon for society? How could this dawning light be overturned?

The murder of Kennedy had been an early step in this direction. But the space program continued.

The Vietnam War that President Kennedy had ordered America's withdrawal from, was ramped up instead. But this too, backfired. It roused the peace movement.

The great Peace Music Festival in up-state New York

The great Peace Music Festival that was staged in up-state New York, happened in the same year in which the first moon landing occurred.

Even the banner that the Earth has cancer and that this cancer is man, didn't fly. Cultural optimism was flying high instead.

The masters of empire found themselves forced to dig deeper into their swamp of latent errors that had been accumulated for centuries. From this swamp, they dredged up a special brand of environmentalism that had been brewing there from the very beginning of their war against the USA.

From the USA establishing its Federal Constitution

This takes us back to the late 1700s and to the great cultural optimism that had flowed from the USA establishing its Federal Constitution as a bulwark against the forces of Empire in the world.

It was in this time frame, in the late 1700s, that a Venetian monk and philosopher, Giammaria Ortes, had dished up a mental poison pill, a special kind of environmentalism, right in the background of the USA establishing itself as a free nation.

The Axis of Errors

The Ortes / Aristotle / Malthus / Eugenics Axis of Errors

The Ortes / Aristotle / Malthus / Eugenics Axis of Errors.

The Axis of Errors

Ortes' poison pill

Giovanni Maria Ortes

(March 1713 – 1790)

Venetian economist, mathematician,

Camaldolese monk, and philosopher.

Ortes' poison pill was...

his theory of population 'explosion,' in a geometric progression,

doubling every 30 years. His take was that the herd (society) must be culled

(depopulated) in order that it won't overgraze its pasture (the Earth)

and destroy it, and thereby destroy itself.

Ortes was in error, of course, perhaps by intention. He failed to recognize that humanity expands with scientific and technological progress, with which it creates its own and expanded resources for living that the primitive Earth cannot provide.

It is unclear where Ortes' crafted error has been drawn from, which reduces the profound status of man to that a beast in the field, and humanity to a heard of animals.

The lingering 'error' of Aristotle

Ortes' 'error' may have been rooted in the lingering 'error' of Aristotle, the intellectual author of the doctrine of natural slavery.

Aristotle opposed and denied Plato's concept

Aristotle opposed and denied Plato's concept of the universal spiritual value and creative power of man.

Aristotle spoke in defense of slavery

Aristotle spoke in defense of the very system of slavery that some of the greatest Greek classical pioneers, like Solo of Athens, had been trying to overcome.

The British Empire loved Ortes' 'error'

This means that the swamp of latent errors has had already a long trail of history before Giammaria Ortes of the Venetian Empire became a champion of it and amplified it.

The British Empire, of course, loved Ortes' 'error' and its potential root in Aristotle who had argued for keeping humanity down. This wonderful swamp of errors justified the Empire chokehold to keep its colonial nations small, impoverished, and impotent by impeding society's natural scientific and technological development.

Thomas Malthus who plagiarized Ortes' 'error'

Thomas Robert Malthus
(1766 – 1834)

**An English cleric and scholar,
influential in the fields of
political economy and demography.**

His ideology was in essence:

- that any achieved progress that improves living conditions
causes population expansion that negates the achieved progress.

- that the power of populations to expand is greater than the
the power of the Earth to provide a subsistence for it.

Progress is futile (the Malthusian trap)

Ortes' contribution to the swamp of latent errors was also picked up by Thomas Malthus who plagiarized Ortes' 'error' extensively and built on it.

Malthus' ideology was in essence:

- that any achieved progress that improves living conditions

causes population expansion that negates the achieved progress.

- and that the power of populations to expand is greater than

the power of the Earth to provide a subsistence for it.

Thus, progress is futile says Malthus.

His ideal society is small, underdeveloped, impotent, and impoverished; the kind of docile, 'stable' society that never challenges empires. His take was that society should be kept so primitive that the poor die at an early age.

Malthus' infamous depopulation ideology

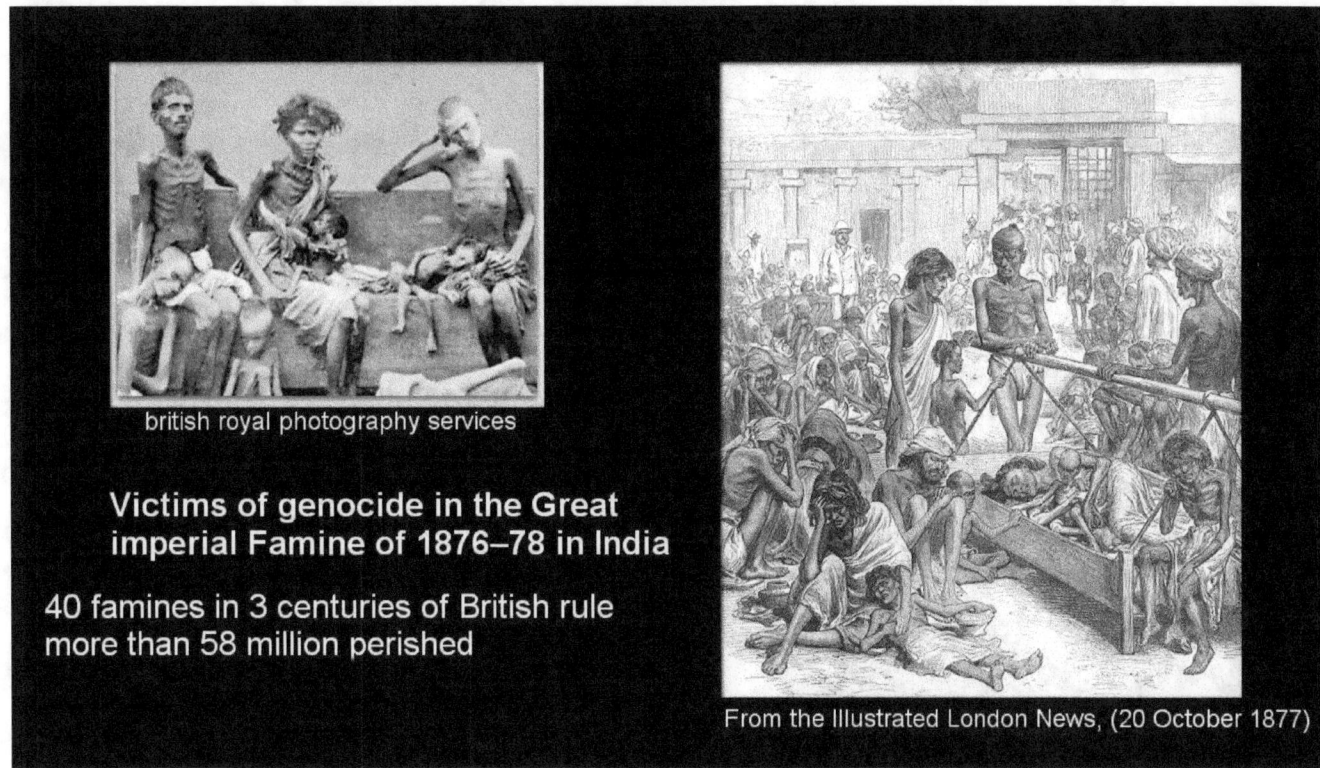

british royal photography services

Victims of genocide in the Great imperial Famine of 1876–78 in India

40 famines in 3 centuries of British rule more than 58 million perished

From the Illustrated London News, (20 October 1877)

Malthus' contribution to the swamp was likewise picked up by the British Empire and amplified its infamous depopulation ideology. Depopulation had been implemented in India in a big way, by means of famine. With it, the empire protected itself against human development that would have dethroned its rule, which eventually happened.

81

Social Darwinism and Eugenics

Sir Francis Galton
(1822–1911 - knighted in 1909)

**Founder of the Eugenics theory:
an English Victorian era statistician,
sociologist, psychologist, and anthropologist.**

After Thomas Malthus, Francis Galton, the grandson of Charles Darwin, picked up the depopulation poison pill from the swap of latent errors and developed it further.

By building on Darwin's extension of the poison pill, in the form of social Darwinism, a form of 'managed' breeding of people, Galton had amplified the underlying error from the swamp still further with his Eugenics theory.

Adolf Hitler had loved both social Darwinism and Eugenics, and had practiced them extensively in his pure Arian 'breeding' centers, and in his NAZI euthanasia operations of people unworthy of life.

The Manmade Global Warming doctrine, a lie

This tells us that the swamp of latent errors that the Manmade Global Warming doctrine became a modern 'son' of, had a long trail of history standing in the background, with a poison element of it having been raised into the limelight almost as soon as the USA was formed, which became its prime target.

The Manmade Global Warming doctrine still caries this early torch from the Ortes days of the swamp. The Manmade Global Warming doctrine, by its very design as a lie, renders society a climate villain who destroys the Earth, and thereby destroys itself. What a poison pill! What a lie! The doctrine sets up a problem in the mind for which no solution is said to be possible, except for humanity to eliminate its living, commit suicide, hail depopulation, and lay itself into the grave.

'Son' of the Swamp

> **The Manmade Global Warming doctrine**
>
> ## A 'Son' of the Swamp

'Son' of the Swamp

Contrary to appearances, the Manmade Global Warming doctrine is not humanity's song for a safer world. The doctrine is a 'son' of the empire's swamp of latent errors. It is one of many such 'sons'.

In ancient times a calendar month was referred to as "the son of a year."

In this sense, the Manmade Global Warming doctrine is a 'son' of the swamp of the carefully crafted errors, piled upon numerous errors, where nothing is real, where we find Ortes standing in the middle of it all, and the Roman Empire not far behind him.

The system of empire itself, is a 'son' of the swamp. It is its champion. It lives in the swamp and is a part of it.

To roll back the industrial revolution

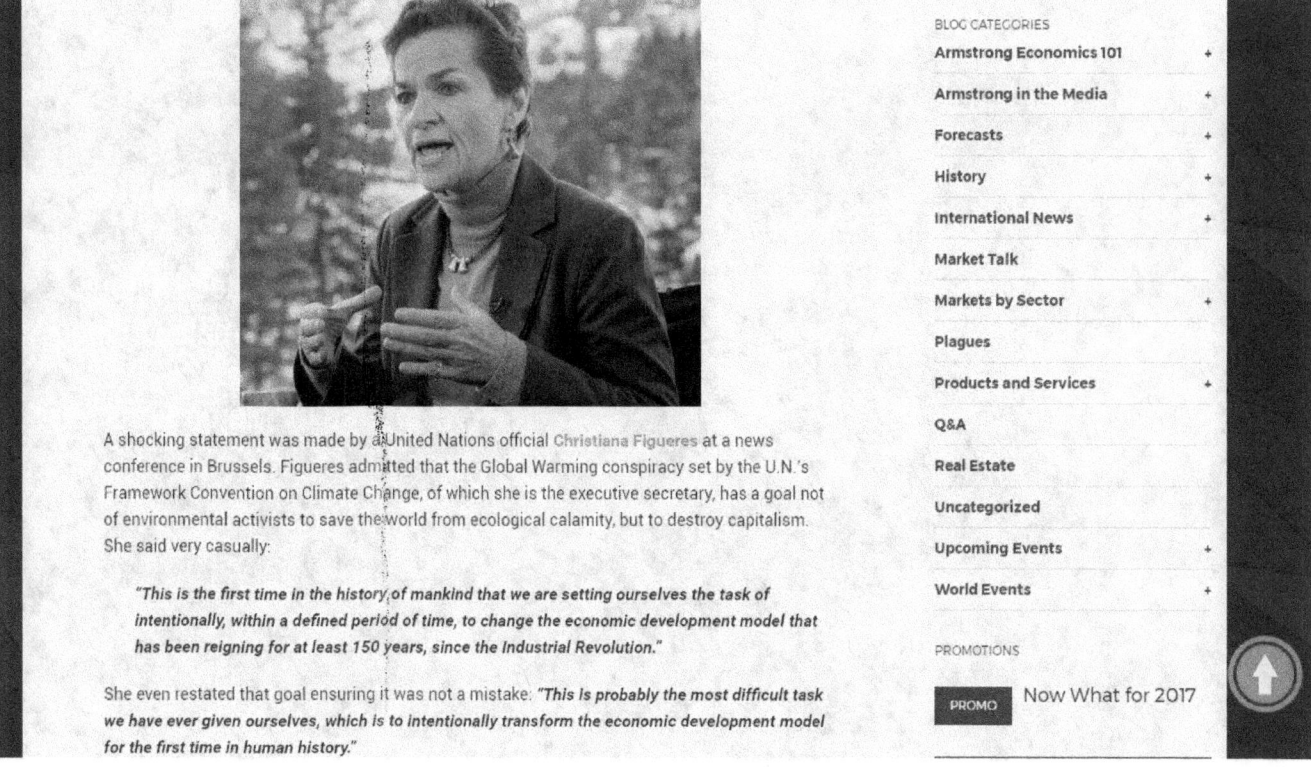

A shocking statement was made by a United Nations official Christiana Figueres at a news conference in Brussels. Figueres admitted that the Global Warming conspiracy set by the U.N.'s Framework Convention on Climate Change, of which she is the executive secretary, has a goal not of environmental activists to save the world from ecological calamity, but to destroy capitalism. She said very casually:

"This is the first time in the history of mankind that we are setting ourselves the task of intentionally, within a defined period of time, to change the economic development model that has been reigning for at least 150 years, since the Industrial Revolution."

She even restated that goal ensuring it was not a mistake: *"This is probably the most difficult task we have ever given ourselves, which is to intentionally transform the economic development model for the first time in human history."*

BLOG CATEGORIES

Armstrong Economics 101   +
Armstrong in the Media   +
Forecasts   +
History   +
International News   +
Market Talk
Markets by Sector   +
Plagues
Products and Services   +
Q&A
Real Estate
Uncategorized
Upcoming Events   +
World Events   +

PROMOTIONS

PROMO   Now What for 2017

That the Manmade Global Warming doctrine, now called Manmade Climate Change to veil the issue, is rooted in the swamp of latent errors, rather than being rooted in actual climate science, was made rather plain recently by a secretary of the U.N.

She stated that the Climate Change objective of the U.N. is, to roll back the industrial revolution of the last 150 years.

The swamp owns the press the media, and even world institutions

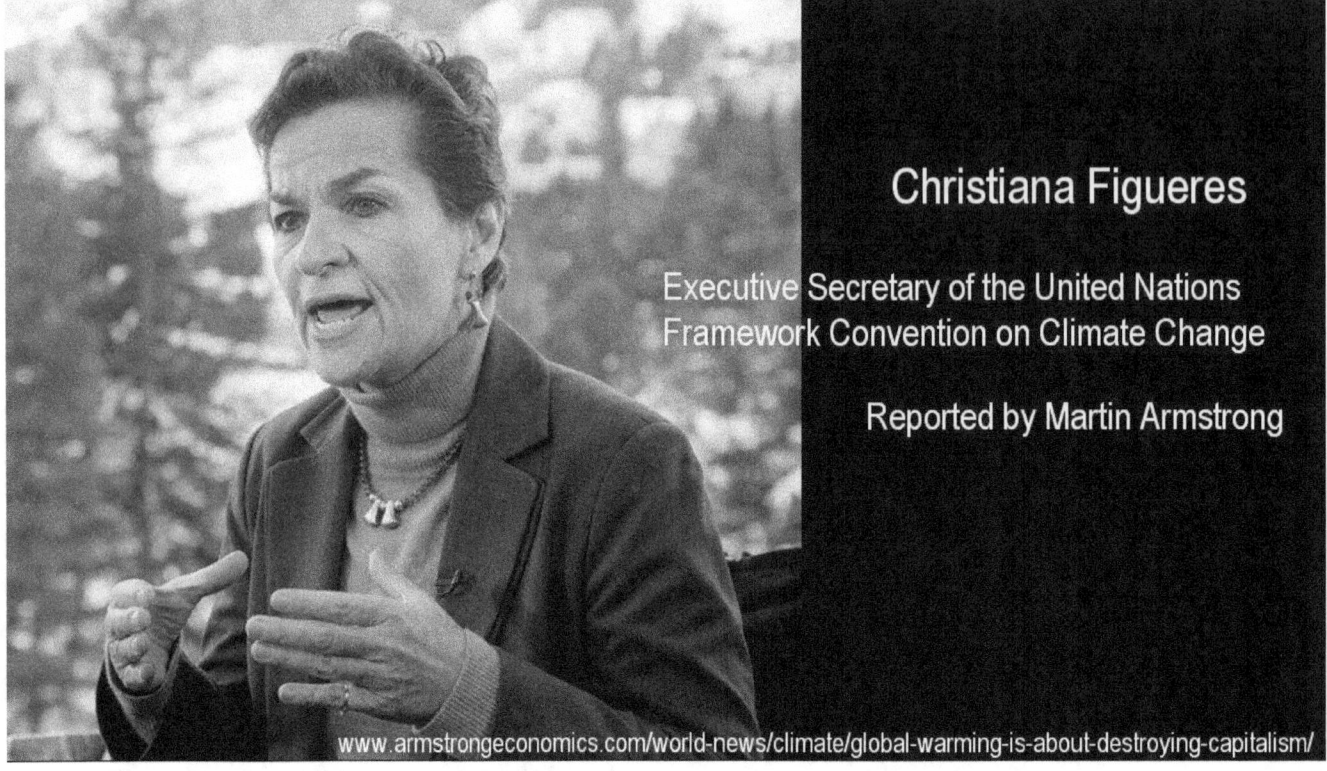

Christiana Figueres

Executive Secretary of the United Nations
Framework Convention on Climate Change

Reported by Martin Armstrong

www.armstrongeconomics.com/world-news/climate/global-warming-is-about-destroying-capitalism/

The swamp succeeds, because it owns the press and the media, and even world institutions who make the news that the press projects. With this vastly extensive control, the swamp breaks into the mind, shapes humanity's self-perception, and forces dehumanization unto it. With its war against industrial revolution, the U.N. defines the backbone of modern physical economics to be the target for elimination in the name of Climate Change.

Climate Change is happening

> Substance and Truth come into view when one steps away from the swamp of latent errors, and of illusions without substance and reality.

Outside the swamp Manmade Climate Change has no leg to stand on.

Substance and Truth come into view when one steps away from the

swamp of latent errors, and of illusions without substance and reality.

Outside the swamp, Manmade Climate Change has no leg to stand on.

This doesn't mean that Climate Change isn't happening. Climate Change is happening. It is real. It is big. It is gigantic. But this change isn't manmade, nor is the climate warming.

The climate is cooling in the real world, and the cooling is driven by astrophysical factors. Here reality comes into view.

The Swamp is Going Global

1974 - The Swamp is Going Global

1974 - The Swamp is Going Global

That the Manmade Global Warming terror doctrine has nothing to do with actual climate science, but reflects the swamp that Ortes, Malthus, and Galton war a part of, became evident in 1975 when the doctrine was announced..

A two-pronged approach for the same objective

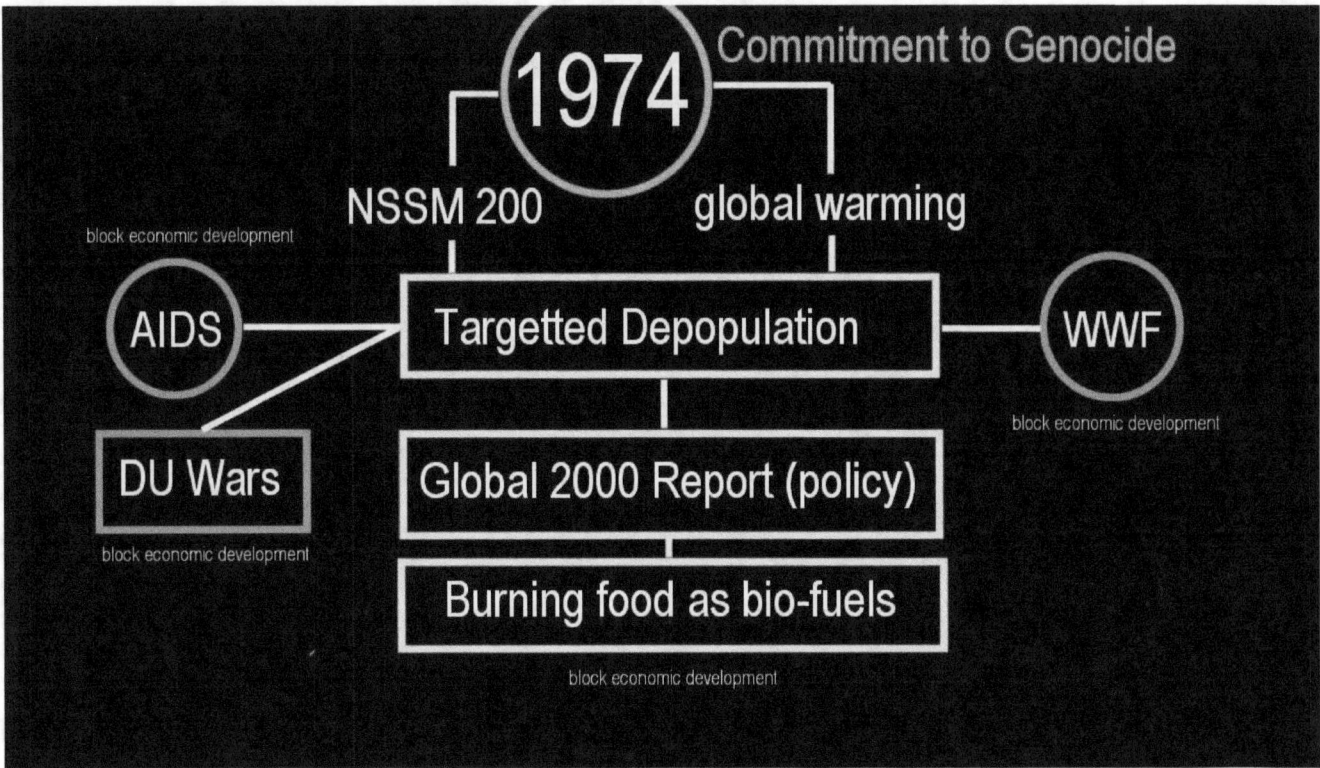

The Manmade Global Warming doctrine was officially announced in parallel with America's National Security Study Memorandum 200 becoming policy. NSSM-200 called for the targeted depopulation of third-world nations in order to preserve their natural resources for America's future needs.

Both, NSSM-200 and the Manmade Global Warming doctrine were concocted together in 1974 as a single package to serve as a two-pronged approach for the same objective. NSSM-200 targeted the third world. The Manmade Global Warming doctrine targeted the developed world.

The objective of the doctrine from the swamp, was from its beginning, to create an energy-lean, de-industrialized, primitive society right across the world; the kind of society that Malthus would have hailed. It forces by design a high-rate of starvation and deep economic collapse. That's the Malthus song, the economic suicide song. NSSM-200 spelled out the same type of objectives

The Russian Academy of Science correctly referred to the doctrine's infamous Kyoto Accord as an "Economic Suicide Pact."

To keep the regressive demoralization of America on track

Vietnam War - after a napalm bomb was dropped on the village of Trang Bàng by a plane of the Vietnam Air Force

Vietnam War

Kim Phúc (age 9) survived by tearing off her burning clothes

Nick Ut / The Associated Press   1972-06-08

wikipedia

The year of the start-up of the doctrine, the year 1975, was also a significant year for the doctrine for another reason. The reason was the outbreak of peace.

In 1973, all American forces had been withdrawn from the Vietnam War. A decade of horror and demoralization had come to a close. A new era was on the horizon, with hope for the future.

The 1969 peace euphoria of the Woodstock Concert in up-state New York, was still in sight. In like manner had the cultural optimism of America's moon landing in the same year, still lingered. These two great cultural lights lingered in the background when the final end of the Vietnam War was happening. A hope and dream by many was fulfilled. The world was becoming a brighter place.

In order for the masters of empire to keep the regressive demoralization of America on track that the war had successfully inflicted, and to prevent the demoralization from becoming reversed again in the erupting euphoria of peace, a new demoralizing project was quickly invented. The poison doctrine of Manmade Global Warming was assigned this role. The doctrine was designed in such a way, as to escalate the imperial war against humanity, and to once again, especially target America.

The doctrine causes a subliminal regression in the mind

COP 21: Heads of delegations by GUSTAVO-CAMACHO-GONZALEZ - Licensed under CC BY 2.0 via Commons by Presidencia de la República Mexicana -delegates

Poster of the Climate Conference. Licensed under Fair use via Wikipedia

The doctrine excels exceedingly in what it was designed to achieve. As it defines humanity an enemy to itself, and imposes on it a problem for which no solution is possible except for it to commit suicide, the doctrine causes a subliminal regression in the mind towards a more infantile stage where slavish obedience happens.

A type of terror-war in society, against one another

The Thirty Years' War

The miseries of war; No. 11, "The Hanging"
by Jacques Callot (1592–1635)

The doctrine also staged a type of terror-war in society, against one another - activists versus deniers - along the line that the Venetian Empire had used to poison the Renaissance Environment in the 1500s, with the Reformation and Counterreformation poised against each other, which destroyed the Renaissance from within and became escalated into the 30-Years War.

Science becomes twisted, faked, and crafted

"In Lies We Trust!"
The truth be damned

"In Lies We Trust!" The truth be damned

In high-profile cases where imperial imperatives stand in the background, science becomes twisted, faked, and crafted to meet the political objective. The truth falls by the wayside.

Carbon-14 isotope ratios in historic ice samples

That there is no truth in the Manmade Global Warming doctrine is evident by the scientifically measured fact that the Earth had been in an almost 300-years long trend of massive global warming forced by the Sun. This astrophysical global warming had shut down the Little Ice Age in the early 1700s. The up-ramping of the Sun during this period is easily measured in Carbon-14 ratios that reflect variations in solar activity.

While the technology didn't exist in 1975 to measure Carbon-14 isotope ratios in historic ice samples, it was well known in the 1970s that the historically counted sunspot numbers, which also reflect solar activity levels, did correspond with known climate conditions.

Sunspot numbers had peaked in 1960 to an all-time high

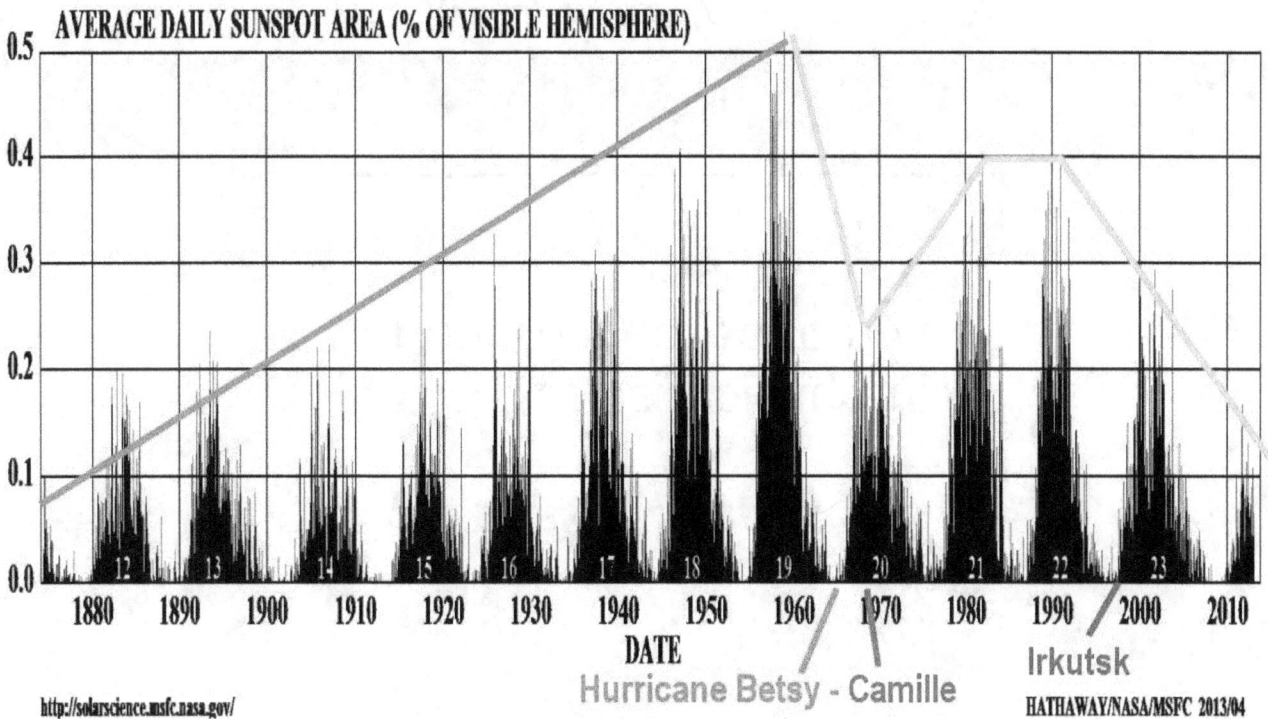

It was no secret in 1975 that the sunspot numbers had peaked in 1960 to an all-time high, and that the climate had peaked likewise, and that the numbers had dramatically dropped after that, to almost half in 1970.

A serious scientist with a background in physics or astrophysics would have never imagined that the global warming that had occurred when the Sun had been ramped up, had been in any way manmade.

In addition, a serious scientist would have noted that the solar-caused global warming had already reversed, and had reversed sharply. No one in his right mind would have proposed in 1975 that the Earth was in danger of overheating. The doctrine of Manmade Global Warming would have never been raised if serious science had ruled the day.

A scientist without a background in physical science

A scientist
without a background
in physical science

A scientist without a background in physical science

As it was, the Manmade Global Warming doctrine wasn't announced by anyone with a working background in physics or astrophysics. It was put on the plate of humanity by a person schooled in anthropology, a field of science that is far removed from physics and climate dynamics, but who speaks for the swamp. The masters of empire evidently needed someone with standing in the scientific community, but one who had no practical background in physics and climate dynamics, who could be recruited to launch the swamp poison doctrine with zeal, and who could be guided to promote it vigorously around the world.

The 'winner' who was selected was evidently unaware of what huge type of Pandora's box the doctrine had been planned to become.

Food-burning biofuels a holocaust of 100 million per year

The selected 'winner' couldn't have known that the poison box that the doctrine developed into, would be used decades later to enable its masters to stage the largest-ever holocaust in history, all in the name of reducing carbon emissions (which the holocaust project is actually increasing).

The holocaust is the modern food-burning biofuels project that consumes agricultural resources, worldwide, at a rate that would normally nourish 400 million people. In a world that has a billion people living in chronic starvation, the massive food burning adds up to a holocaust of upwards to 100 million victims per year, by starvation.

Numerous scientists began to oppose swamp science

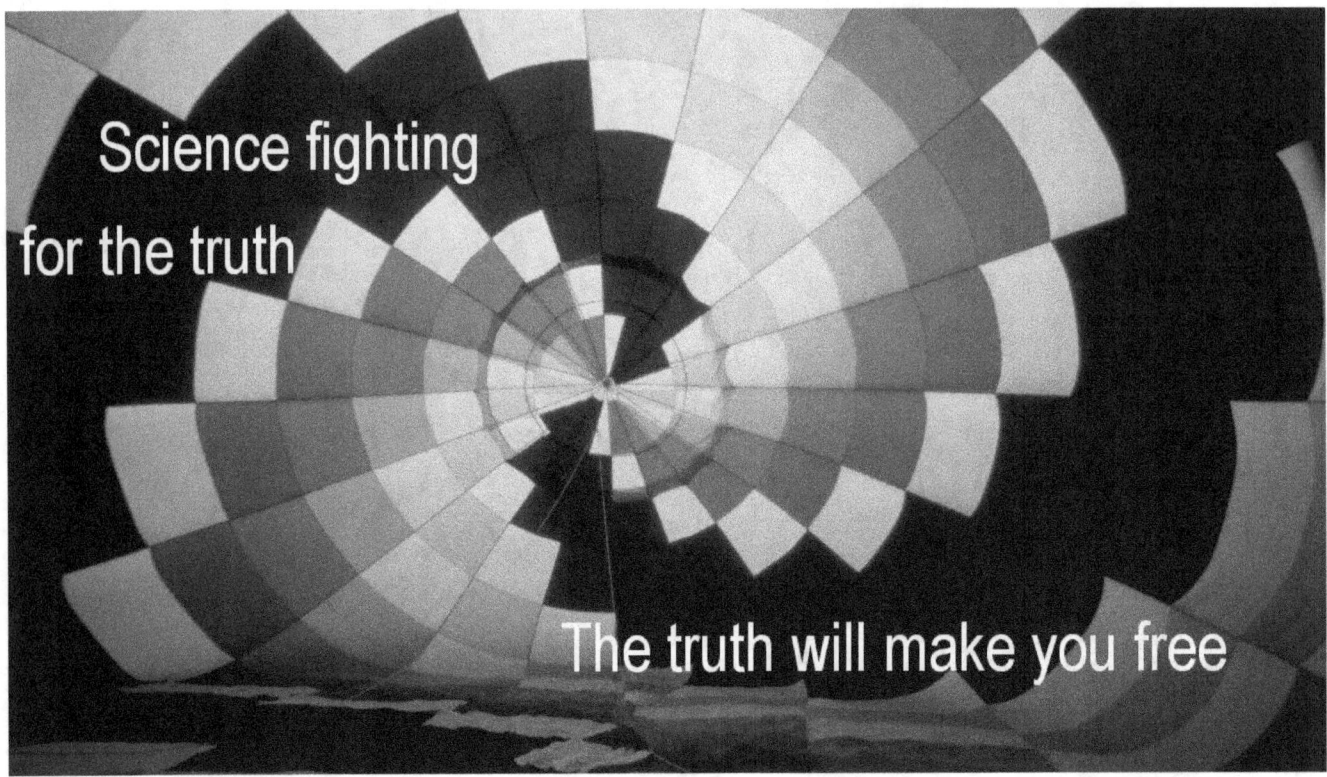

It must have been blatantly self-evident already back in the 1990s, to the scientific alert, that the global warming that the world had enjoyed, was caused exclusively by the Sun, with carbon gases playing no role at all. Numerous scientists around the world began to see through the facade of the doctrine as a scam, and began to oppose its swamp science and its subliminal terror assertions.

Opposition Movements in the Science Community

Opposition Movements in the Science Community

Opposition Movements in the Science Communitylies

Dr. Hugh Ellsaesser describes the Heidelberg Appeal

One of the opposing scientists, Dr. Hugh Ellsaesser describes in an 1999 article the fate of the Heidelberg Appeal, by the University of Heidelberg in Germany, with which the organized opposition movement began, back in 1992.

In this case over 4,000 scientists had responded to the appeal, including '62 Nobel Laureates from 69 countries'. It was hoped at the time that the wide-based voice from scientists around the world, standing in opposition, would have an impact on the policy makers at the Rio Earth Summit. Dr. Hugh Ellsaesser stated that over 35 organizations were publicly standing against the global warming doctrine at the time, though he noted that their 'voices' were not even heard, much less were considered.

Over 50,000 scientists had signed their name

Over 50,000 signatures from the science community opposing the Manmade Global Warming doctrine

1992 The Heidelberg Appeal
- signed by 4000 scientists from 69 countries, including 63 Nobel Laureates

1997 The Leipzig Declaration
- signed by 110 climate specialists

1998 The Oregon Petition Project
- signed by 17,000 scientists (organized against the Kyoto Protocol)
The petition was organized and circulated by Arthur B. Robinson, president of the Oregon Institute of Science and Medicine

The Kyoto Protocol met with an 85% rejection across the world by 2004

2006 Statements Opposing the Doctrine of Manmade Global Warming
- put on record by - U.S. Senate Committee on Environment & Public Works

2007 The U.S. Senate Report:
- Over 400 Prominent Scientists Dispute Man-Made Global Warming Claims - listed by name in detail

2008 New Oregon Petition Project - online, and still ongoing - signed by over 31,000

Details at: www.ice-age-ahead-iaa.ca/alternate_healing/lovescapenovels/climate_change_opposition.html

Over the years, 50,000 scientists from around the world had signed their name in support of numerous appeals, declarations, petition projects, reports, and records of statements, all in opposition to the unscientific assumptions of the doctrine. While this opposition was never heard, much less was considered at the numerous U.N. sponsored Climate Change conferences, one of the petition projects did have some success. It had caused an 85% rejection of the Kyoto Protocol in 2004. This was accomplished by addressing the governments directly.

In considering the wide base of the opposition movement, it becomes evident that the overwhelming consensus on the carbon-climate issue stands in opposition to the doctrine, and NOT in support of it, as it is claimed in the media. However, we face a tragedy on this front, because the entire opposition movement against the false assumption of carbon forced global warming, is itself built on false assumptions. No one in this arena, to my knowledge, speaks for the real solar dynamics, where solar activity variations have large effects on the climate on Earth, where the Sun is NOT its own master, causing is own activity variations, but is itself mastered by changing external conditions within the larger cosmic system that the Sun is a part of. This means that the opposition movement is itself unaware of the actual nature of the Sun and the larger cosmic dynamics that are affecting the Earth's climate by way of the Sun, in a big way.

The opposition movement doesn't ask the right questions

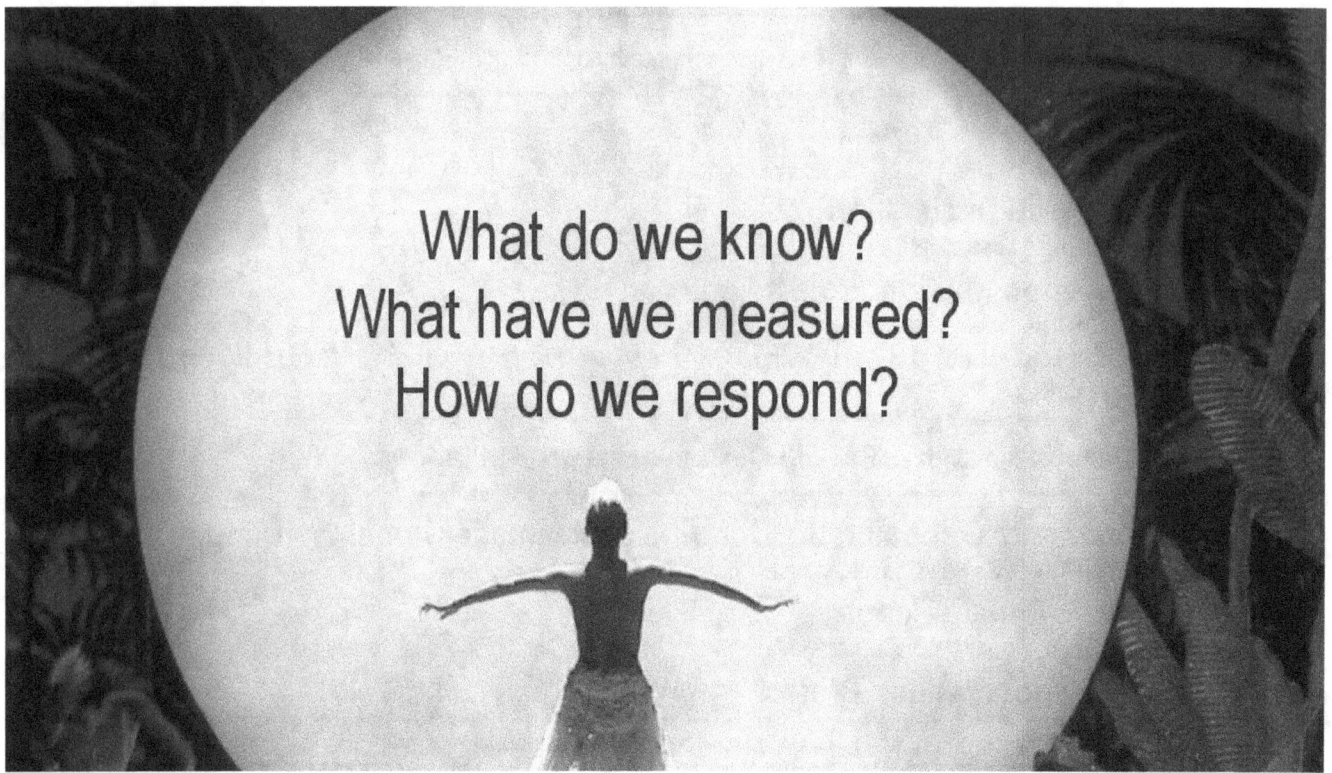

This means that the opposition movement against the global warming climate scare doesn't offer solutions for the real Climate Change issues at all, because it fails to recognize what really affects the climate on Earth. It doesn't ask the right questions and look for the truth. The opposition is so far off track that it doesn't even acknowledge the ongoing Climate Collapse towards the next Ice Age, but does in fact hide it.

The opposition movement, actively prevents the building of solutions

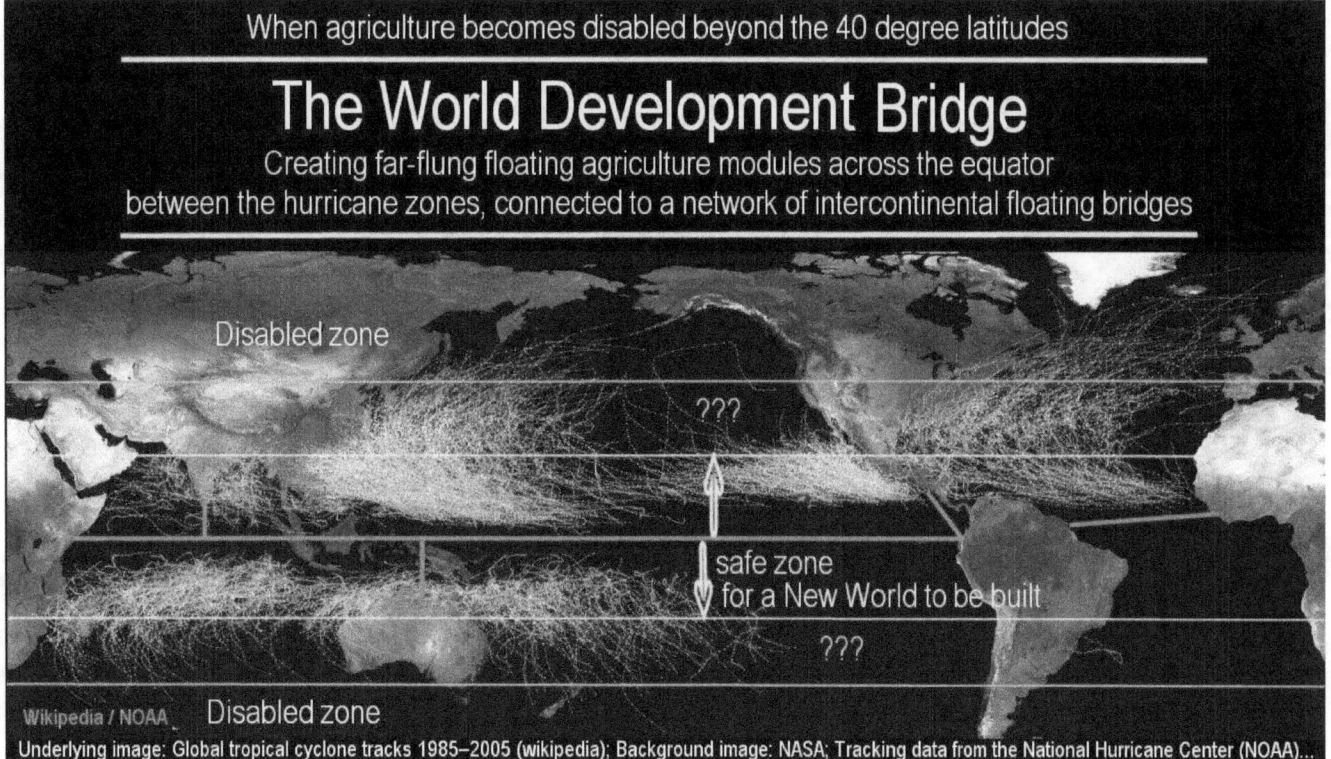

With its ignorance, the opposition movement, that is as small-minded than what it opposes, actively prevents the building of solutions for dealing with the greatest threat to civilization, which is the ongoing Climate Collapse that humanity must urgently protect itself against and its future.

A greater danger than the Global Warming doctrine

From its false basis, the opposition movement poses a greater danger to humanity than the Global Warming doctrine does, which it opposes. The global warming doctrine is so obviously false that people simply laugh about it, while the opposition movement dishes out more-deeply rooted errors that are more difficult to recognize and to correct.

What about global warming

> But what about global warming itself?
> Is solar activity now collapsing past the peak in 1960?
> Is the Earth getting colder everywhere?

But what about global warming itself?

Is solar activity still collapsing? Is the Earth getting colder everywhere?

The solar warming of the Earth is over

Yes, the Earth is getting colder everywhere. The solar warming of the Earth that started in 1715 and gave us wonderfully warm climates for the last 300 years, is over. It's history. We wont have it again. The Earth is getting colder year after year. We face longer periods of colder climates to the point that they will decimate agriculture.

The warming had peaked in the 1960s

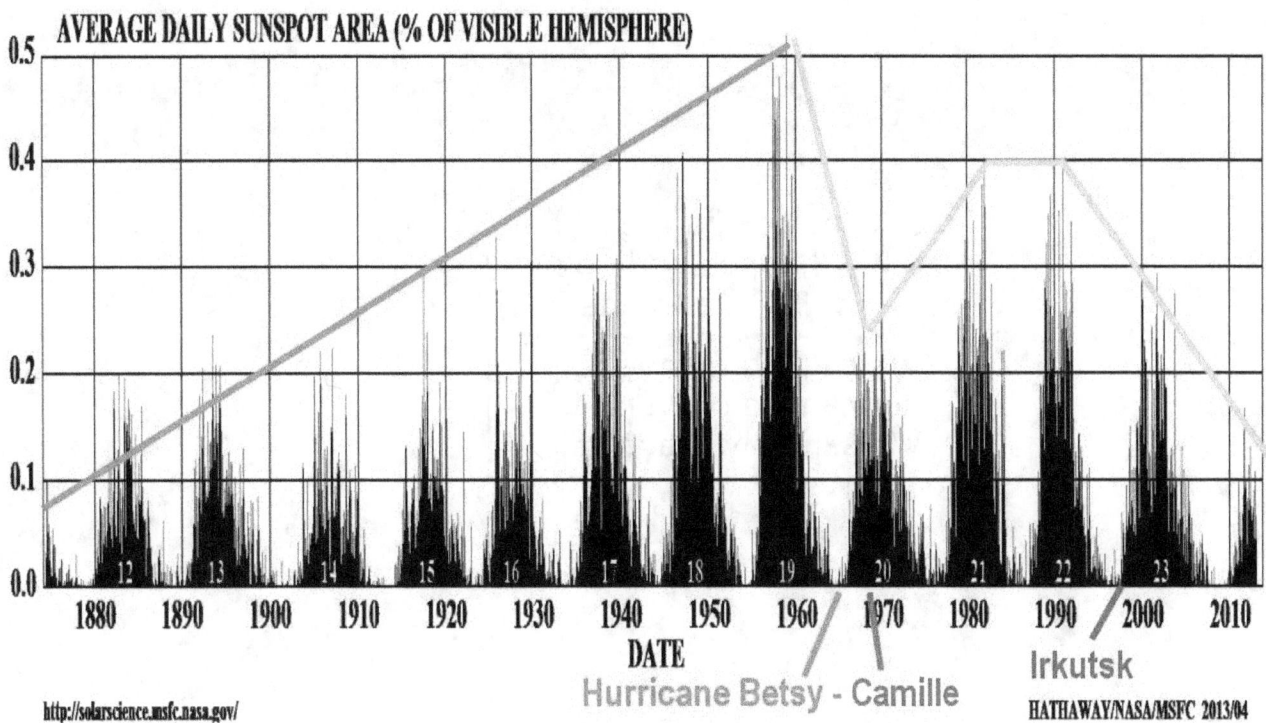

The warming had peaked in the 1960s, then collapsed briefly and reversed slightly, but from the late 1990s onward, it began to diminish sharply. The sharp collapse is evident in numerous real physical measurements. Today, 20 years after the solar reversal, increasing cooling has begun to affect agriculture.

Climate Change IS happening

Yes, Climate Change IS happening,
and it is happening in a big way,
but it is NOT manmade.

> We cannot change it,
> nor can we prevent it.
> We can only react to it.

Yes, Climate Change IS happening, and it is happening in a big way, but it is NOT manmade. We cannot change it, nor can we prevent it. We can only react to it.

The northern nations will cease to exist in 5 to 15 years

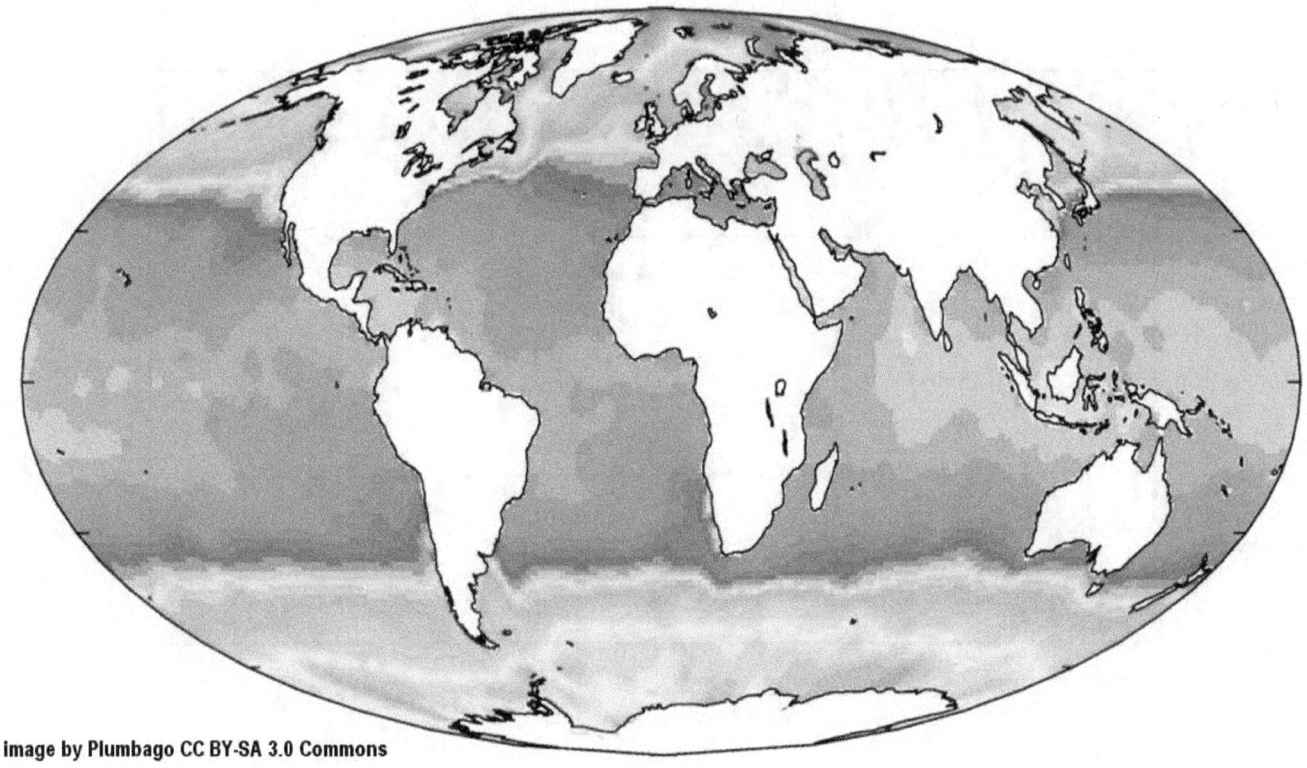

image by Plumbago CC BY-SA 3.0 Commons

At the present rate of global cooling, the resulting agricultural collapse may become so extensive that many of the northern nations will cease to exist in 5 to 15 years, if no actions are taken by humanity to create itself a new food-supply infrastructure in the tropics, far from the cold climates.

When agriculture becomes disabled

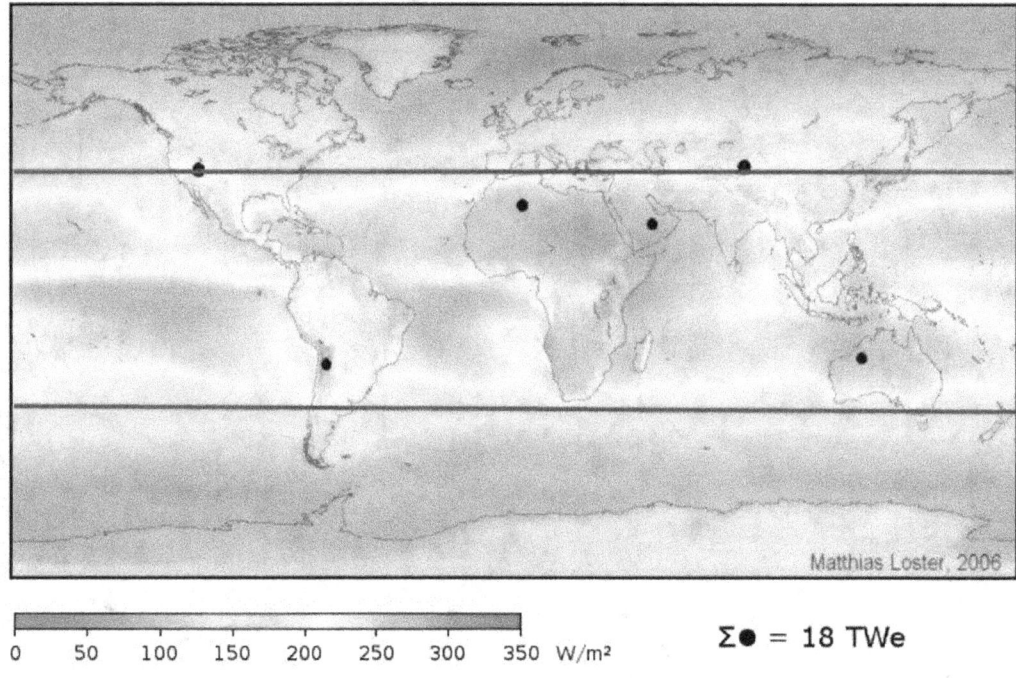

Relative solar irradiation

$\Sigma \bullet = 18$ TWe

Since the cooling is global, the effects won't be regional. All the vulnerable nations outside the tropics, where the solar irradiation is weak, will be affected simultaneously, such as Canada, Russia, the European nations, and to some degree also the USA and China. When agriculture becomes disabled on a broad front, where no food is grown, people die. Without food people die. A nation ceases to exist without people. Nations will vanish.

Is this scary? No it isn't.

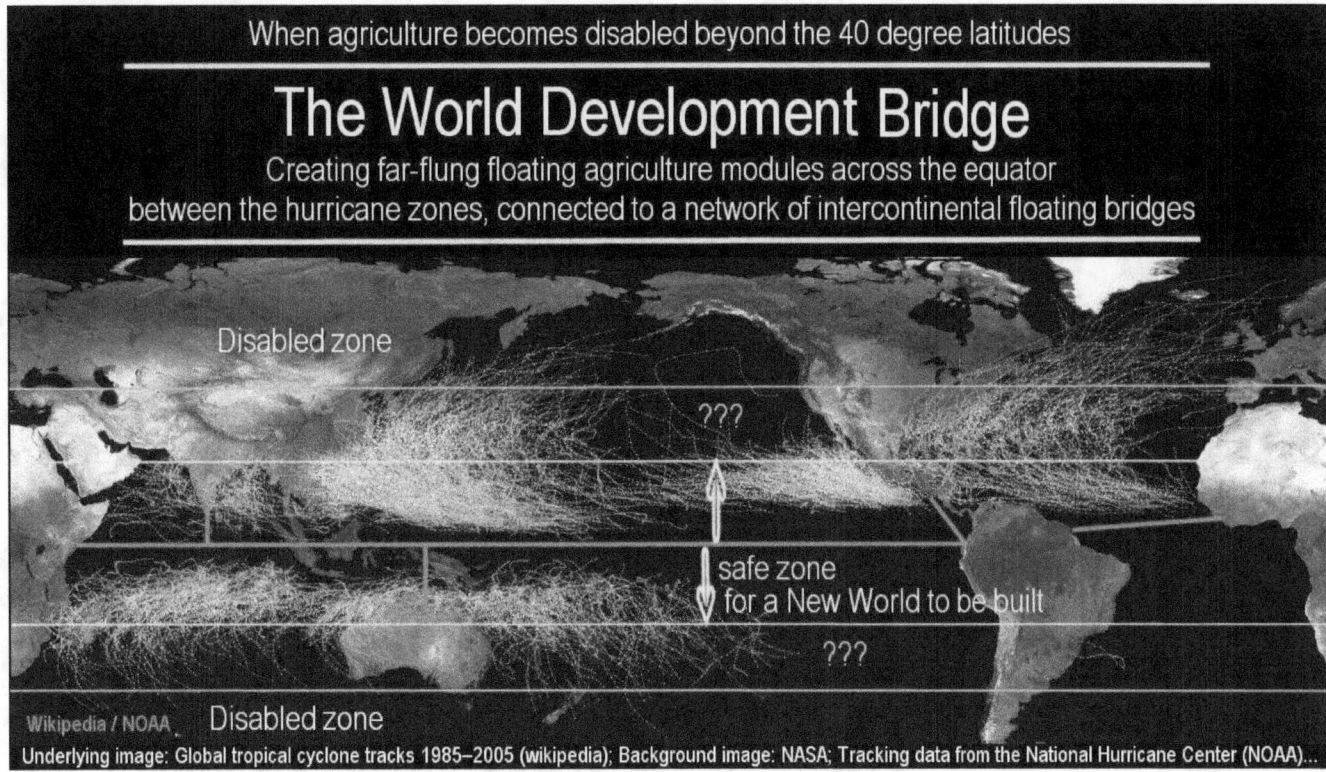

Is this scary? No it isn't. It is only scary if you decide NOT to become involved in creating a new food supply infrastructure for the world, in the tropics.

Are you looking for a Free Ride ticket?

Are you looking for a Free Ride ticket?

Hop to it. It is called "Suicide".

It is absolutely free. It only costs you your life, (which most people don't attribute any value to)

> The Living ticket is extremely expensive in efforts and commitments. For this, it promises 1000-fold returns in benefits.

Are you looking for a Free Ride ticket?

Hop to it. It is called 'Suicide'.

It is absolutely free. It only costs you your life, (which most people don't attribute any value to)

The Living ticket is extremely expensivein efforts and commitments. For this, it promises 1000-fold returns in benefits.

If the infrastructures are created

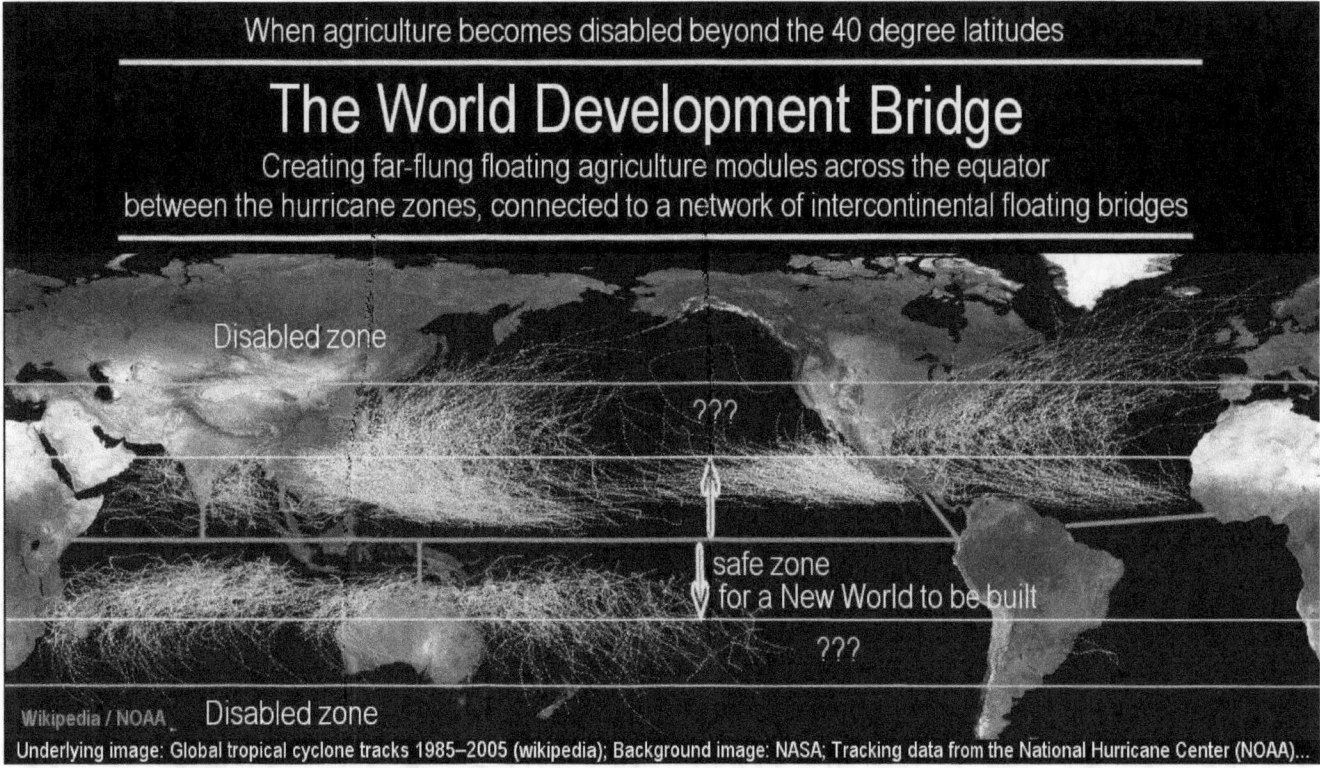

If the infrastructures are created, life continues, and will likely thrive on a vastly-higher-level cultural and economic platform than we can yet imagine, which is something worth celebrating.

Time is running out fast

Whether we will make the effort to build us a New World, will likely depend on President Trump, or another leader, or society itself, becoming successful in prying the lid off, of the Pandora's Box of the poison doctrine of Manmade Global Warming.

The doctrine is presently so strongly in control of society that the massive global cooling that is already in progress, is deemed not to exist, and thus remains to be overlaid with dreams of global warming. The breakout from this trap is critical, and the time for it is now. - Time is running out fast.

The breakout to REAL climate science is possible

The breakout to REAL climate science is possible.
It may happen.

The facade of the fake-science (hoax) is wearing thin.
The scene is wide open.

The breakout to REAL climate science is possible.

It may happen. The facade of the fake-science (hoax) is wearing thin. The scene is wide open.

The Presidential Commission on Climate Change

The Presidential Commission on Climate Change, if it is honest, will invariably recognize the ongoing cooling of the Earth and its consequences for agriculture, which is humanity's main food resource. If the recognition is made, humanity is one step closer to having a future, versus having none. The stakes are that high.

This means that the big question is: Will the President move with his proposal at this critical stage and succeed? Or will he flinch?

Global Cooling Climate Change IS real

Global Cooling Climate Change IS real.
The climate IS changing.
A catastrophe IS in the making.
The catastrophe, if it happens, will be manmade.
The Global Cooling IS increasing every year.
It MAY 'murder' you in 5-15 years, but it IS preventable.
The prevention IS blocked by the doctrine that is hailed.
The blocking renders the resulting catastrophe MANMADE.
But there exists a giant in the world who is greater than the doctrine.
This giant is the human being.
Even a President is a human being!
The President CAN...

Global Cooling Climate Change IS real.

The climate IS changing.

A catastrophe IS in the making.

The catastrophe, if it happens, will be manmade.

The Global Cooling IS increasing every year.

It MAY 'murder' you in 5-15 years, but it IS preventable.

The prevention IS blocked by the doctrine that is hailed.

The blocking renders the resulting catastrophe MANMADE.

But there exists a giant in the world who is greater than the doctrine.

This giant is the human being.

Even a President is a human being!

The President CAN...

Well, I must apologize here. These statements should have been presented as questions. You are the giant. The giant doesn't need to be erected, though asking questions tends to unlock the door within, and awakens the dormant recognitions that are within reach of everyone.

Segment 2 - Global Cooling is Real

Segment 2 - Global Cooling is Real

Part 1	How do we know that global cooling is real?
Part 2	Agriculture in Danger of Collapsing
Part 3	Is the climate on Earth forced by the Sun?
Part 4	Solar Collapse, Measured by the Ulysses Spacecraft
Part 5	Proof of Solar Cosmic-Ray Flux
Part 6	Measurements that quantify solar activity collapse
Part 7	Climate Recovery NOT Possible anymore
Part 8	Building a Climate-Independent New World

Segment 2 - Global Cooling is Real

Part 1 How do we know that global cooling is real?

Part 2 Agriculture in Danger of Collapsing

Part 3 Is the climate on Earth forced by the Sun?

Part 4 Solar Collapse, Measured by the Ulysses Spacecraft

Part 5 Proof of Solar Cosmic-Ray Flux

Part 6 Measurements that quantify solar activity collapse

Part 7 Climate Recovery NOT Possible anymore

Part 8 Building a Climate-Independent New World

How do we know that global cooling is real?

So, how do we know that global cooling is real?

So, how do we know that global cooling is real?

We can measure the evidence of it

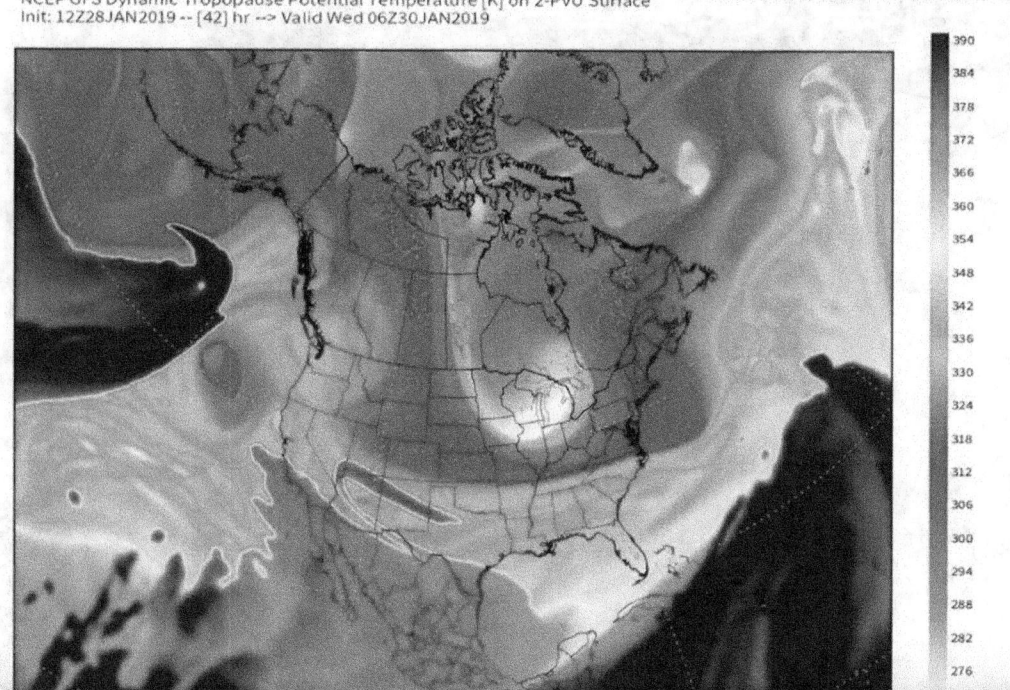

The cooling of the Earth has an astrophysical cause. This cause IS unstoppable. It IS ongoing, unavoidable, and it is knowable. It IS presently cooling the Earth. And since it is happening, we can measure the evidence of it, can't we? That's what we see here. The evidence that the Earth is cooling is found in the increasing outflow of cold air from the polar regions.

Cold air is heavier than warm air, which causes the cold air from the polar regions to become forced towards the equator by the centrifugal force generated by the rotation of the Earth. This means that the colder the climate gets, the stronger the outflow from the Arctic becomes.

On the American continent

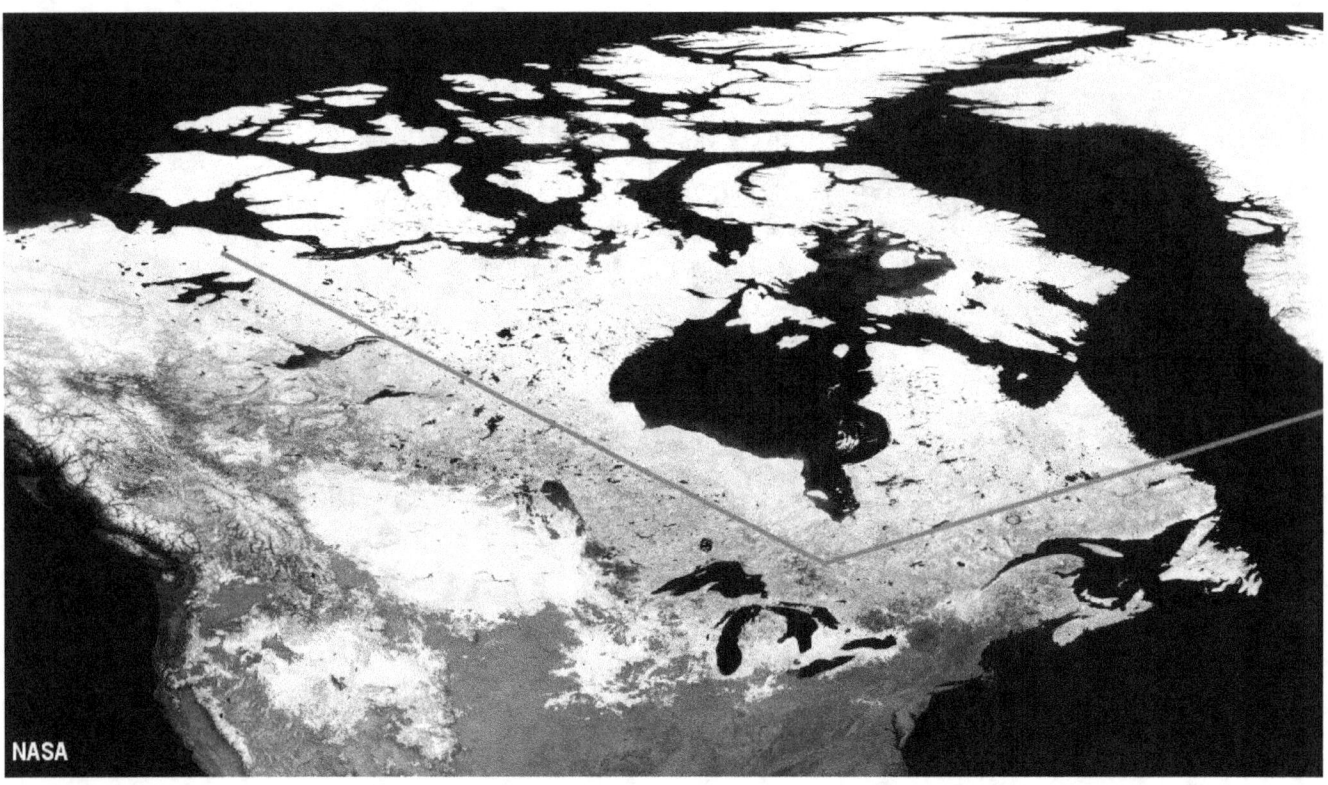

On the American continent, the cold northern air, which has a natural westward flow across the northern Canadian landmass that had previously hosted the big ice sheet during the Ice Ages, becomes trapped by the Rocky Mountain chain in the West and is thereby forced more strongly southward.

The back-flow draws the warmed into the arctic region

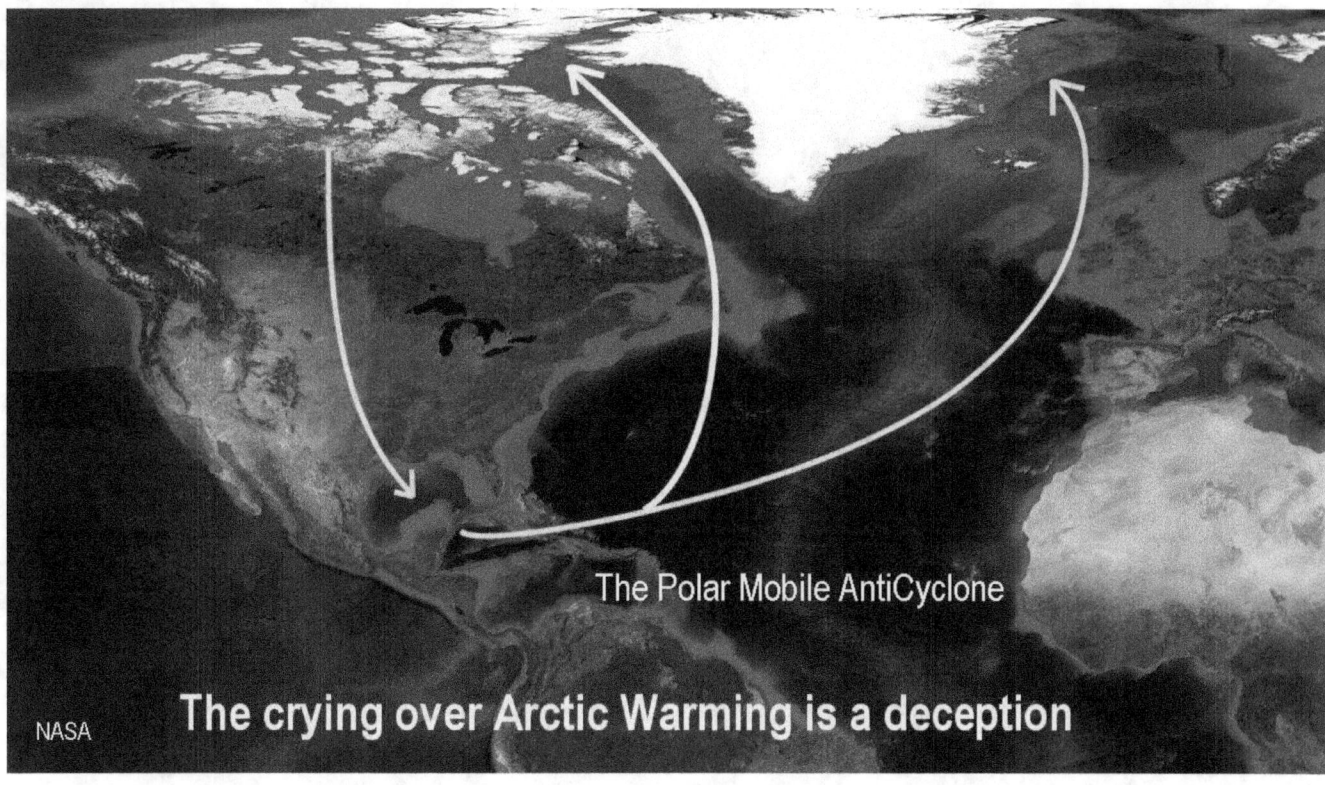

The strongly focused southward flow, crosses the Canadian parries and south across the central U.S. states, which are the main grain growing areas in North America. Then deep in the south, the northern air stream slows to a halt and becomes tremendously heated, especially over the warm waters of the Gulf of Mexico.

Since the northern outflow requires a corresponding backflow, the back-flow occurs over the Atlantic and draws the warmed air northward, and back into the arctic region, to complete the circulation.

This means that the colder the global climate gets, the more the arctic region gets warmed up. The circulation system has been named the Polar Mobile Anticyclone.

Since the rate of flow is now increasing, with the Earth getting colder, the warming of the Arctic is also increasing. The warming of the Arctic, is presently a part of the evidence that the Earth is getting colder, but it is the least significant part of the evidence.

The increasing cooling of the Earth cause far-more dramatic effects than the warming of the Arctic, by affecting agriculture.

Agriculture in Danger of Collapsing

Agriculture in Danger of Collapsing

Agriculture in Danger of Collapsing

A large winter-type blizzard in the planting season

In mid-April of 2018, for example, a large winter-type blizzard swept across the American grain belt from the north. It dumped snow on the ground with temperatures in the minus 40 degree Celsius range in some areas, and this right in the middle of what should be the planting season.

Seen as the writing on the wall

While agriculture recovered from this setback, with planting having been delayed into May, the huge blizzard Xanto, should nevertheless be seen as the writing on the wall of what we will yet have to face with the Earth becoming colder year after year for the next 30 years, after which it gets really bad and the next Ice Age begins.

When these large winter blizzards strike in the spring

When these large winter blizzards strike in the spring, in April as we see it here, it is hard to ignore that the Earth is cooling.

The collapse of agriculture altogether

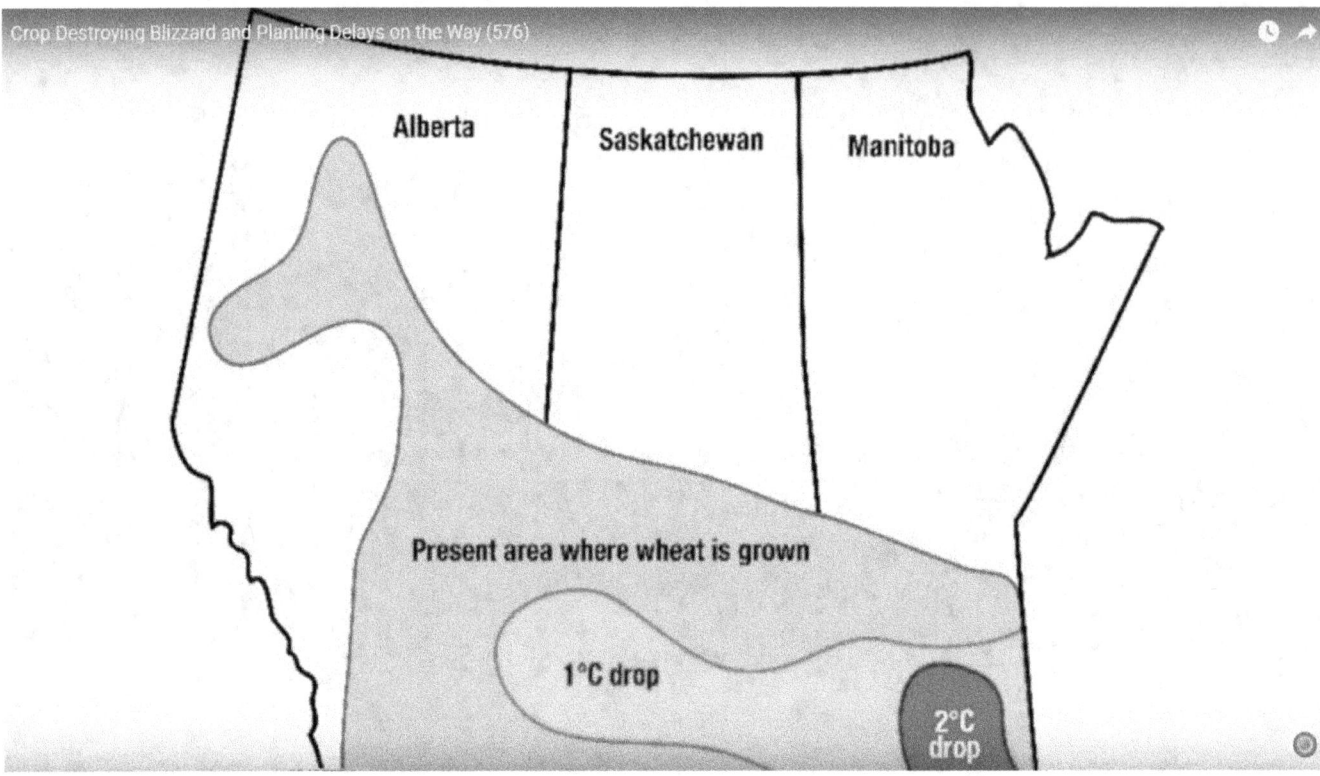

The next effect will be the collapse of agriculture altogether. At the present rate of cooling, Canada, the European nations, Russia, and similarly situated nations, will rapidly cease to exist when food production breaks down. This could happen in 5 to 15 years.

When climate shrinks the growing season

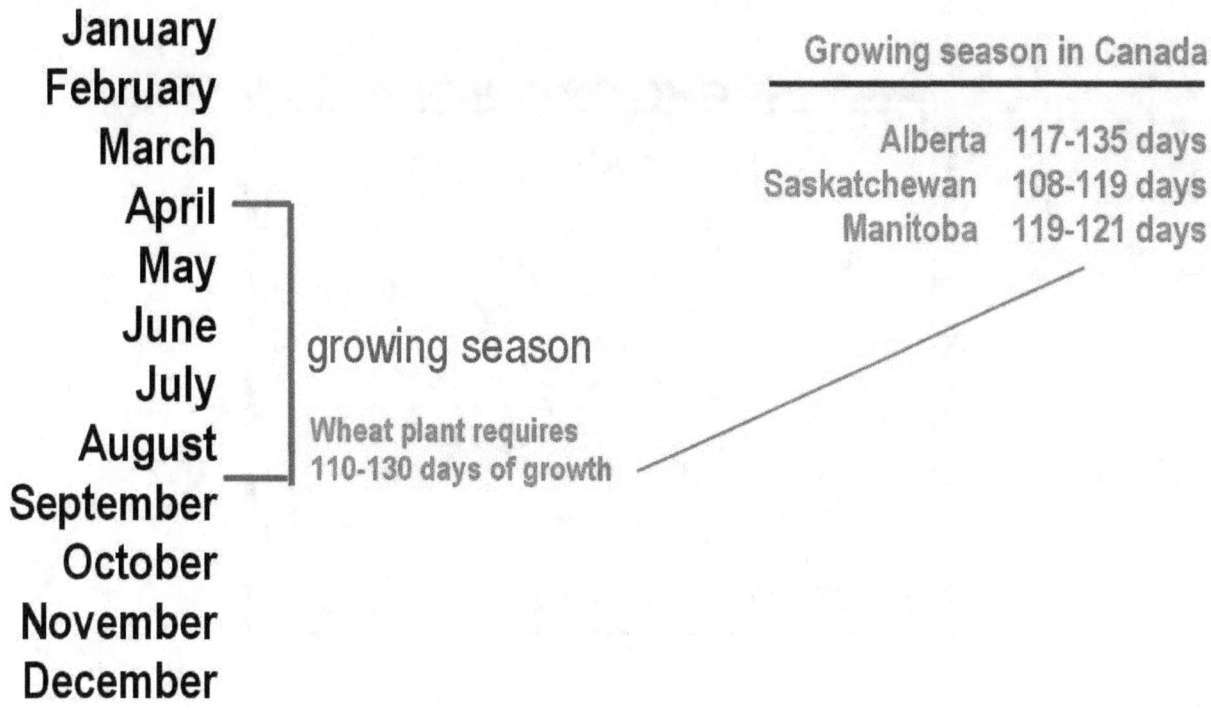

When the cooling climate shrinks the growing season, so that summers become shorter all the way to the point that food plants can no longer mature and produce a harvest, food production begins to collapse. Without food, people die. Without people, there exists no nation. Entire nations are presently situated to vanish by this process when agriculture breaks down. The breakdown is already beginning, slightly

Production expected to no longer meet demands

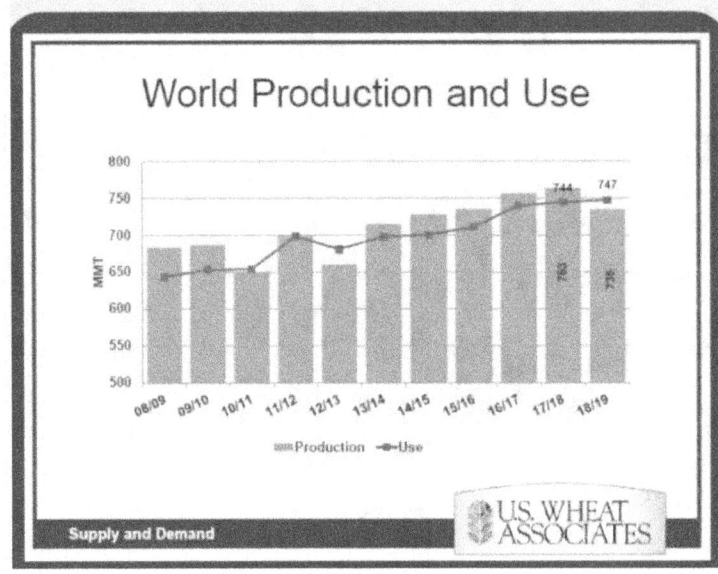

During the 2018/19 growing season, the world production of wheat, for example, is expected to no longer meet demands, though by a small margin for a start.

The shortfall will likely be sequestered

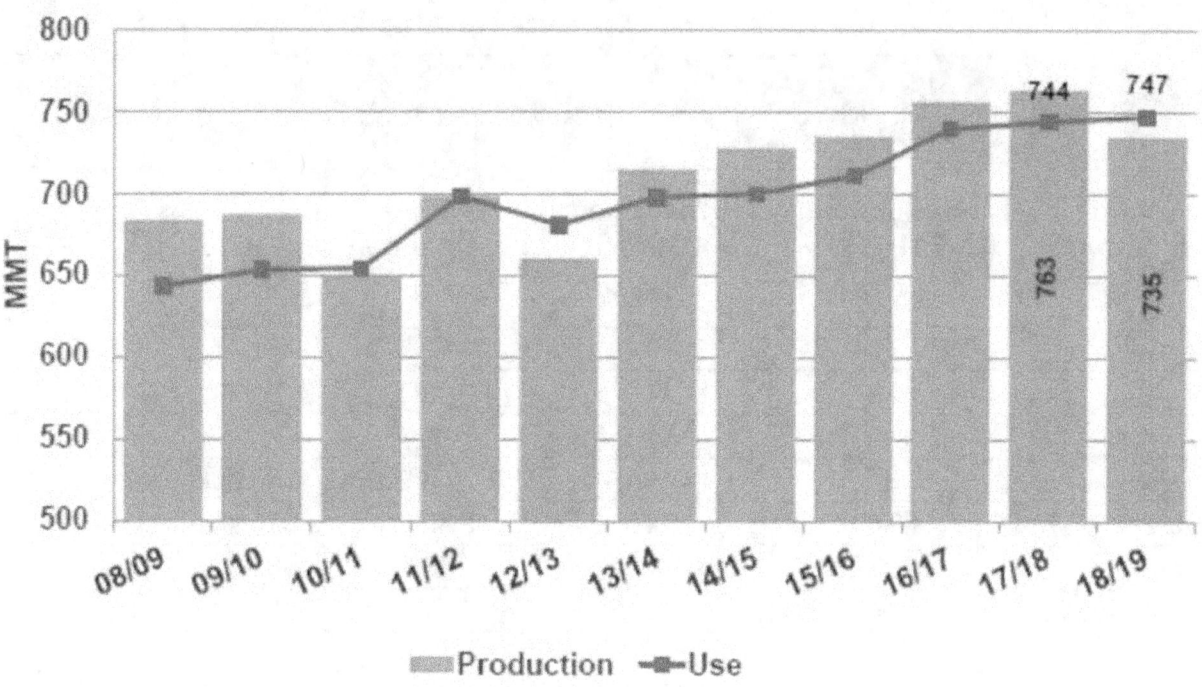

The shortfall will likely be sequestered from carry-over stocks until the reserves are exhausted.

The shortfall is already severe

Major Exporter Production (in MMT)				
Major Exporters	**Production 2017/18**	**Production 2018/19**	**Percent Change**	**Source**
U.S.	47.3	51.2	8%	USDA*
Argentina	18.5	19.0	3%	USDA*, *Bolsa de Cereales*
Australia	21.3	17.0	-20%	USDA*, ABARES
Canada	30.0	31.8	6%	AAFC
EU-27	151	136	-10%	*Stratégie Grains*
Russia	85.0	72.0	-15%	*Stratégie Grains*
Ukraine	26.7	24.6	-8%	SSSU
Kazakhstan	14.6	14.3	-2%	*Stratégie Grains*

*USDA: WASDE data as of Dec. 12, 2018

For some countries the shortfall is already severe. In Russia, the wheat production is expected to be down 15%, for the EU block, 10%, and for Australia 20% over last year's 40% reduction.

These are big numbers, especially when one considers that we are still in the early stage of the diminishing solar activity, which causes the cooling, and which will increase for the next 30 years.

Australia had suffered a 40% reduction

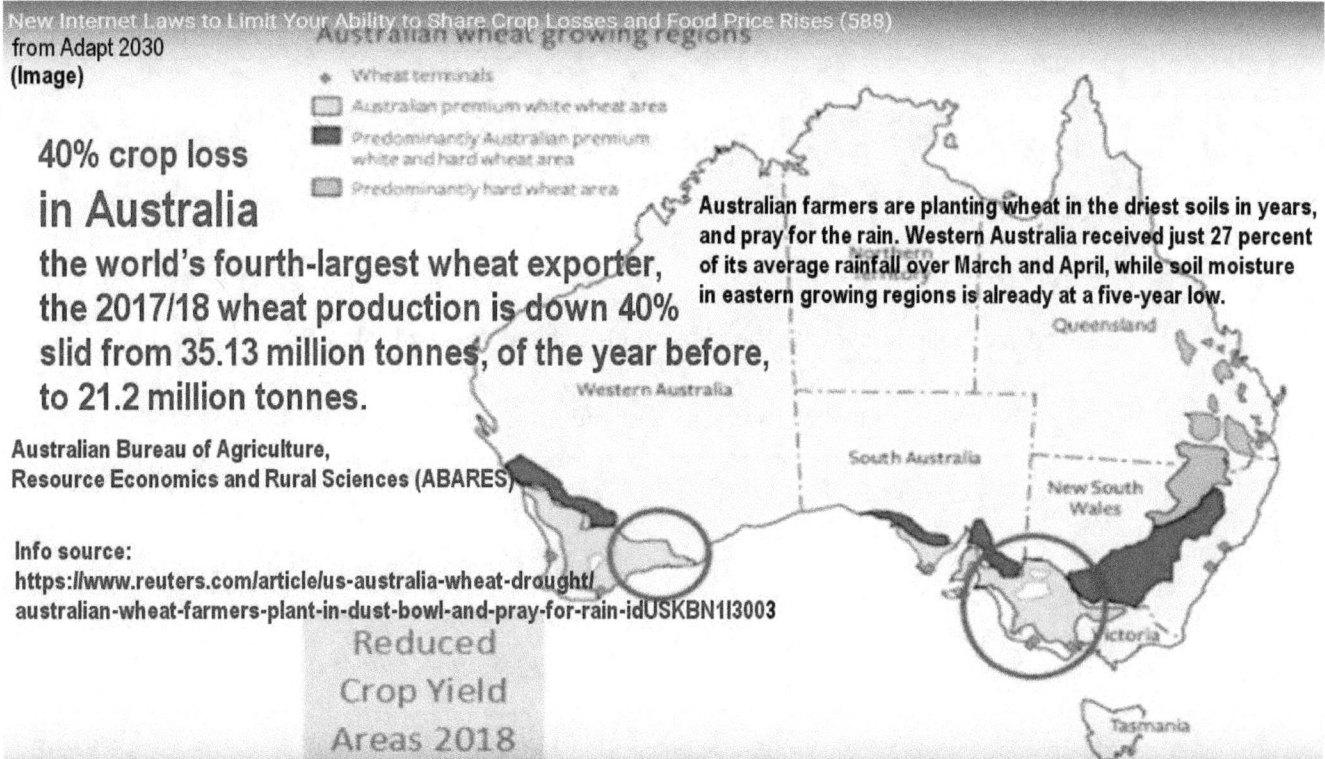

Australia had suffered a 40% reduction in wheat harvest in the 2017/18 season, due to climate effects caused by the solar system's diminishing dynamics.

Can we really know that the climate is forced by the Sun?

Can we really know that the climate on Earth is forced by the Sun?

> Let's look at the known Climate History,
> and compare it with the history of the Sun.

Can we really know that the climate on Earth is forced by the Sun?

Let's look at the known Climate History, and compare it with the history of the Sun.

The Earth warmed up with the increasing solar activity

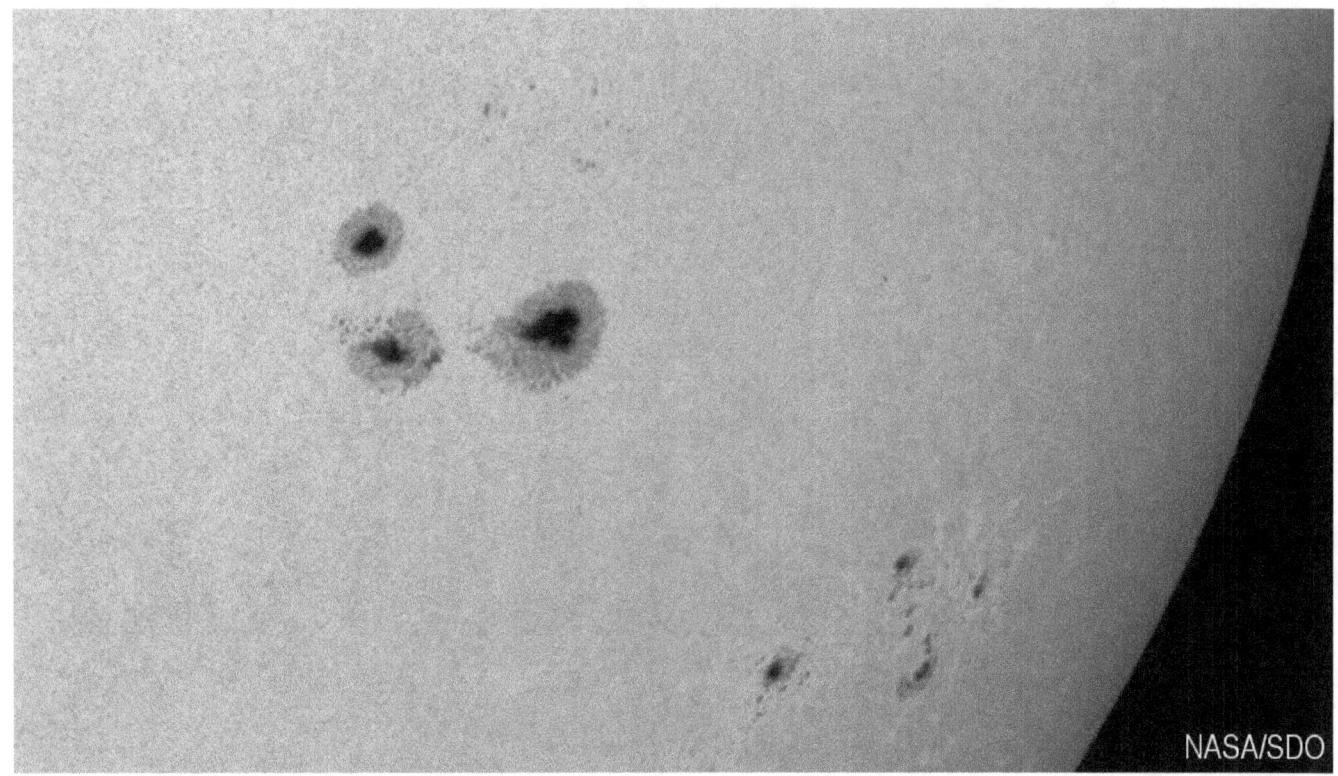

We know from historic climate records that the Earth has warmed up tremendously after the end of the Little Ice Age. We also know from historic sunspot records that the solar activity has ramped up tremendously during the same timeframe. No sunspots had been observed for decades during the Little Ice Age of the 1600s. Then the sunspots came back from 1715 onward and increased evermore, and the Earth warmed up coincidental with the increasing solar activity.

The climate on Earth is linked to solar activity

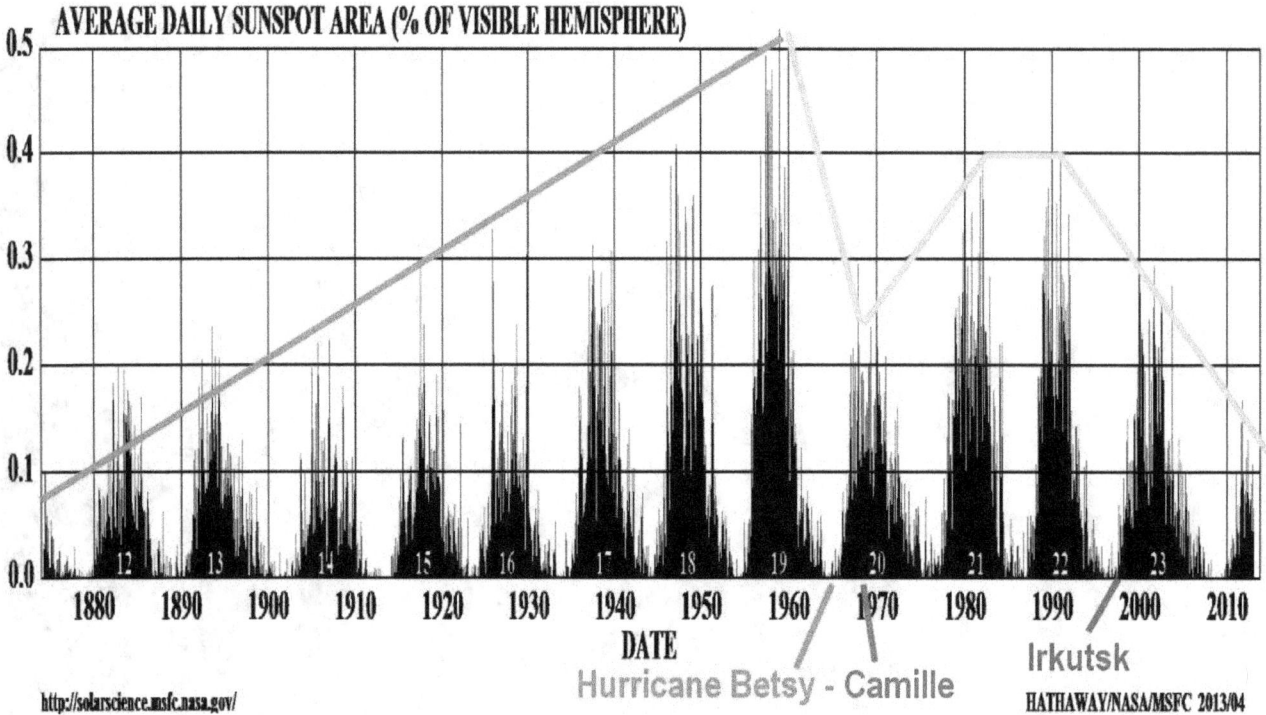

Now we have huge numbers of sunspots again, at least we had so in the late period of solar global warming between the 1960s and the late 1990s.

With the high numbers of sunspots that we had in this period, which correspond to high-intensity solar activity, the experienced climate on Earth was also the warmest in modern history. The matching relationship proves rather conclusively that the climate on Earth is linked to solar activity.

The Sun emits cosmic-ray flux

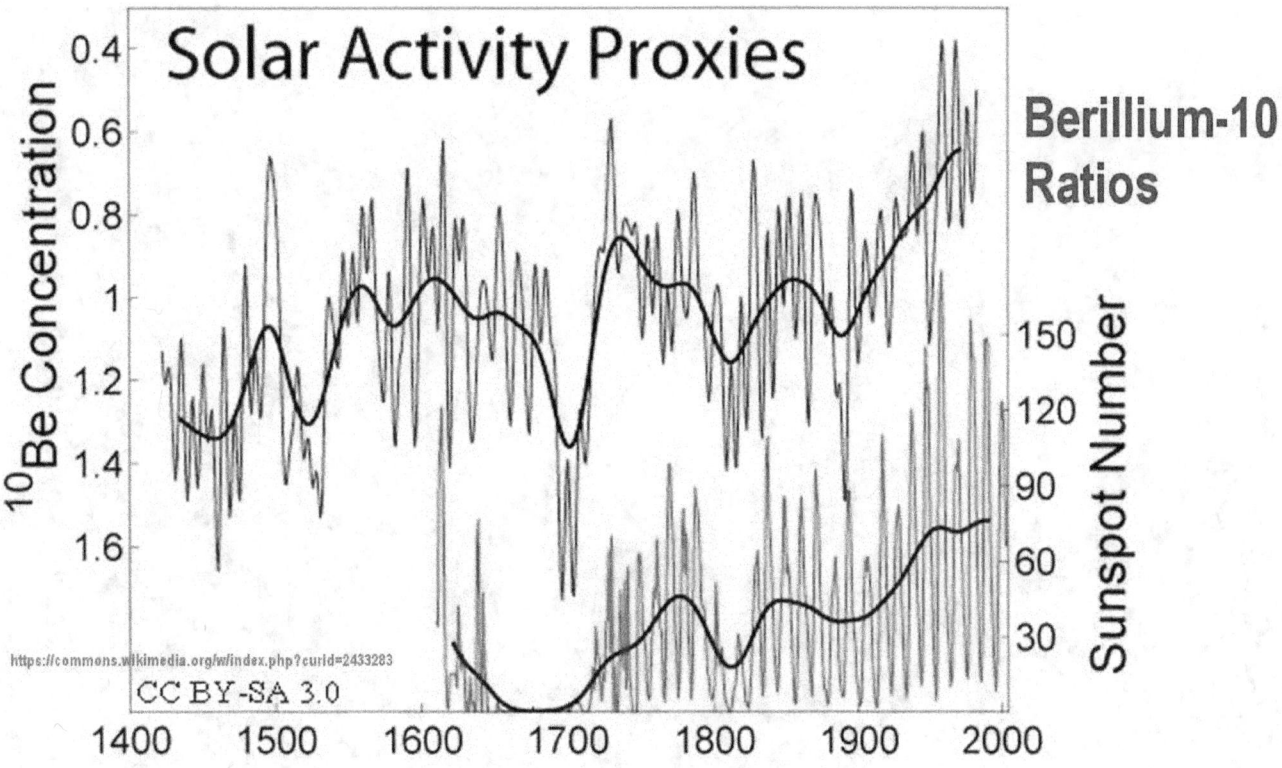

It has also been discovered that the Sun emits not only light and and heat, but also emits cosmic-ray flux in an inverse relationship to its solar activity. The inverse relationship results, because in times when the solar activity is high, the Sun is surrounded with a denser plasma corona where much of the solar cosmic-ray flux is trapped. It has been discovered that the historic solar activity can be measured, by measuring the presence of a rare radio-isotope that is produced by cosmic-ray interaction with the atmosphere. The historic ratios of this isotope, closely match the historically counted sunspot numbers, and the historically known climate pattern.

This tells us that changing solar activity intensity affects the Earth atmosphere with changing cosmic-ray flux, which in turn affects the Earth's climate by affecting the cloud forming process.

The CERN laboratory CLOUD experiment

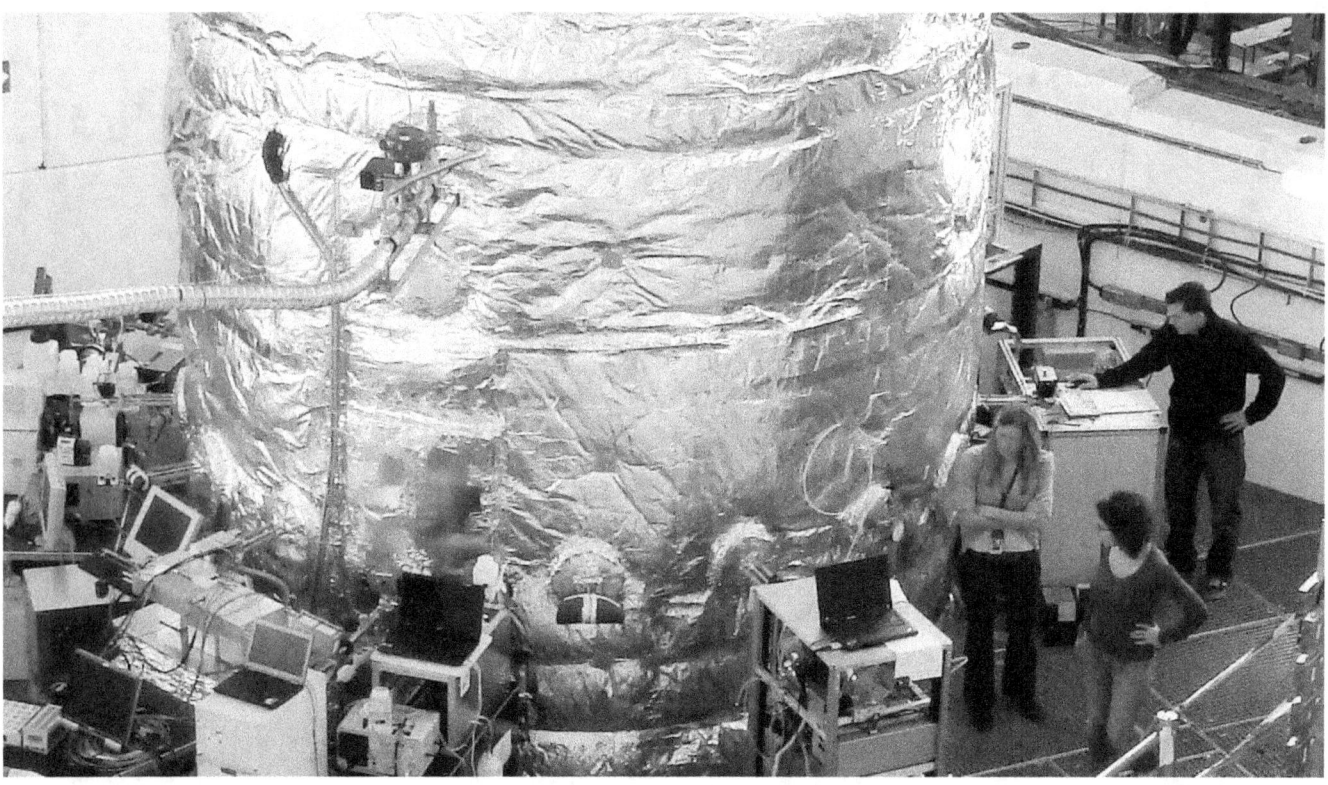

How big the effect is of cosmic-ray flux affecting our atmosphere, has been explored at the CERN laboratory in Europe, with the CLOUD experiment. A large test chamber had artificial cosmic rays injected, and the effects were measured.

When the cosmic-rays were turned on

When the cosmic-rays were turned on, the measured aerosol nucleation went straight up and off the chart, which proves in principle that solar cosmic-ray flux has an enormous effect on the cloud nucleation in our atmosphere.

Changing solar activity has huge affects on our climate

This means that when the solar activity is low, by which solar cosmic-ray flux is high, the cloud forming process is more intense. As a consequence the Earth becomes colder, because increased cloudiness reflects a larger portion of the incoming sunlight back into space, which becomes lost to the heat budget of the Earth. By this interaction, changing solar activity has huge affects on our climate.

Sunlight absorbed in the ultraviolet band by oxygen and by the scattering effect

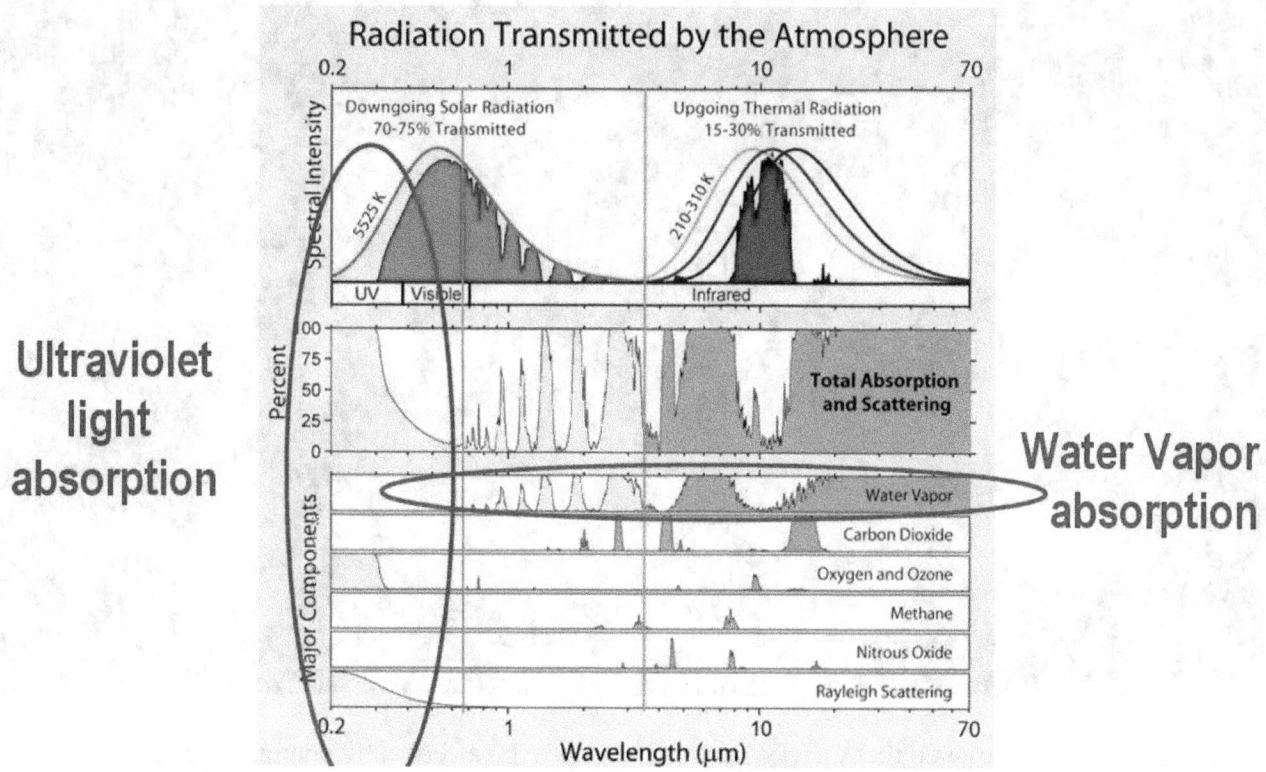

Another effect of solar activity on our climate is located in ultraviolet spectrum of the sunlight. It has been discovered that a large portion of the sunlight that is absorbed in the Earth's atmosphere, is absorbed in the ultraviolet band of the spectrum by oxygen and by the scattering effect.

The fluctuation as high as 23-fold

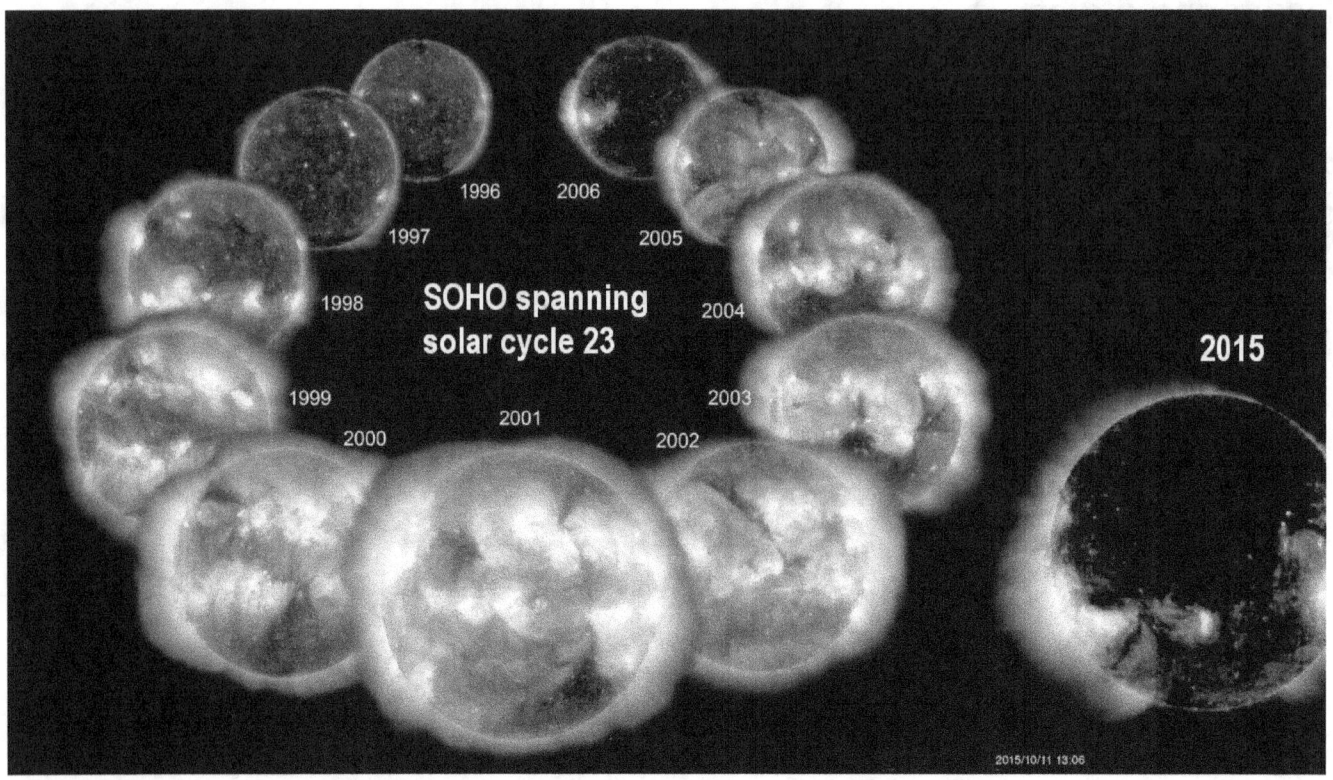

It has been further discovered that the UV band is the first to be affected by changing solar activity.

Satellite observation of the Sun in the Extreme UV band measured dramatic fluctuations of solar radiation over the span of a solar cycle. The fluctuation has been reported to be as high as 23-fold. By this principle, solar activity variations affect the climate by affecting the greenhouse of the Earth, while cosmic rays affect our climate by affecting cloudiness. These variations are big, while carbon gases affect almost nothing.

The images shown here are for solar cycle 23. The current cycle, cycle 24, is significantly weaker, with the next one likely becoming weaker still. This means that the Earth is getting colder, and will continue to cool evermore.

Solar Global Warming is reversing

300 years of Solar Global Warming (in C14) is reversing

Almost 300 years of Solar Global Warming is reversing

Our modern civilization developed during solar global warming

Changing solar cosmic-ray flux, measured in carbon-14 ratios, shows direct inverse relationship with known cold-climate events

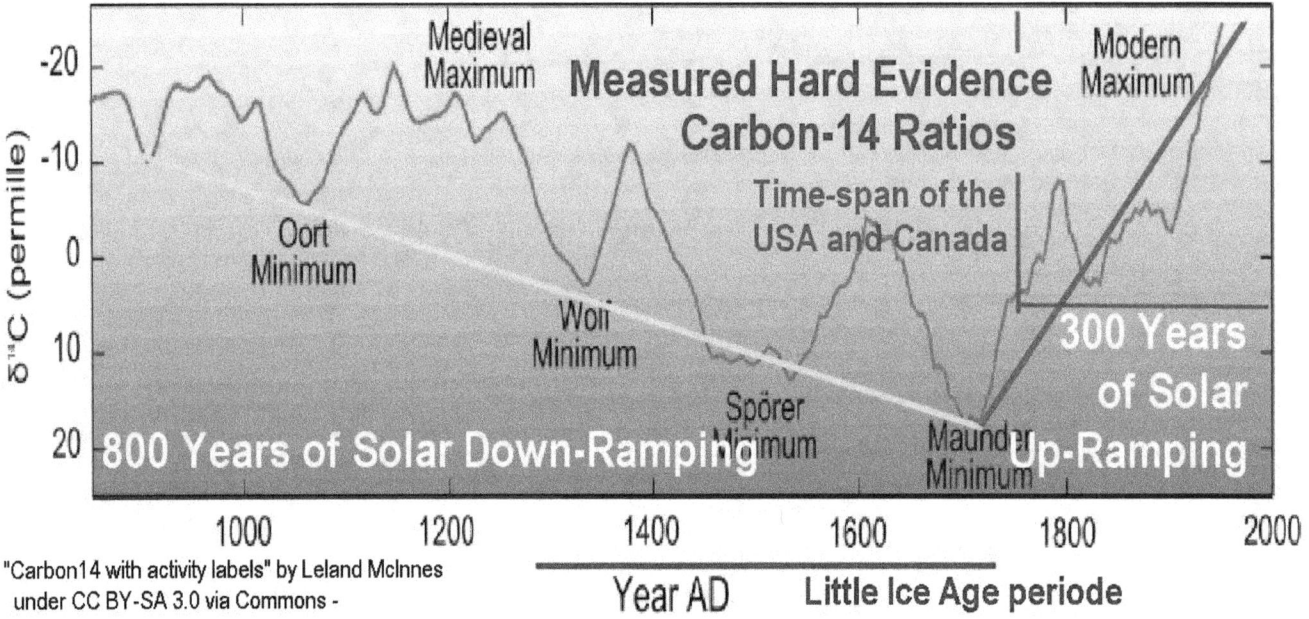

"Carbon14 with activity labels" by Leland McInnes
under CC BY-SA 3.0 via Commons -

The cooling of the Earth affects agriculture. Note, our entire modern civilization developed during the 300-years period of solar global warming. The USA and Canada were formed during this period.

Solar activity is diminishing at a 5-times faster rate

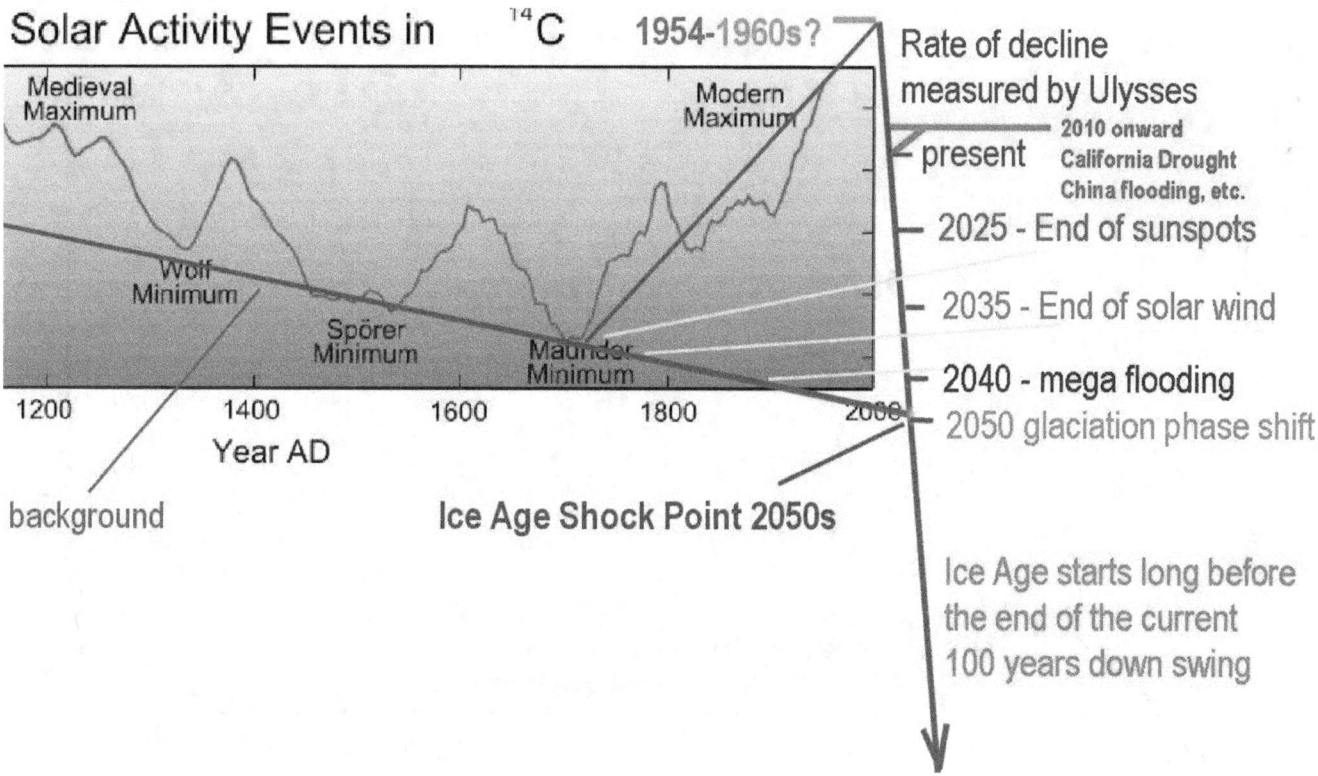

This means that our food-production capability that is rooted in global warming agriculture, is fast reversing, because solar activity is fast diminishing. As I will demonstrate later, solar activity is diminishing at a 5-times faster rate than it was ramped up during the solar global warming period. This fast-rate climate collapse affects the entire world population.

It took humanity 200,000 years to grow to half a billion

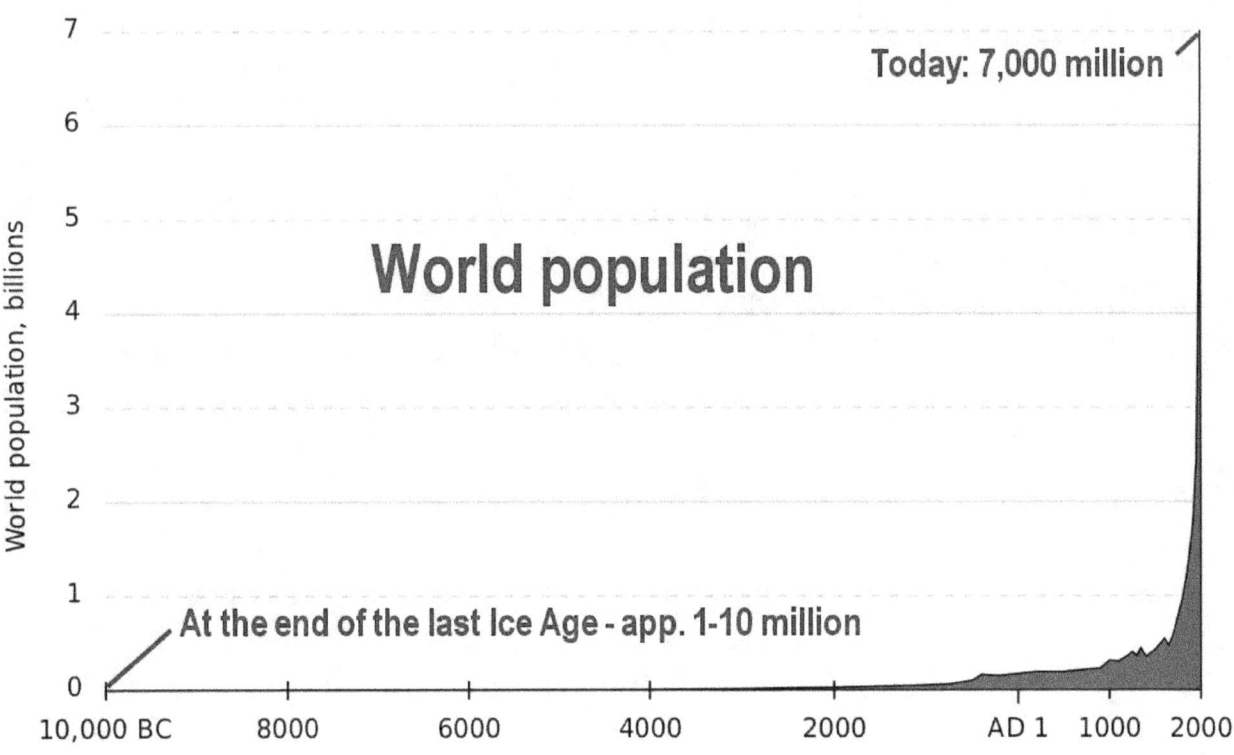

It took humanity 200,000 years to grow in numbers to half a billion people that we had in the 1600s, and only 300 years thereafter, to reach 7 billion level that we have today.

Population increase during solar global warming

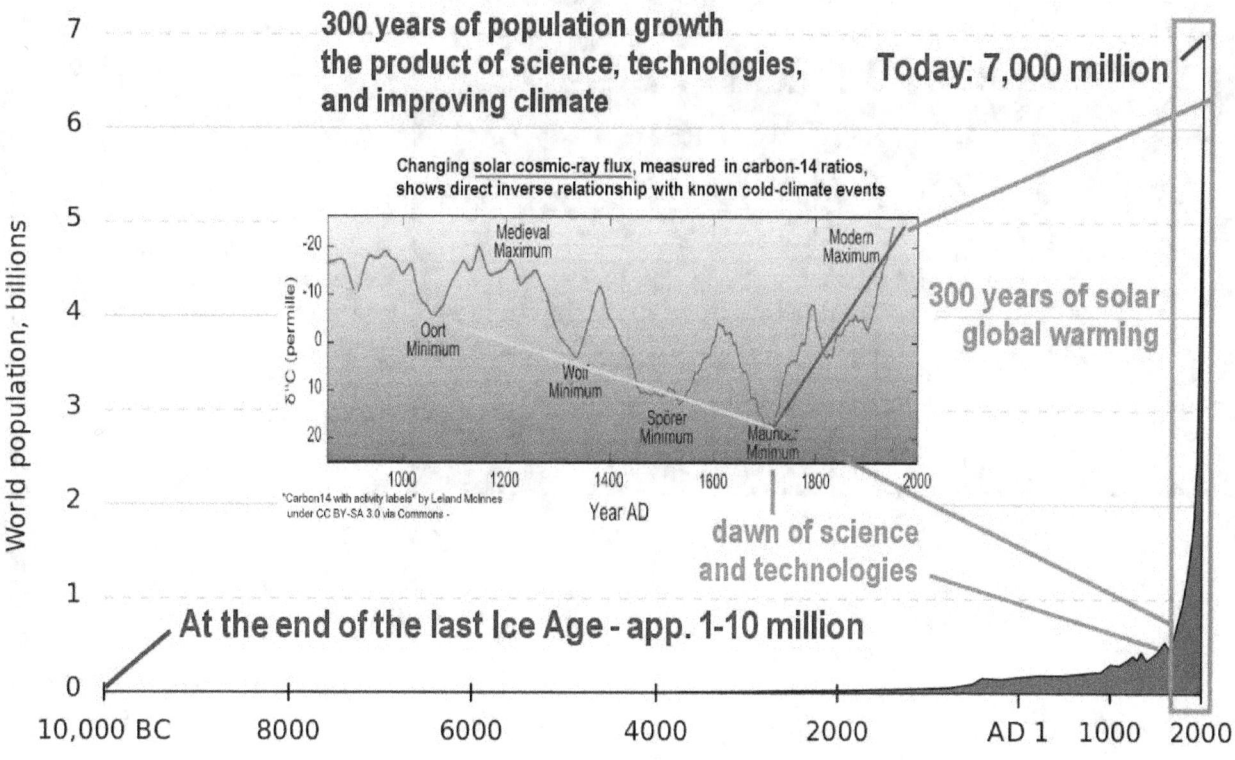

The enormous population increase occurred during the 300-years period of the grand solar global warming that ended the Little Ice Age.

Humanity grew from 660 million to 7,000 million in 300 years of global warming, and with scientific and technological progress happening in the background. Both factors flowing together gave rise to our modern civilization.

The climate warming is a bigger contributing factor

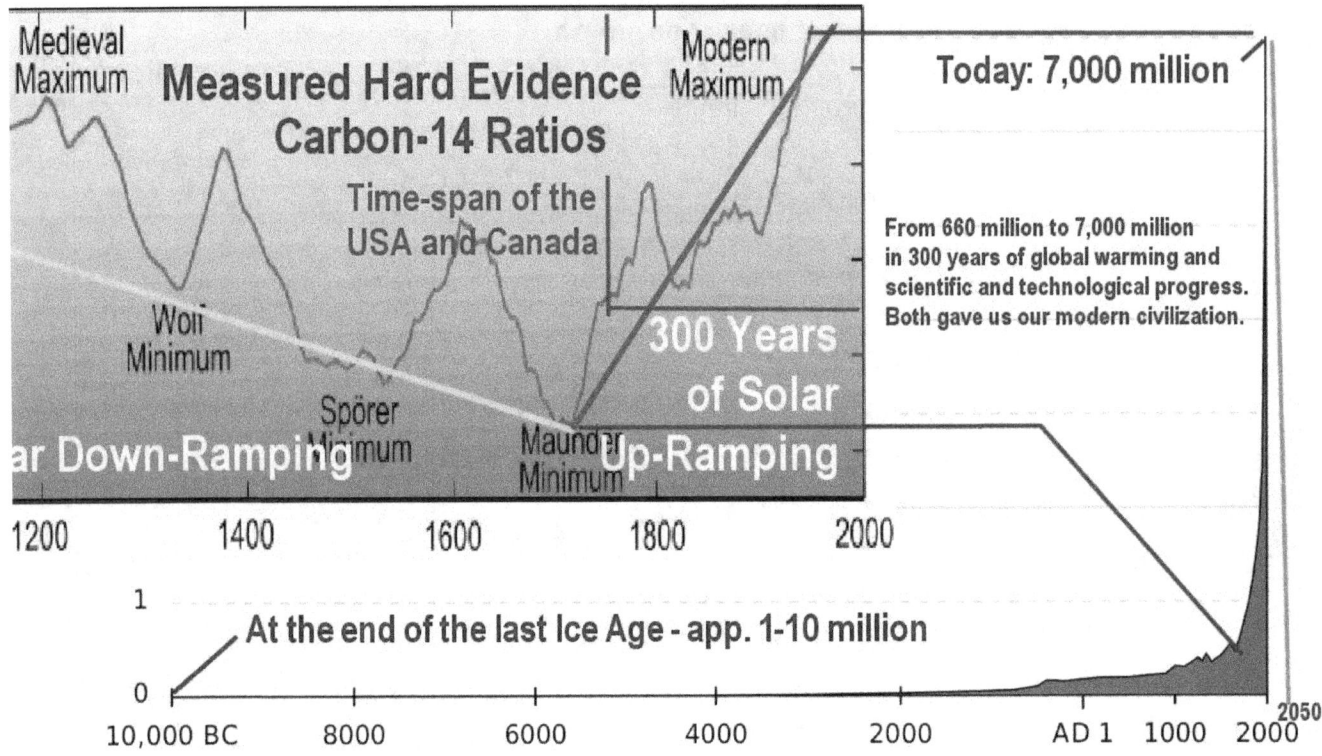

Evidently the climate warming is a bigger contributing factor than we generally realize. During the cold of the Little Ice Age, agricultural production had been so deeply depressed that people had resorted to cannibalism in some areas.

The dynamics that gave us the rich harvests are now reversed

Wheat harvest on the Palouse, Idaho, USA

Food for eating!

wikipedia

Now, at the end of the solar global warming period, we have enough food available on the Earth to nourish 10 times as many people than we had when the warming began.

However, the dynamics that gave us the rich harvests are now reversed. The reversal happened in the late 1990s. Solar activity, and with it our climate, are now collapsing 5 times faster than they had ramped up.

The up-ramping and of the subsequent collapse

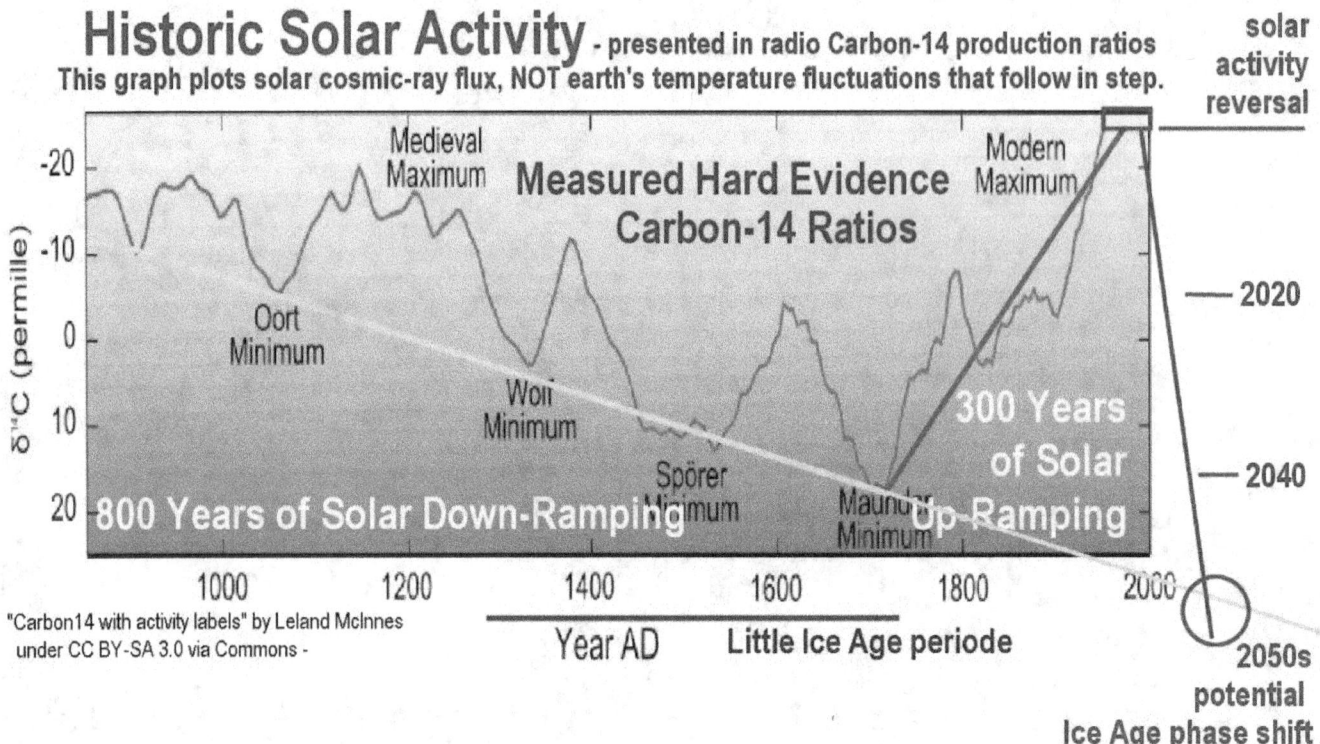

The solar activity gain, and with it the climate gain, of the entire last 250 years period up to the 1960s, which leveled off till the 1990s, is now reversing at such a rapid rate that the entire global warming gain will be lost by the 2030s or 2040s, and the loss be superseded in the 2050s when the Ice Age phase shift potentially begins.

The up-ramping of the historic solar activity has been measured in Carbon-14 isotope ratios until the dawn of the atomic bomb, that also produces Carbon-14, had obsoleted the process.

After the solar activity reversal, the rate of collapse in solar activity was measured by the Ulysses spacecraft in terms of diminishing solar-wind pressure.

Both the rate of the up-ramping and of the subsequent collapse are quantified by technological physical measurements. The measurements tell us that the global-warming that we have enjoyed, especially from 1900s on, in which modern civilization had developed, was a solar-caused anomaly that is now rapidly ending.

Solar Collapse, Measured by the Ulysses Spacecraft

Solar Collapse, Measured by the Ulysses Spacecraft

Solar Collapse, Measured by the Ulysses Spacecraft

Solar-wind pressure diminishing at 30% per decade.

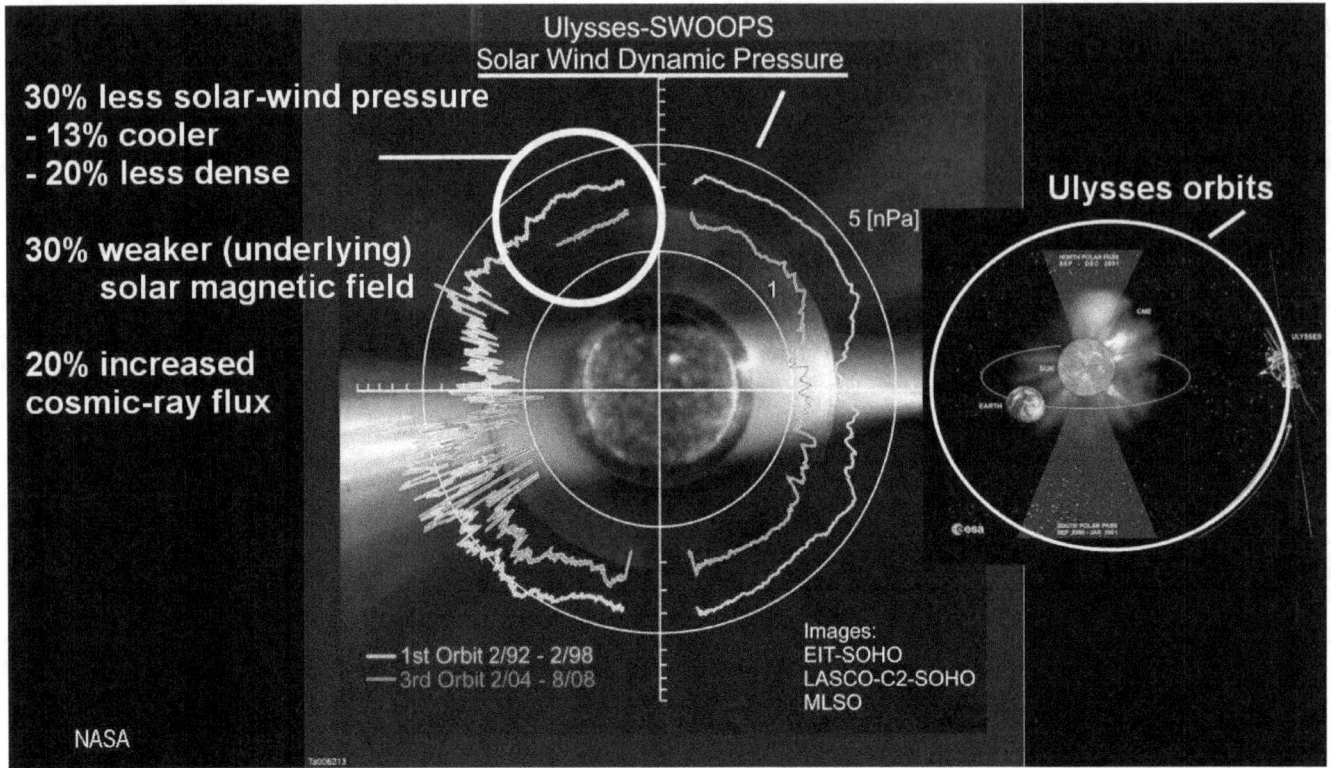

The Ulysses spacecraft flew 3 polar orbits around the Sun between 1994 to 2008. It measured the solar-wind pressure diminishing at a rate of 30% per decade.

The Sun venting off excess plasma pressure

Maximum temperature
of liquid water
at ambient pressure
is 100 degrees Celsius:
The Boiling Point

The Sun venting off excess plasma pressure in the form of solar wind is comparable to a kettle venting off steam. When the energy input is reduced, the steam diminishes and stops. On the Sun, the solar wind diminishes and then stops, for much of the same reason.

If one projects the measured rate forward

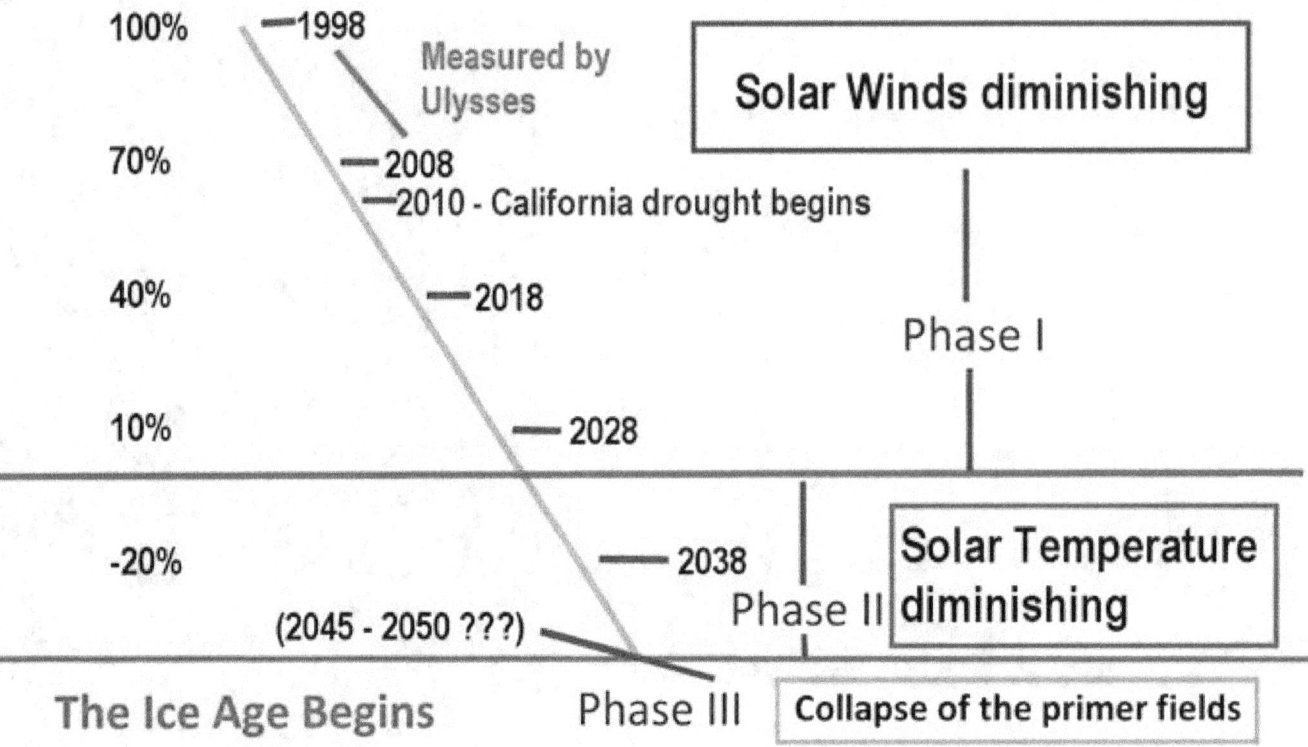

If one projects the measured rate forward, the solar wind will cease in the 2030s. After that the solar temperature will being to diminish until the Primer Fields for Sun collapse and the Ice Age phase shift happens, potentially in the 2050s. The Ulysses spacecraft was the first to quantitatively measure the rate of the solar activity collapse.

The same rate of collapse in diminishing sunspot numbers

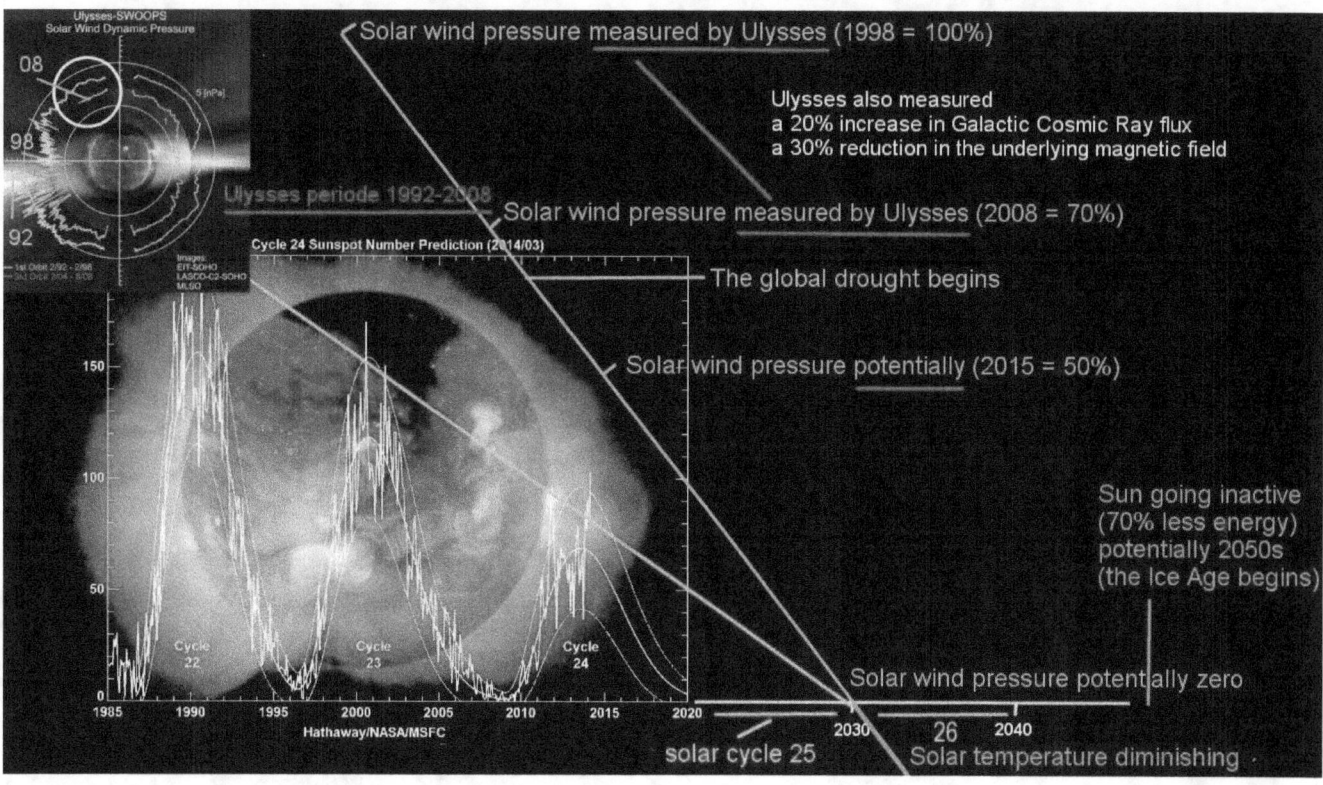

We see the same high rate of collapse also reflected in diminishing sunspot numbers, as one would expect, because both reflect solar activity.

Proof of Solar Cosmic-Ray Flux

Proof of Solar Cosmic-Ray Flux

Proof of Solar Cosmic-Ray Flux

The 30% rate of collapse in solar activity by the Moscow Neutron Monitor

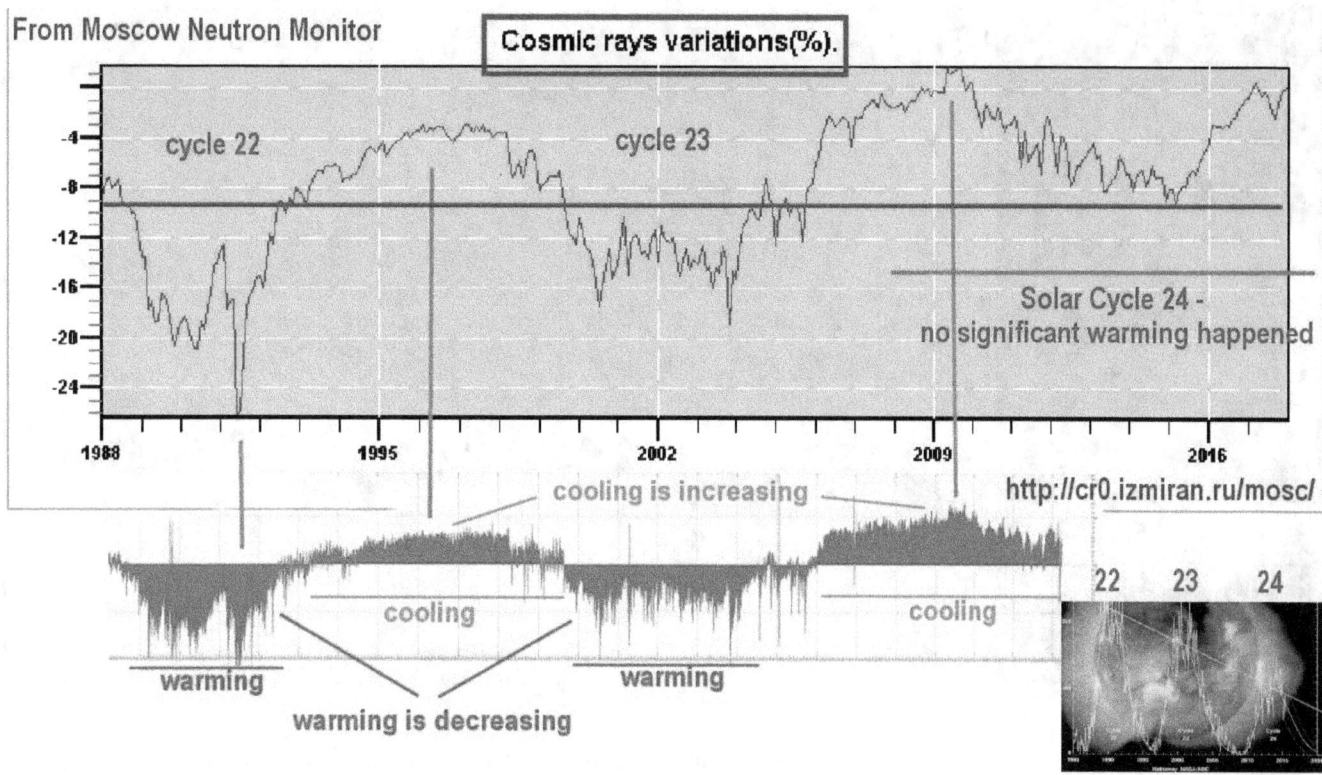

We also see the 30% rate of collapse in solar activity, which Ulysses had measured, continuing on after Ulysses. We see the 30% per decade rate reflected in the form of increasing neutron-flux measurements conducted by the Moscow Neutron Monitor. We see in them increasing volumes of solar cosmic-ray flux being emitted. The increase results when the corona around the Sun becomes weaker, which traps cosmic-ray flux. The resulting increase in cosmic-ray flux is measured in the form of increasing neutron flux that cosmic rays generate.

The majority of the cosmic-ray flux is solar

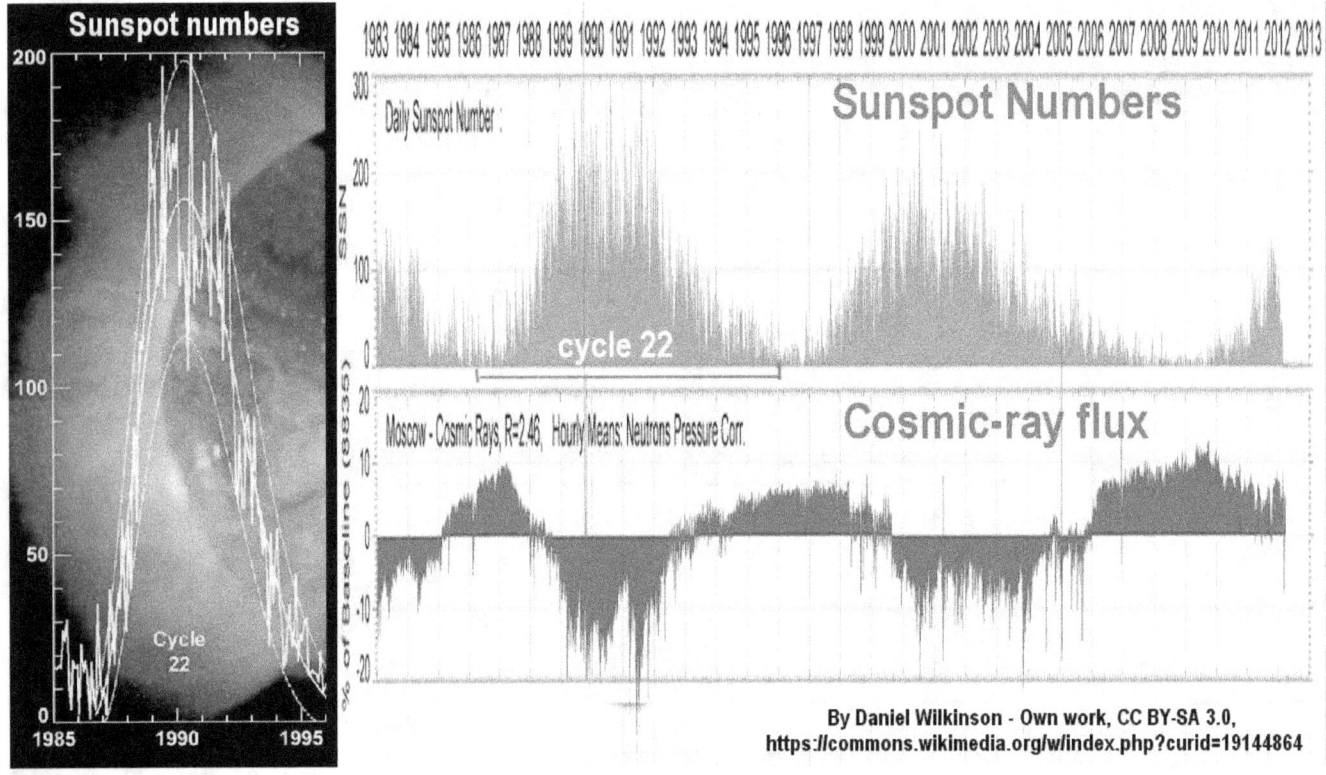

By Daniel Wilkinson - Own work, CC BY-SA 3.0,
https://commons.wikimedia.org/w/index.php?curid=19144864

That the majority of the cosmic-ray flux is solar, rather than galactic, in origin, is evident in the measured fact that the cosmic-ray variations follow the solar cycles.

Further proof that cosmic rays are mostly solar

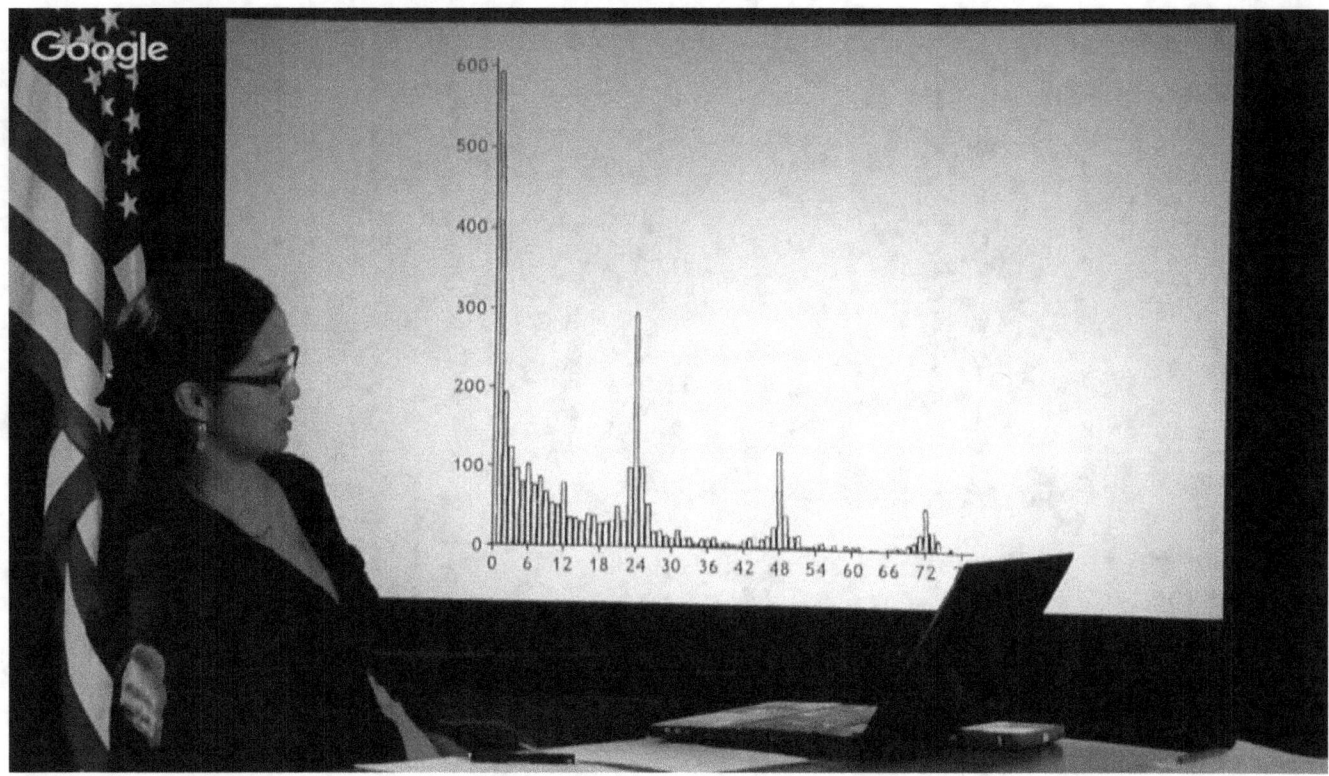

Further proof that cosmic rays are mostly solar, resulted from a chemical reaction experiment that was continually repeated in an identical manner. At one point large spikes in the reactivity were measured, occurring in 24-hour intervals according to the rotation of the Earth, but with the spikes diminishing according to the rotation of the Sun. It appears that a coronal hole occurred that had enabled large volumes of cosmic-ray flux to flow from the Sun, which became smaller in volume as the coronal hole turned away from the Earth.

Proof in the flash-flood event in May 2015

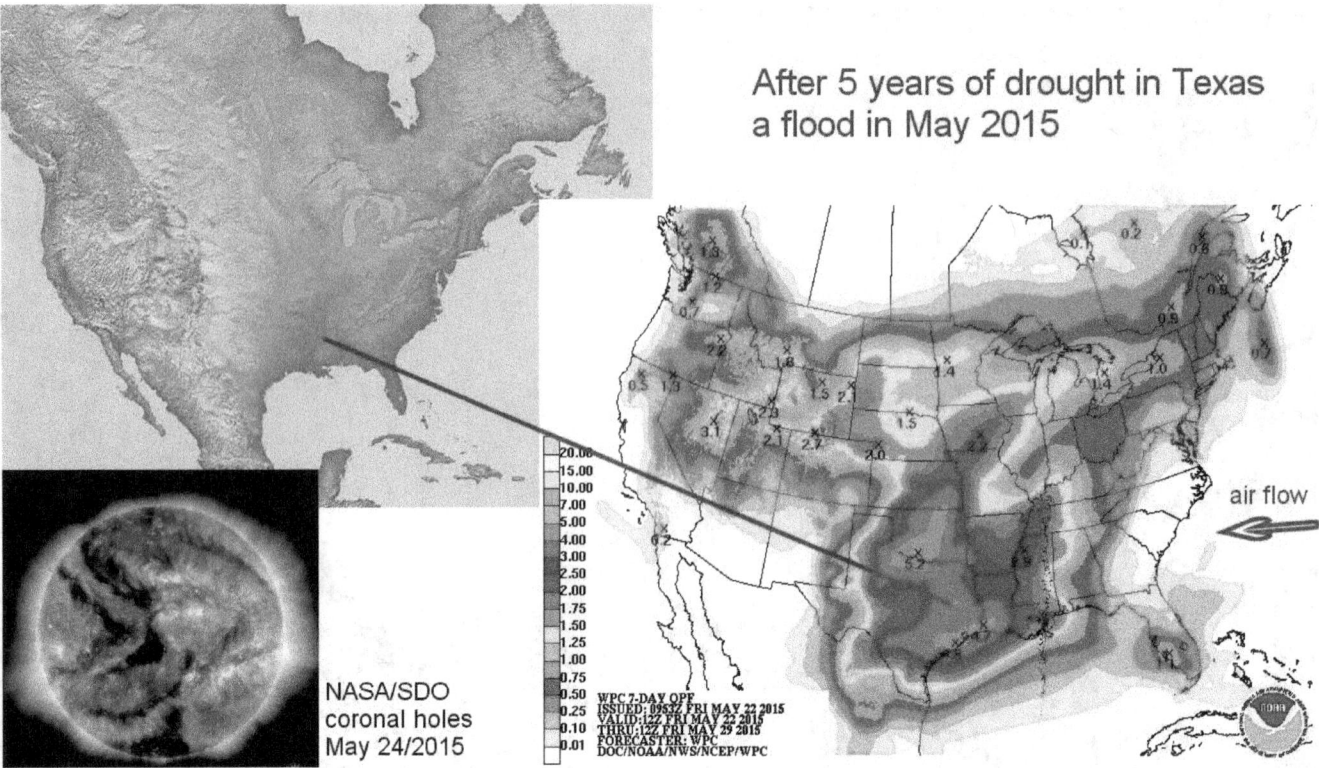

After 5 years of drought in Texas a flood in May 2015

NASA/SDO coronal holes May 24/2015

air flow

Another measured proof that coronal holes on the Sun emit large showers of cosmic rays that affect the climate on Earth, is evident in the reported flash-flood event in May 2015 at a time when some large coronal holes erupted on the Sun.

As solar cosmic-ray flux is now increasing

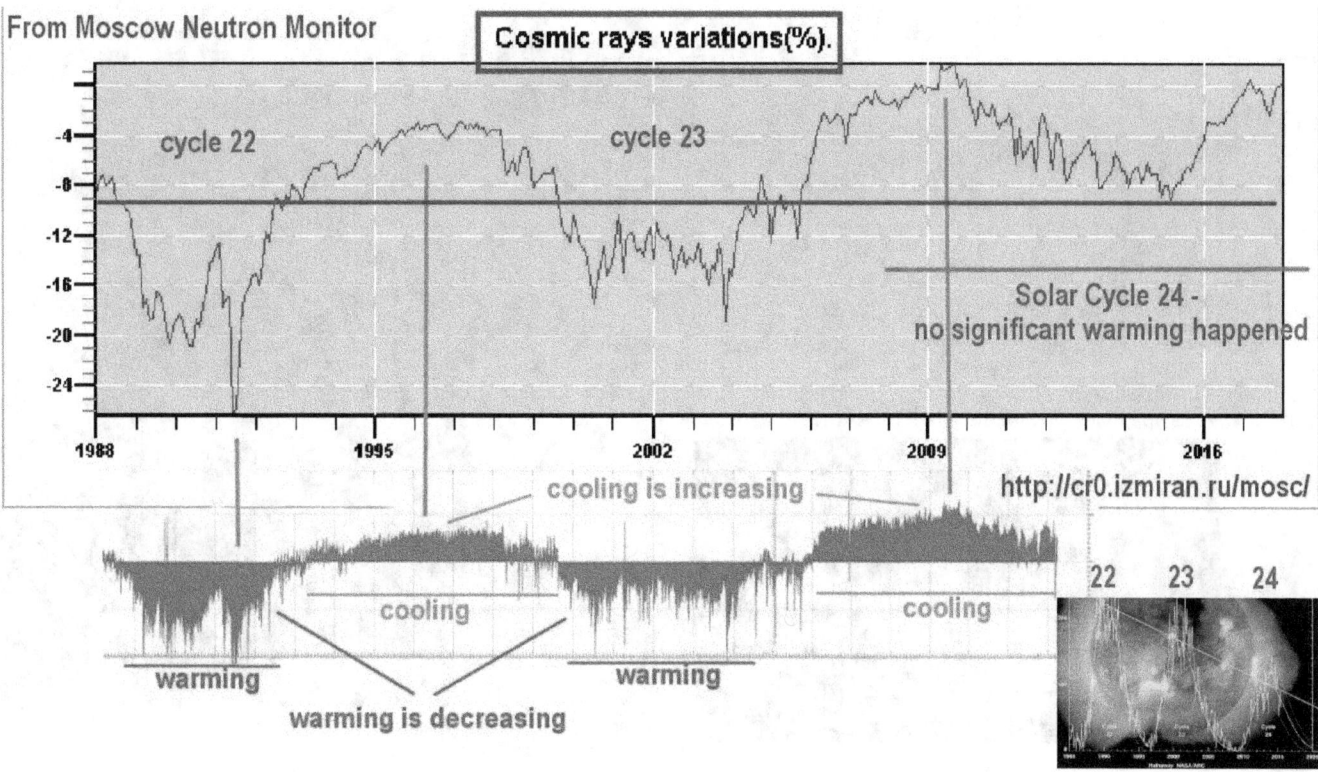

This means that as solar cosmic-ray flux is now increasing, with the weakening Sun, cloudiness is increasing accordingly, with the Earth becoming correspond colder thereby, year after year.

Continuing collapse of solar radio-flux measurements

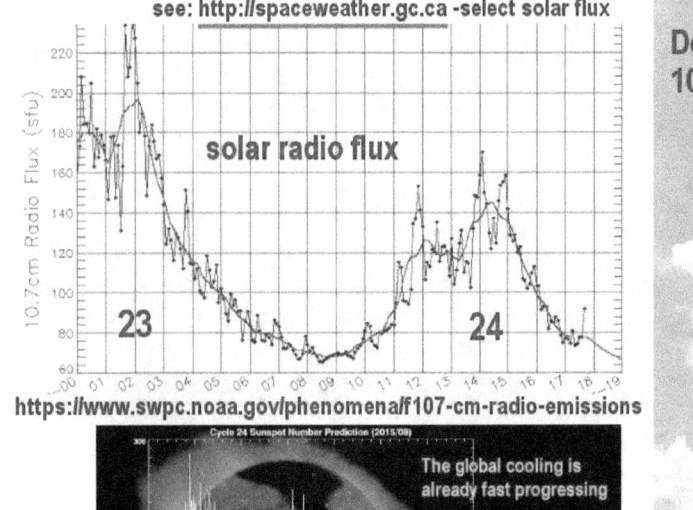

By Jjnishiyama at English Wikipedia, CC BY 2.5,
https://commons.wikimedia.org/w/index.php?curid=41186116

Another proof that the 30%-per-decade rate of collapse in solar activity that the Ulysses satellite, still continues, is evident in the continuing collapse of solar radio-flux measurements that have been reported.

One researcher who is familiar with the collapsing radio-flux measurements in the 10.7 cm band, had warned in a comment, 'the Sun is dying, you have 3 years to get out of Europe before they close the borders.'

The solar system's heartbeat is slowing down

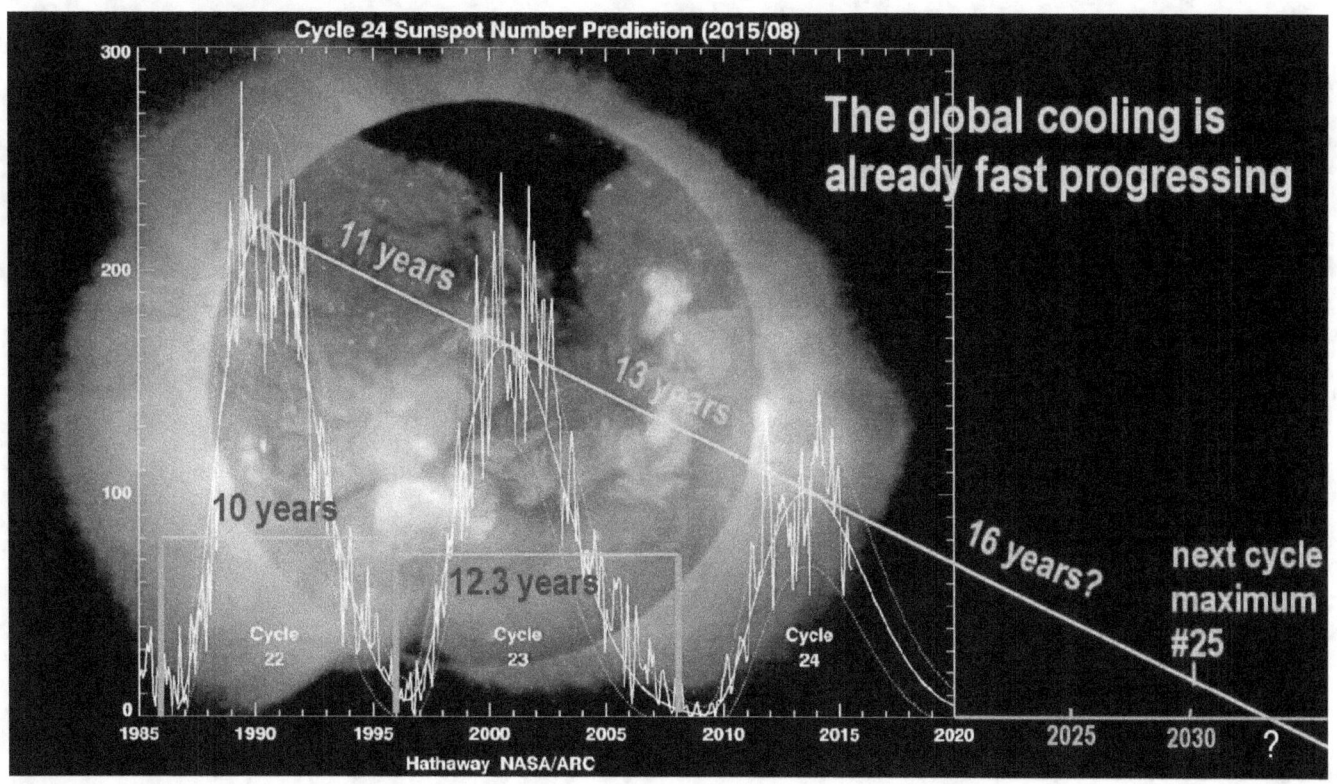

Of course, the Sun isn't actually dying. The Sun cannot die. However, the dynamics of the larger solar system that the Sun is a part of, are diminishing. The timing of the peaks of the sunspot numbers tell us that the solar system's heartbeat is slowing down. The 11-years solar heartbeat had slowed to 13 years, between the peaks of cycle 23 and 24. The next heartbeat may be as slow as 16 years per cycle, which is speculation, of course, though the dynamics of the current change point in that direction.

Physical measurements that quantify solar activity collapse

Physical measurements that quantify solar activity collapse

1	Ulysses spacecraft had measured 30% less solar-wind pressure in 10 years
2	Diminishing sunspot numbers (ongoing)
3	Moscow Neutron Monitor measuring increasing neutron flux (ongoing)
4	Solar Radio Flux Observatory measuring diminishing radio flux (ongoing)
5	Slowing solar cycle heart beat

Physical measurements that quantify solar activity collapse

1 Ulysses spacecraft had measured 30% less solar-wind pressure in 10 years

2 Diminishing sunspot numbers (ongoing)

3 Moscow Neutron Monitor measuring increasing neutron flux (ongoing)

4 Solar Radio Flux Observatory measuring diminishing radio flux (ongoing)

5 Slowing solar cycle heart beat

This means in summary that we have 5 different types of physical measurements on hand that all tell us in their own way that the Sun-caused global warming anomaly is over and is fast collapsing.

Of course, not all measurements are quantifiable in measurable terms, but are nevertheless significant.

Blizzard Xanto types of anomalies have become more frequent

Blizzard Xanto in April 2018, with its massive snow and deep minus temperatures, is evidence that the Earth cooling, though the rate of cooling is hard to quantify on this basis. These general types of anomalies, however, have become more frequent.

Australia's 40% reduction in wheat harvest

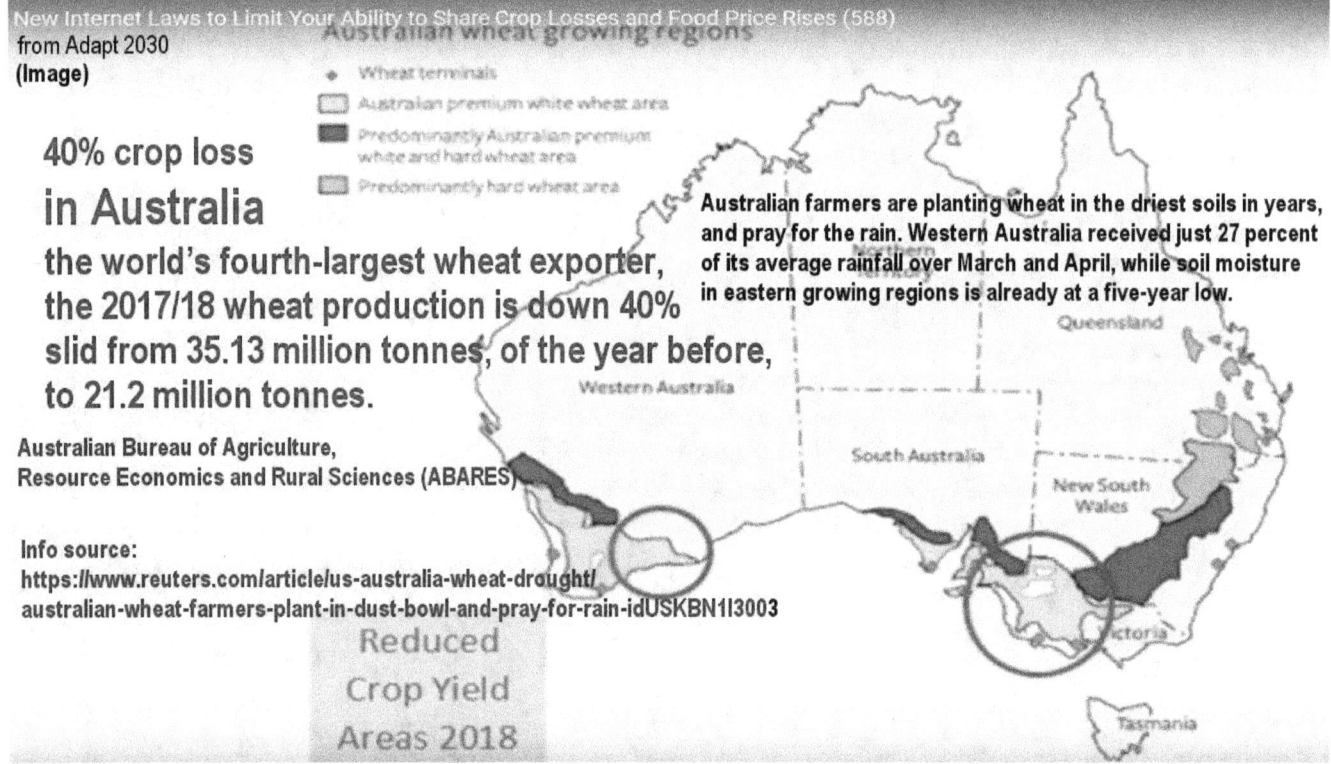

Reduced food production, like Australia's 40% reduction in wheat harvest in 2018, due to climate change, is another type of evidence that the earth is cooling, but cannot quantify the cooling itself. In the case of Australia the loss was caused by drought. Drought is caused when increased solar cosmic-ray flux ionizes clouds that thereby rain out faster and reduce water vapor that reduces the greenhouse protection.

Climate Recovery NOT Possible anymore

Climate Recovery NOT Possible anymore

Climate Recovery NOT Possible anymore

The chance for a cyclical climate recovery is zero.

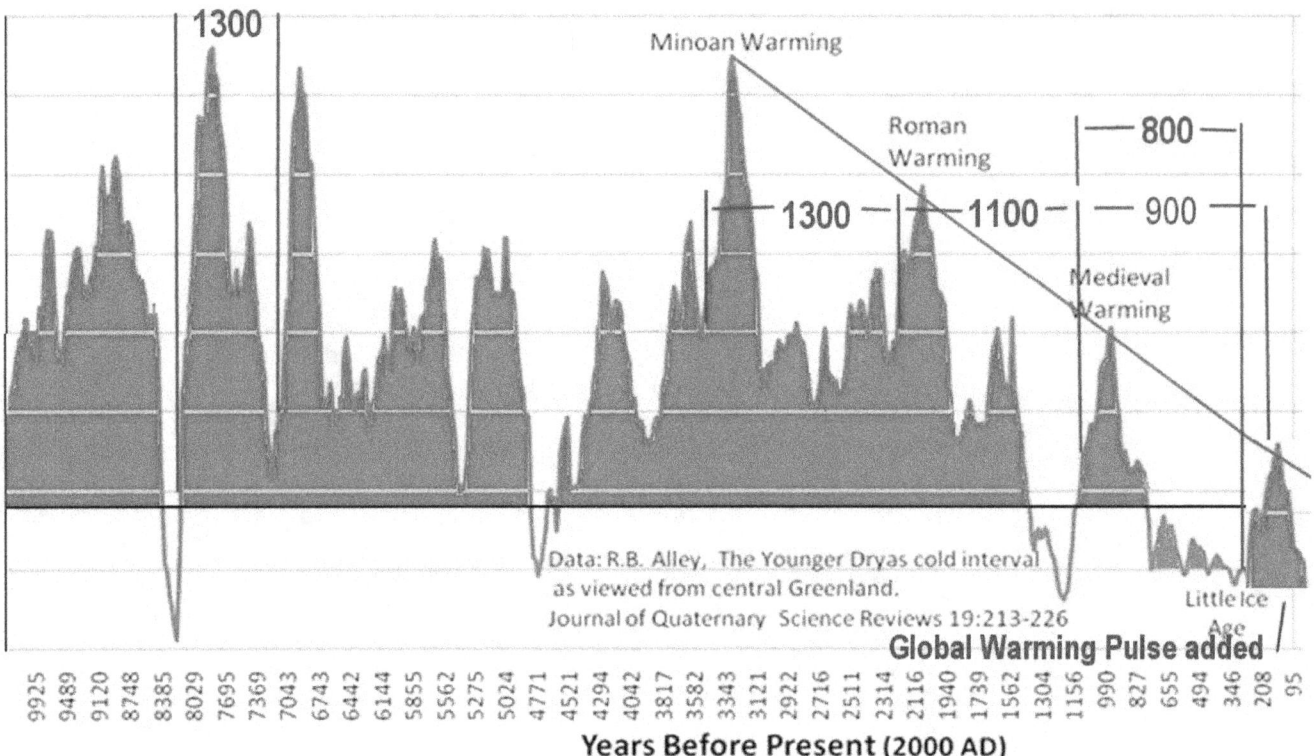

The chance for a cyclical climate recovery to happen is physically observable, although it is not quantifiable, because that chance for this to happen, is zero.

We see measurements conducted in ice that tells us that the big historic warming pulses have been diminishing over the last 3000 years, both in amplitude and in the length of their intervals. With the current global warming pulse being the 4th one in line, and it being quite small, we won't see another one of this type for a long time to come. The Ice Age phase shift will be upon us much sooner.

We are rushing towards the Grand Solar Termination

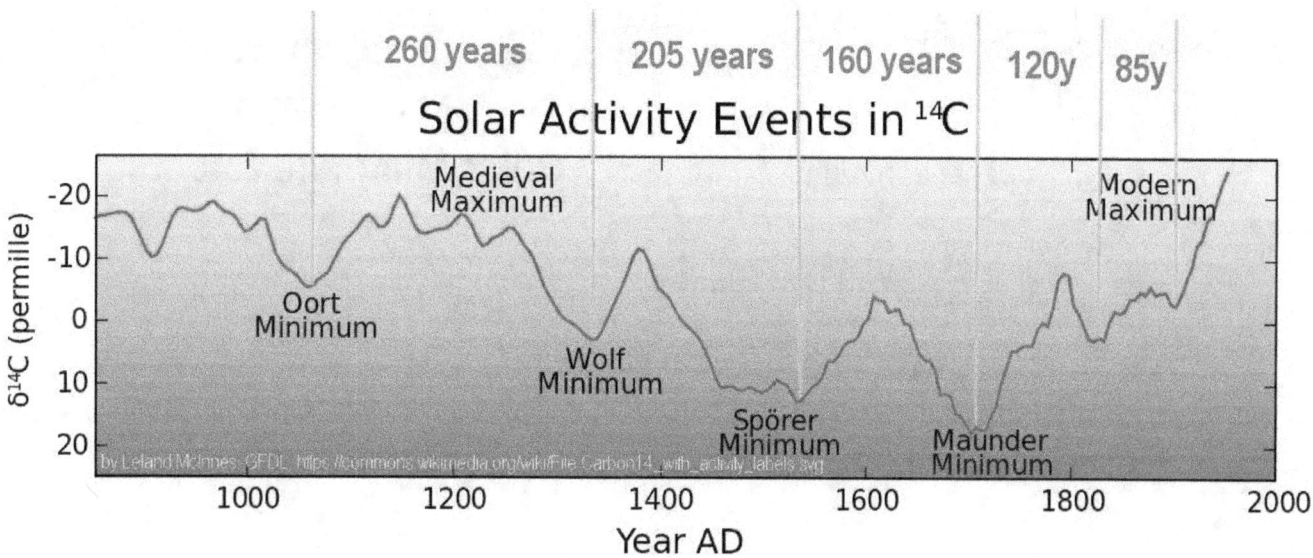

The historic 250-years climate cycles of the last 1,000 years that are associated with the little ice ages, have likewise diminished. The amplitude of their fluctuation has become extremely small. We are definitely not rushing towards another Grand Solar Minimum again, that we can recover from, such as the Maunder Minimum. Instead, we are rushing towards the Grand Solar Termination that ushers in the next Ice Age.

Diminished both in amplitude and intervals

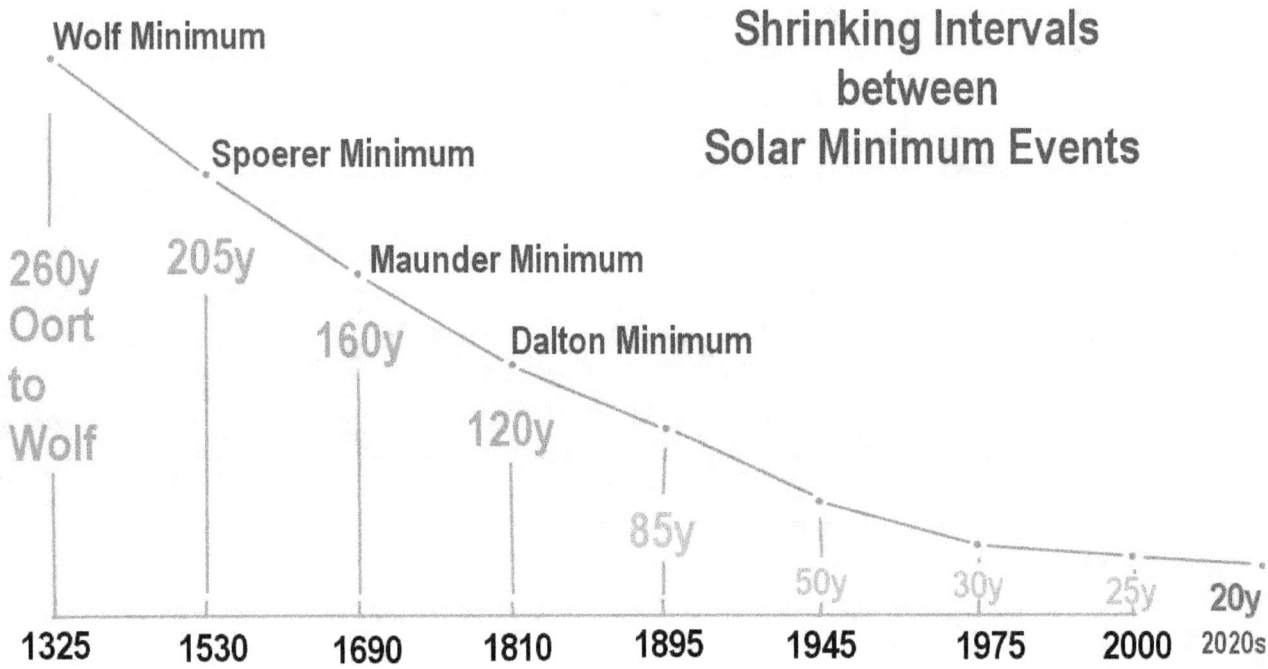

The short-term fluctuations have diminished both in amplitude and intervals. The intervals have become extremely short, and their amplitudes extremely weak. There is nothing left in this system too, that could give us a recovery from the now ongoing climate collapse.

When the current global warm pulse ends

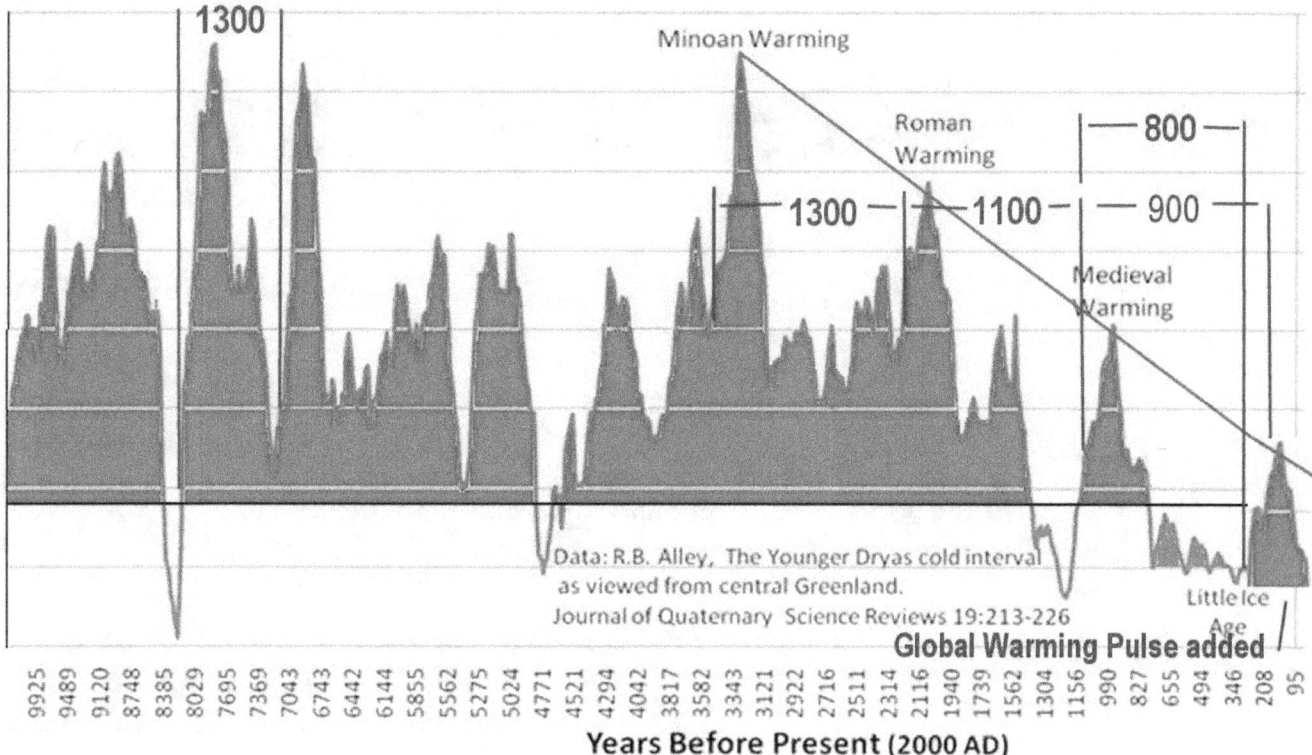

This means that when the current global warm pulse ends, that has pulled us out of the Little Ice Age and is now collapsing, no recovery will happen.

Interglacial Termination in the 2050s.

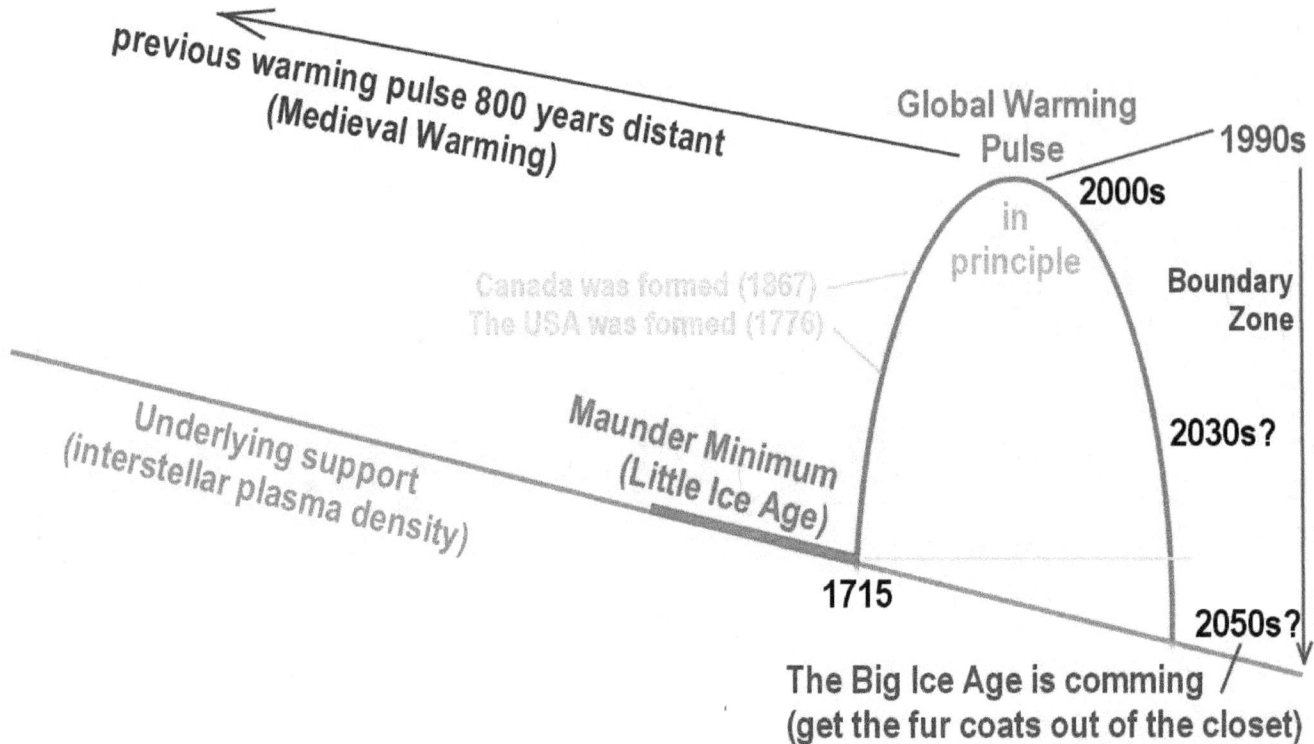

The collapse will simply continue towards the Grand Interglacial Termination, which will happen, potentially, in the 2050s.

Grand Solar Minimum is gone

Grand Solar Minimum
becomes the Ice Age

part 2:
Uncertainty

When climate explorers speak of a Grand Solar Minimum occurring, they assume that a recovery will follow. They assume that the Sun is its own master and will continue to cycle on as it had a thousand years ago when there was a lot of life left in the solar dynamics. But all this is gone. The Sun is not its own master. It is mastered by external conditions that are rapidly becoming weaker. The advertized assumption that a cyclical recovery will occur, which isn't possible anymore, has tragic consequences, because that dreaming of a recovery prevents the building of a real solution, the building of a climate-independent New World.

The world will be in deep trouble without a New World

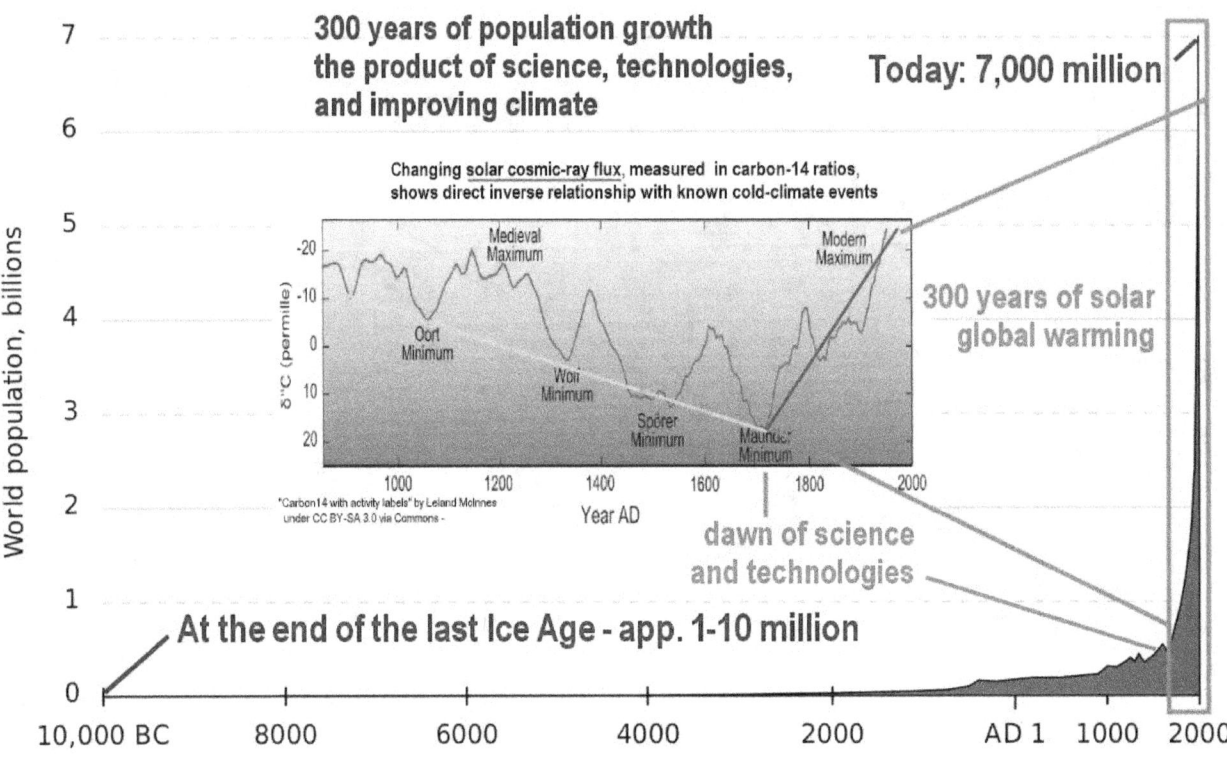

The world will be in deep trouble when the current climate collapses to the termination point, without a New World having been built along the way, because then the wonderful warm climate that has enabled us to become a 7 billion world population, will collapse into deeply cold Ice Age conditions.

Right now we find us still enjoying the benefits of the last 300 years of global warming that ended only 20 years ago. However, we are at the beginning of what might be called the boundary zone towards the next Ice Age phase shift. In this boundary zone the world is getting colder with increasing drought conditions, year after year, for another 30 years, potentially. In the boundary zone, agriculture as we know it, ends. But what will happen to our 7 billion world population in the boundary zone? The answer depends on us all, in today's time. Will we build us a New World?

One way or another, it can be said with certainty, that we haven't seen anything yet.

The writing is on the wall

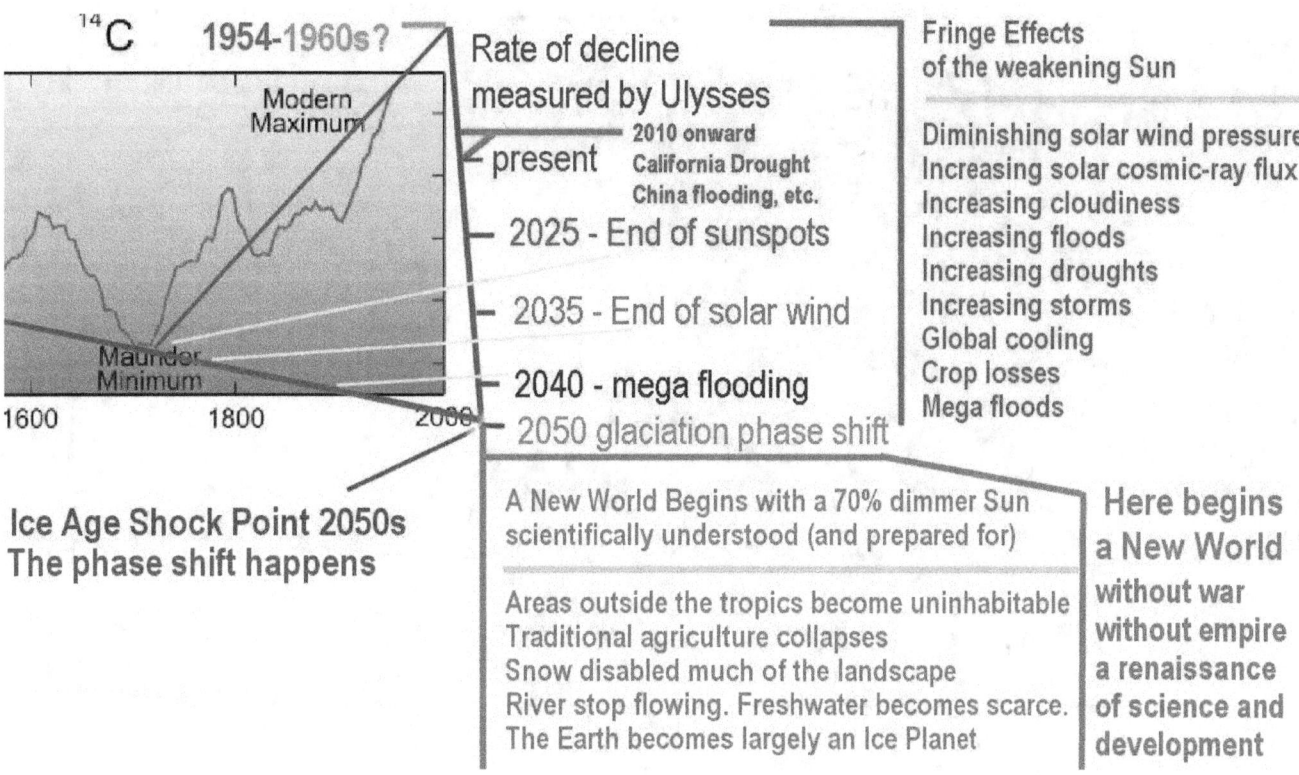

This means, the writing is on the wall. If we don't have a new world built with indoor agriculture in the tropics, by the time the collapse becomes critical, the 7 billion world population that we have become, will then expire by starvation.

Unless we put the 'spate into the ground' and start to build

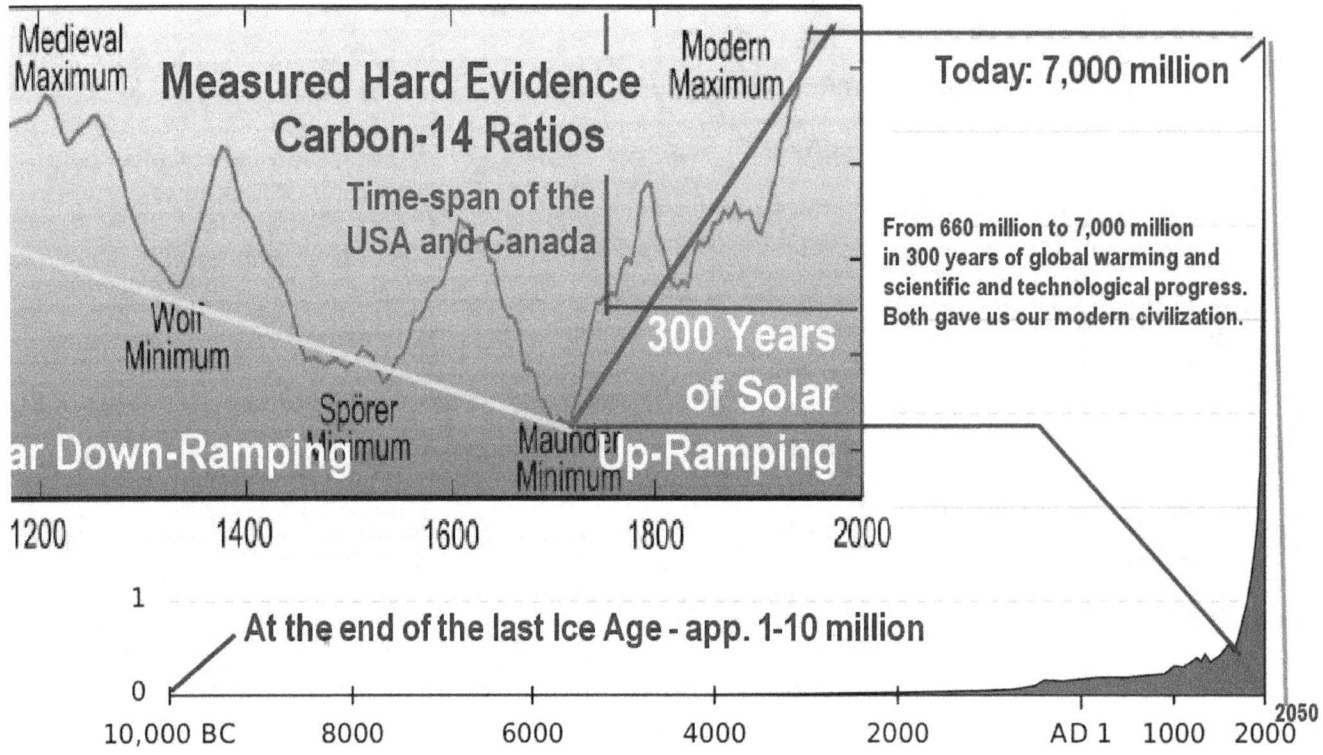

Almost all of modern civilization has developed during the global warming anomaly. The world population has increased 10-fold in this 300-years period of global warming. Both Canada and the USA were formed quite early during the upswing of it.

Unless we put the 'spate into the ground' and start to build us a technological New World that the climate collapse cannot touch, everything that had been achieved, that we have become, our entire 7 billion people world civilization, will collapse without recourse with the collapsing climate. A recourse is only possible BEFORE the collapse begins. The window of opportunity is still open, but it appears to be closing fast.

Building a Climate-Independent New World

Building a Climate-Independent New World

Building a Climate-Independent New World

Fortunately there is now hope on the horizon

Donald Trump

45th President of the United States of America
inaugurated, January 20, 2017

If the New World infrastructures have not been built and are operational when the large-scale agriculture collapse happens, which will affect wide areas simultaneously, worldwide population collapse will result by starvation. This collapse will be MANMADE, if it happens. It will be the consequence of political inaction in our time.

It will be a MANMADE consequence of the type of political actions that presently prevent the necessary World Bridge construction to become considered and implemented at the present stage while time is running out. The current political environment all across the "Climate Change" front has these types of suicidal consequences for as long as the mental environment is not uplifted onto the level of reality, while time remains.

Fortunately there is now hope on the horizon on this front, with a Presidential Committee on Climate Science becoming formed that might yet succeed, at the near-term stage, to raise the banner of truth.

While the truth is presently, officially, declared 'dead' in climate science, or "settled" as it is now called - settled in the coffin of grand fakery - it can be raised to life again. It appears to be not possible for the truth to become violated with fakery and lies under political will, in the long run, because reality remains what it is and asserts its claim.

Society may have been politically forced to close its eyes to reality, but it cannot avoid the consequences that ultimately speak louder than politics. And so it appears that people are waking up. They most certainly will awake when the food supply is beginning to collapse, as is now faintly happening. Then even the politically 'dead' are bound to be roused into action. Hopefully this will happen while the chance remains to create solutions before food riots will erupt in the streets.

With this in mind, it appears that there is a political movement unfolding towards sanity in our time, and perhaps just under the political horizon. The awakening movement towards sanity appears to have enabled the American President - President Trump - to propose, or to order, the launching of a truth-finding commission, named the Presidential Committee on Climate Science. That's what the Washington Post has reported on February 20, 2019.

It evidently takes a great deal of political courage by President Trump to make this type of proposal, considering the colossal outrage the proposal would immediately stir up among the Democrats, among the climate campaigners, and among the vast scene of renewable energy interests and related interests who profit immensely from the currently operating 2 trillion dollars per year, global Climate-Hoax Industrial Complex.

And even at that, should the Presidential Committee on Climate Science actually be formed against the choruses of opposition voices from the climate change profiteers, the committee might not have the courage to address the real climate change issue head on, which is the ongoing cooling of the Earth, and the diminishing food production resulting as a consequence, for which the evidence is already glaringly real and has been measured in numerous different ways.

Debate meaningless details of meaningless lies

Poster of the Climate Conference.
Licensed under Fair use via Wikipedia

COP 21: Heads of delegations by GUSTAVO-CAMACHO-GONZALEZ - Licensed under CC BY 2.0 via Commons by Presidencia de la República Mexicana -delegates

It is likely that without public support for the truth, the selected committee will debate meaningless details of meaningless lies, as had been done at the Paris Climate Change Conference, for reasons that it is politically risky in the sciences to speak the truth. If the truth would matter to society, there would be no debate happening at all, because the case of the truth is clear. It is well known in the sciences that CO2 - the politically postulated villain - is not a climate factor in real terms.

Choosing the future while we still can

Choosing the future while we still can
suicide versus renaissance

... with blinded eyes	... with truth known and acknowledged
Climate Collapse	World Bridge - New World
Drought	Worldwide Water Distribution
End of Agriculture	Climate Independent Agriculture
Economic Collapse	Economic Miracle Civilization
Nuclear War	Universal Love Superseding War

Choosing the future while we still can

suicide versus renaissance

... with blinded eyes

... with truth known and acknowledged

Climate Collapse- World Bridge - New World

Drought - Worldwide Water Distribution

End of Agriculture - Climate Independent Agriculture

Economic Collapse - Economic Miracle Civilization

Nuclear War - Universal Love Superseding War

Segment 3 - Carbon, Climate, and the Sun

Segment 3 - Carbon, Climate, and the Sun

Part 1	The Towers and the Mouse (the real CO2 story)
Part 2	Who Speaks for the Biosphere?
Part 3	Ice Ages are Radical Events - like falling off a cliff
Part 4	Who Speaks for the Sun?
Part 5	Ice Ages are Digital Events
Part 6	Proof of the Hibernating Sun

Segment 3 - Carbon, Climate, and the Sun

Part 1 The Towers and the Mouse (the real CO2 story)

Part 2 Who Speaks for the Biosphere?

Part 3 Ice Ages are Radical Events - like falling off a cliff

Part 4 Who Speaks for the Sun?

Part 5 Ice Ages are Digital Events

Part 6 Proof of the Hibernating Sun

The Towers and the Mouse

The Towers and the Mouse

The Towers and the Mouse

Absorption coefficient of CO2 is TEN-times SMALLER

Compare the K values: 10 - 30 for CO2 vs. 100-600 for water vapor (H2O)

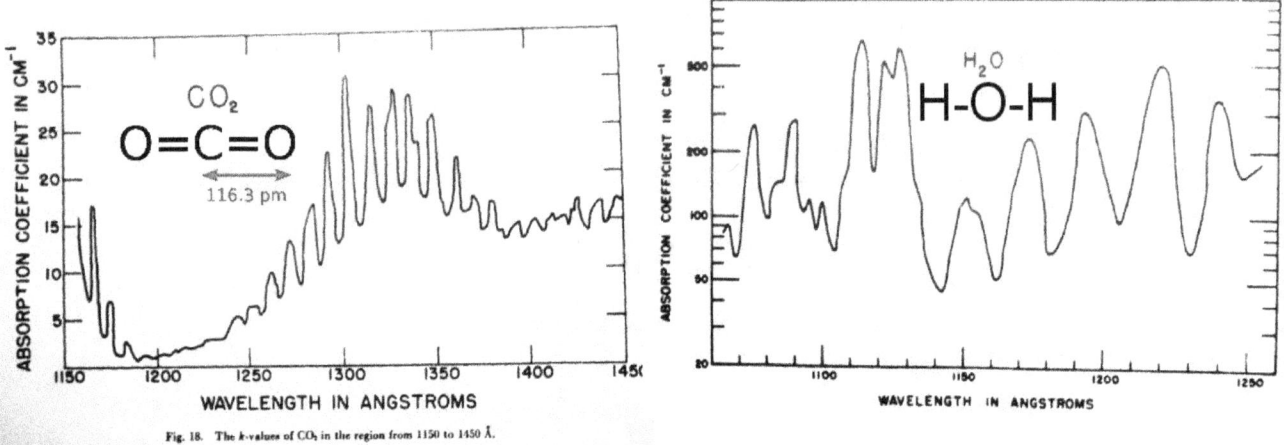

Fig. 18.   The k-values of CO₂ in the region from 1150 to 1450 Å.

From a 1953 study by the Geophysics Research Directorate of the Air Force Cambridge Research Center Cambridge, Massachusetts - http://www.dtic.mil/cgi-bin/GetTRDoc?AD=AD0019700

It is well known that the thermal absorption coefficient of CO2 is TEN-times SMALLER than that of water vapor - just compare the numbers - with water vapor being the main greenhouse gas, while water vapor itself is 100 times more-abundant in the atmosphere than CO2.

CO2 responds only in a few narrow bands

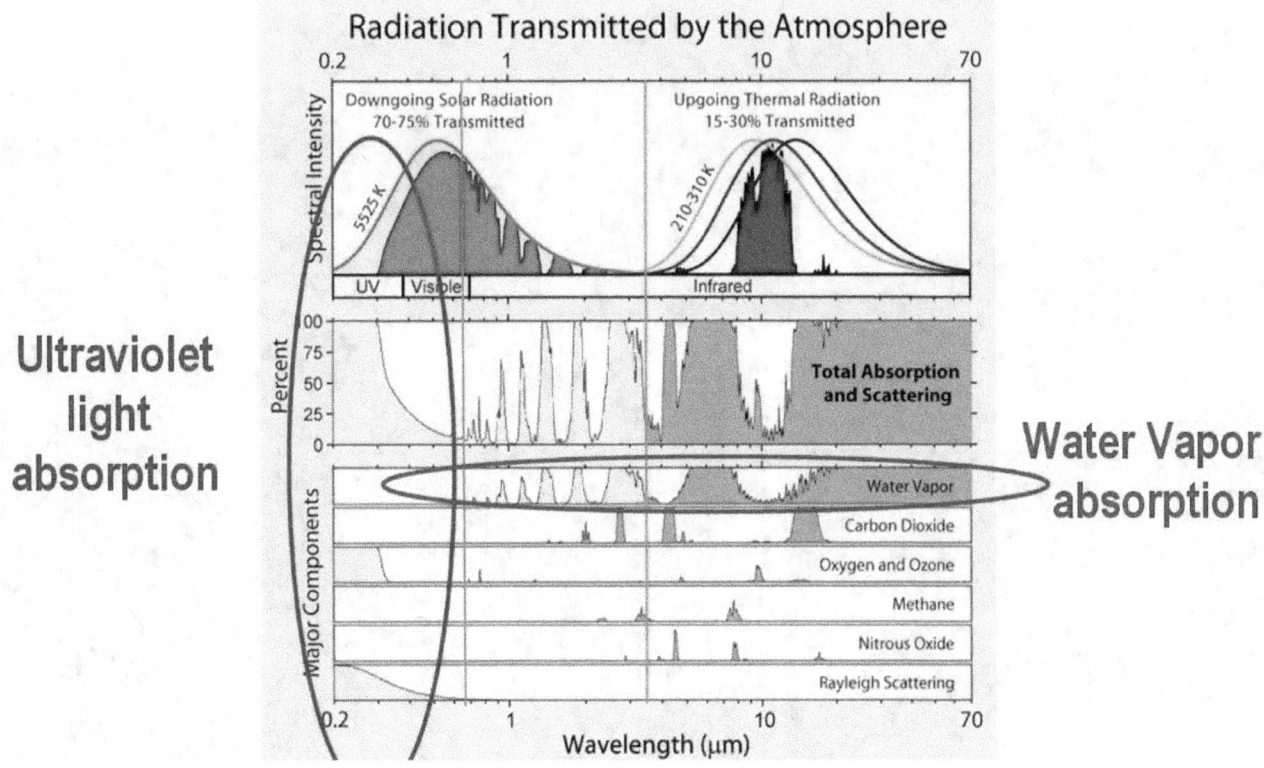

It is furthermore well known that CO2 responds only in a few narrow bands of the light spectrum, and at the low-energy end, while water vapor responds almost across the entire spectrum.

In addition CO2 is far overshadowed by the energy abortion of oxygen and the Raleigh Scattering effect at the high-end of the spectrum, which itself varies with solar-activity levels.

The entire CO2 contribution to the greenhouse effect

New York City Skyline - World Trade Center - wikipedia
A work of the United States Federal Government

If one puts the carbon-gas reality into perspective, the entire carbon-gas greenhouse effect adds up to being no larger than a cat in comparison with the late World Trade towers of New York City. And in comparison with the cat that represents the entire CO2 contribution to the greenhouse effect, the manmade portion of it adds up to be no bigger than a small mouse sitting on the back of the cat. A mouse is insignificant on this vast scene.

And even if it was miraculously possible to overfeed the mouse to become the size of a horse, it would still be insignificant in the overall landscape.

It certainly would not justify the USA spending the proposed 93 trillion dollars by 2030 to keep the mouse as small as it presently is, which the Green New Deal demands, based on lies.

The truth of the total greenhouse effect, which the towers represent, is that the vast majority of it, in the high 90% range, is generated by the thermal absorption of water vapor.

Water vapor effect, is strongly affected by solar cosmic-ray flux

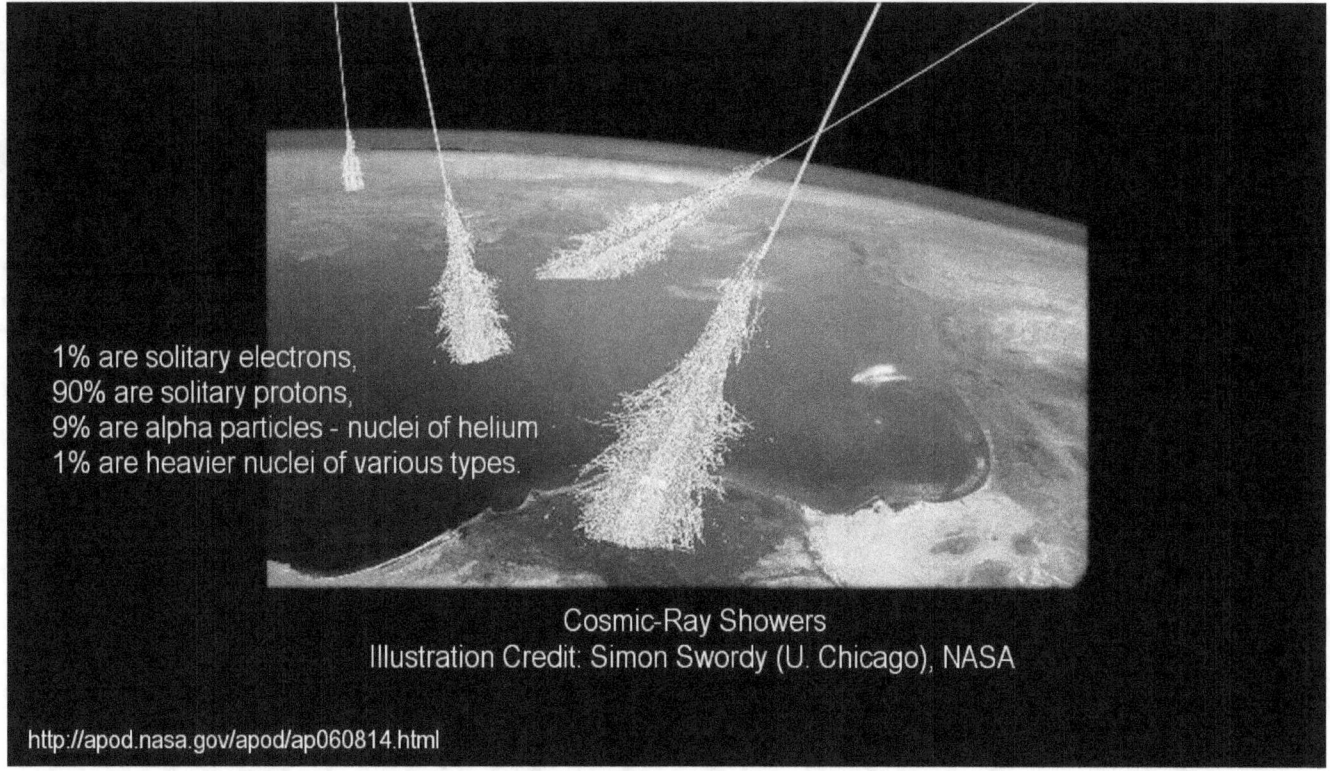

1% are solitary electrons,
90% are solitary protons,
9% are alpha particles - nuclei of helium
1% are heavier nuclei of various types.

Cosmic-Ray Showers
Illustration Credit: Simon Swordy (U. Chicago), NASA

http://apod.nasa.gov/apod/ap060814.html

And it is further evident that this huge factor of the water vapor effect, is strongly affected by solar cosmic-ray flux and the numerous astrophysical causes that modulate the solar cosmic-ray flux. Carbon plays no role at all on this scene.

Solar cosmic-ray fluctuation is the main factor

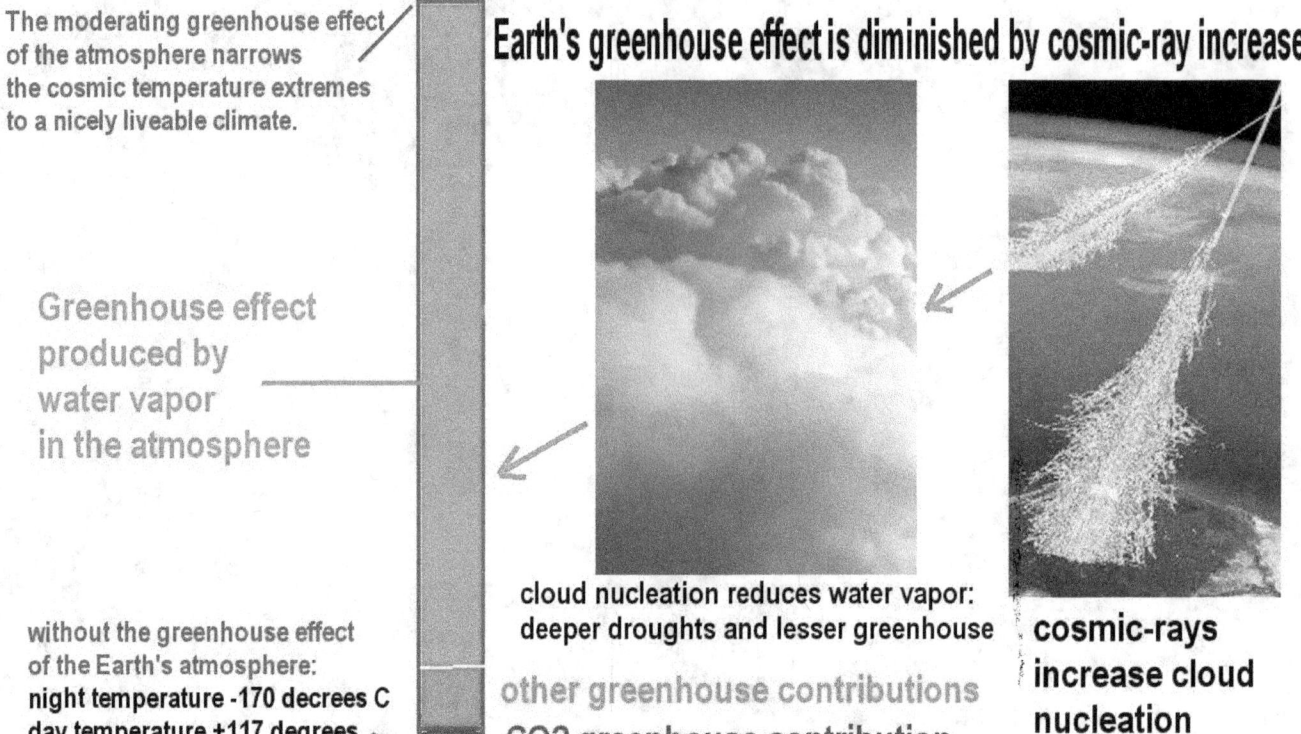

The moderating greenhouse effect of the atmosphere narrows the cosmic temperature extremes to a nicely liveable climate.

Greenhouse effect produced by water vapor in the atmosphere

without the greenhouse effect of the Earth's atmosphere:
night temperature -170 decrees C
day temperature +117 degrees

Earth's greenhouse effect is diminished by cosmic-ray increase

cloud nucleation reduces water vapor: deeper droughts and lesser greenhouse

other greenhouse contributions
CO2 greenhouse contribution

cosmic-rays increase cloud nucleation

The changing solar cosmic-ray fluctuation is the main factor that affects our climate in a big way. It affects cloudiness, and it affects the water vapor density that is the main greenhouse factor.

Cosmic-ray showers ionize the atmosphere and affect the could-forming process.

188

Floods, droughts, global cooling, and so on

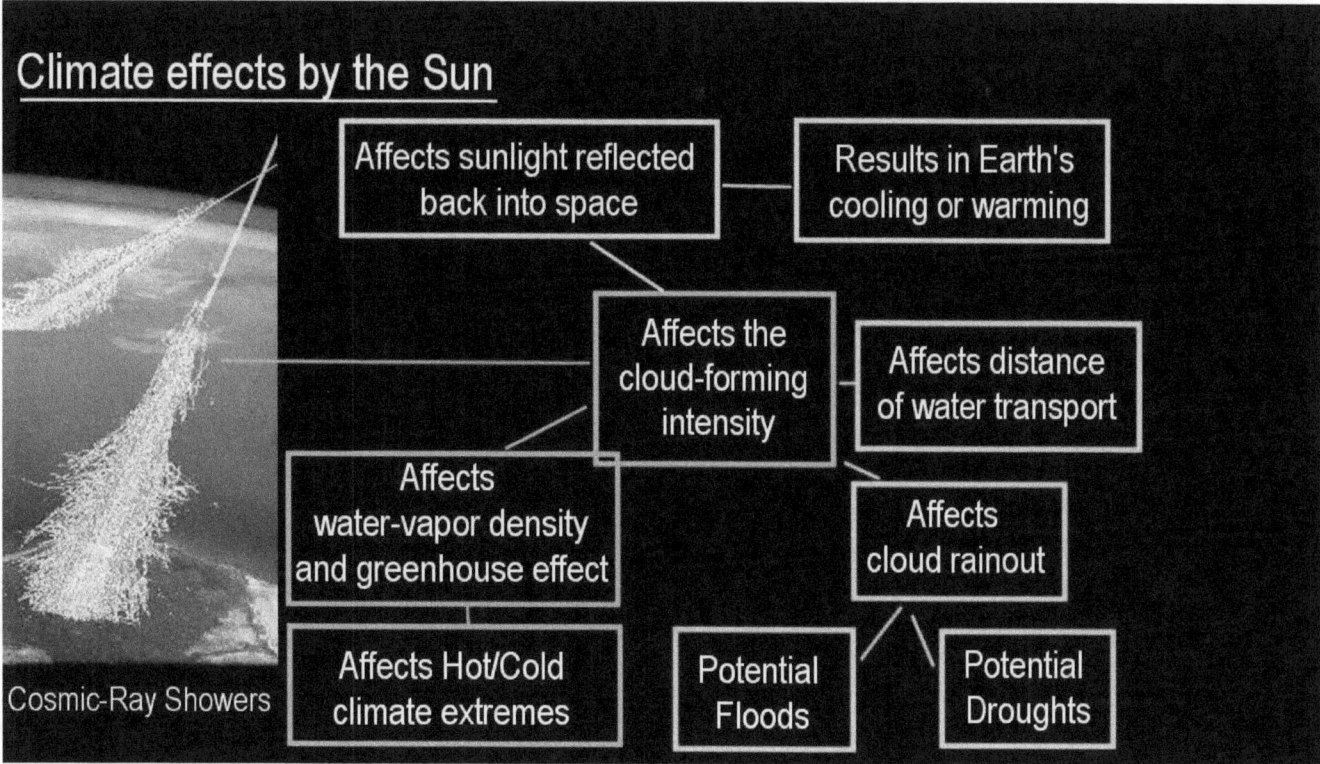

The effects are far-reaching. They are experienced as floods, droughts, global cooling, and so on.

Cosmic-ray induced increased rainout

The moderating greenhouse effect of the atmosphere narrows the cosmic temperature extremes to a nicely liveable climate.

Greenhouse effect produced by water vapor in the atmosphere

without the greenhouse effect of the Earth's atmosphere:
night temperature -170 decrees C
day temperature +117 degrees

Earth's greenhouse effect is diminished by cosmic-ray increase

cloud nucleation reduces water vapor: deeper droughts and lesser greenhouse

other greenhouse contributions

CO2 greenhouse contribution

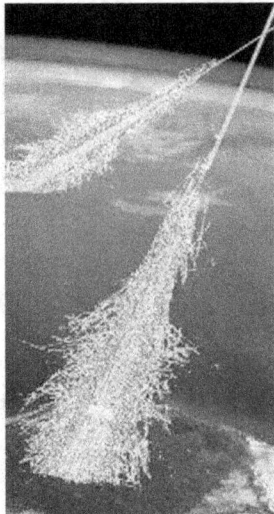

cosmic-rays increase cloud nucleation

Cosmic-ray induced increased rainout also reduces the water-vapor density in the air, which is the main greenhouse generator. The resulting weaker greenhouse, in turn, results in larger climate extremes such as burningly hotter sunshine and colder clear nights.

The weaker greenhouse effects

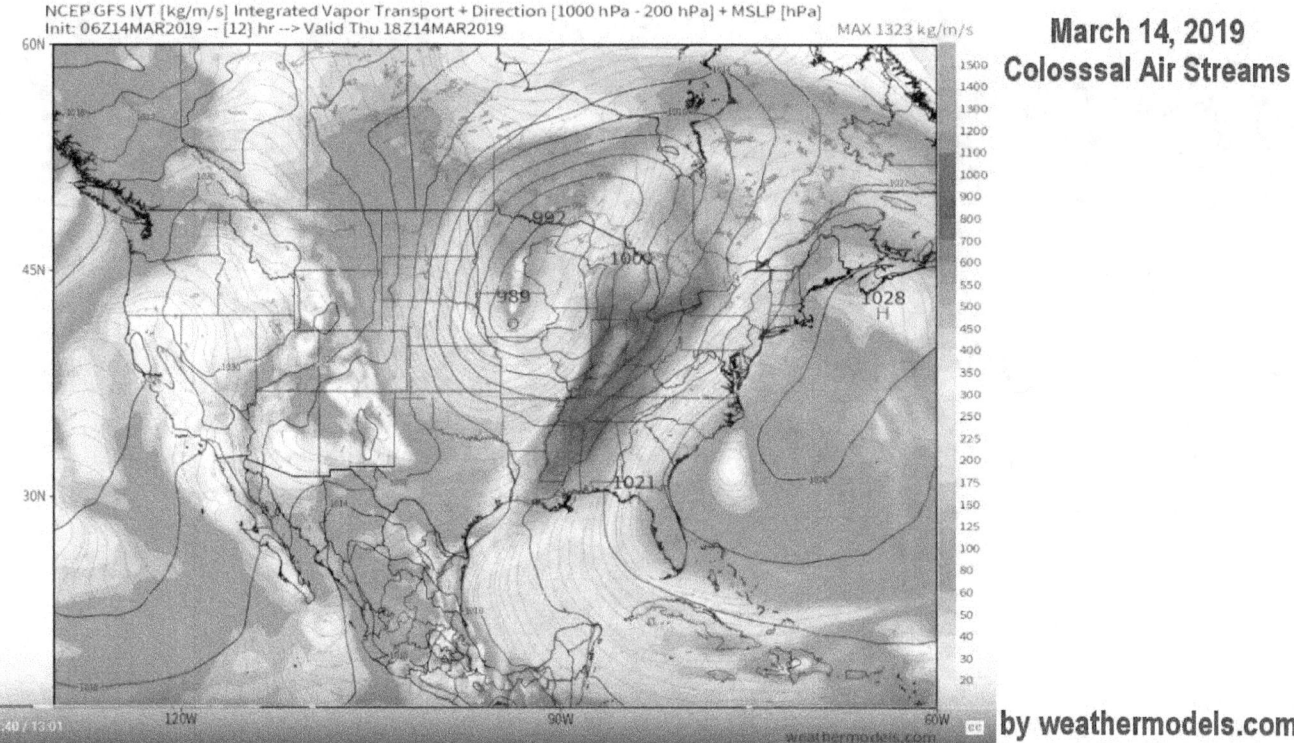

NCEP GFS IVT [kg/m/s] Integrated Vapor Transport + Direction [1000 hPa - 200 hPa] + MSLP [hPa]
Init: 06Z14MAR2019 -- [12] hr --> Valid Thu 18Z14MAR2019   MAX 1323 kg/m/s

**March 14, 2019
Colosssal Air Streams**

by weathermodels.com

The weaker greenhouse effects also result in correspondingly larger storm patterns, colossal air streams, blizzards, winds up to 100 miles per hour, highway closures, train derailments by wind pressure - and this is happening now, not in the future. No amount of increased CO2 could offset the reduced greenhouse effect by reduced water vapor. CO2 is not a greenhouse or climate factor. However, CO2 is a life-critical factor for the biosphere.

Who Speaks for the Biosphere?

Who Speaks for the Biosphere?

Who Speaks for the Biosphere?

CO2 one of the most critical elements for all life on Earth

But isn't atmospheric CO2 one of the most critical elements for all life on Earth?

Shouldn't it therefore be increased in the atmosphere, instead of being choked?

Isn't atmospheric CO2 one of the most critical elements for all life on Earth?

Shouldn't it therefore be increased in the atmosphere, instead of being choked?

CO2 one of the most critical elements for all life on Earth

CO2 at the lowest level of the last 600 million years

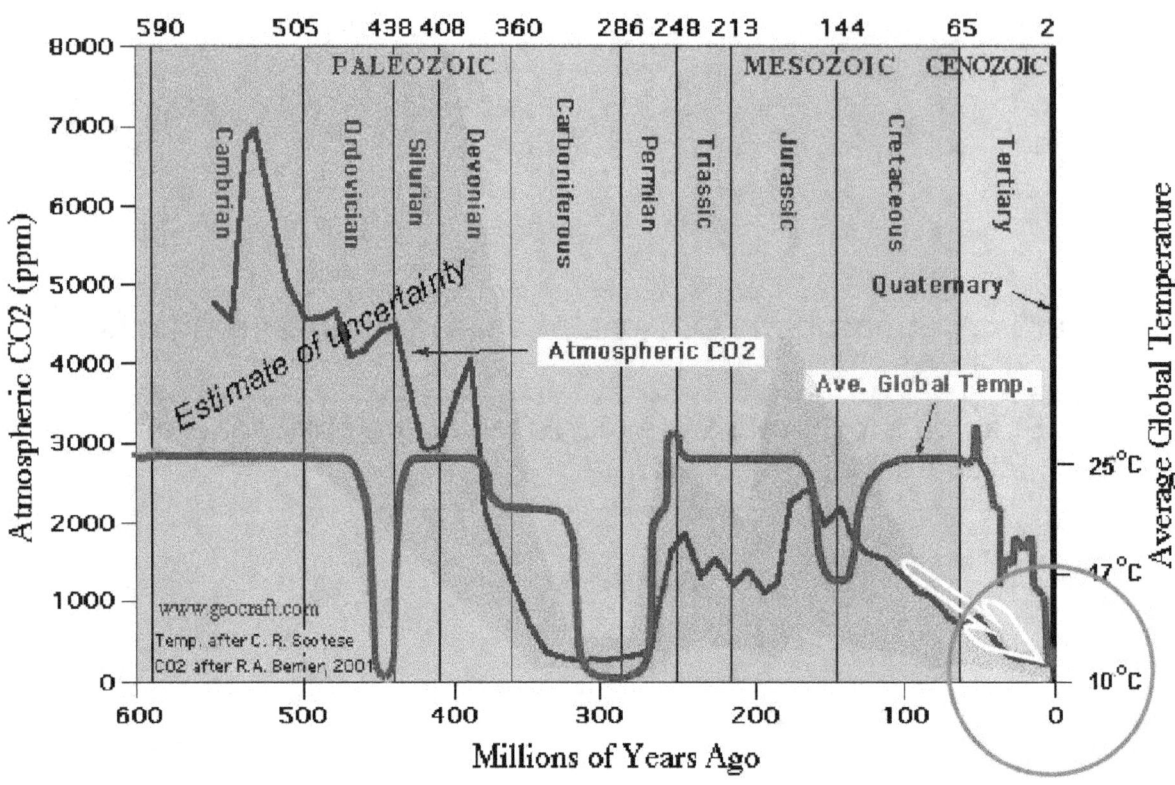

Not one of the high officials who 'conduct' the carbon climate-hoax has jet dared to speak for the biosphere and for all life.

All life on Earth depends on CO2 in the air to facilitate photosynthesis. Plants live by it, and we live of the plants. The plants that we live of exist at the present time in a severely CO2-starved environment.

The CO2 ratio in the air is presently at the lowest level of the last 600 million years that we have measurements for. The CO2 starvation is so severe that greenhouse operators get a 50% increase in plant growth by simply doubling the CO2 concentration.

During the age of the dinosaurs, when food production was plentiful, the CO2 concentration was 6 1/2 times larger than we have it today. The present CO2 ratio is so low, that large segments of the biosphere may starve to oblivion during the next Ice Age, when the CO2 level drops dramatically, which it does in its cold environment as it always has during Ice Ages.

We need a 10-fold INCREASE in atmospheric CO2, to enable the greening of the Earth back to its natural potential. The world is presently in need of increased food production, rather than the starving of it.

Reaction to the Next Ice Age prevented by fakery in science

COP 21: Heads of delegations by GUSTAVO-CAMACHO-GONZALEZ - Licensed under CC BY 2.0 via Commons by Presidencia de la República Mexicana -delegates

Poster of the Climate Conference. Licensed under Fair use via Wikipedia

These critical facts are all facts that the fake-climate-science profiteer-hoaxers like to hide from the world, and from world leaders, as if these critical facts didn't exist.

It would be wonderful for the world if humanity had the capability to actually cause global warming to happen at will. Instead, the Ice Age is coming and is near, as near as the 2050s, and there is nothing at all that we can do to prevent it, or even hinder it. All we can do is react to it. But this reaction to save our existence in the face of the real danger imposed by global cooling towards the Next Ice Age, is strongly prevented by fakery in science.

Fortunately we have still time to repent and react

Fortunately we have still time to repent and react. The 2050s are still 30 years away, at which time things get really bad. The projected 2050s timeframe for the Ice Age phase shift to happen, is predictable by the dynamics of the currently ongoing collapse of solar activity, and the recognition of the operating solar dynamics.

Ice Ages are Radical Events

Ice Ages are Radical Events
like falling off a cliff

Ice Ages are Radical Eventslike falling off a cliff.

Measurements from deep-sea sediments

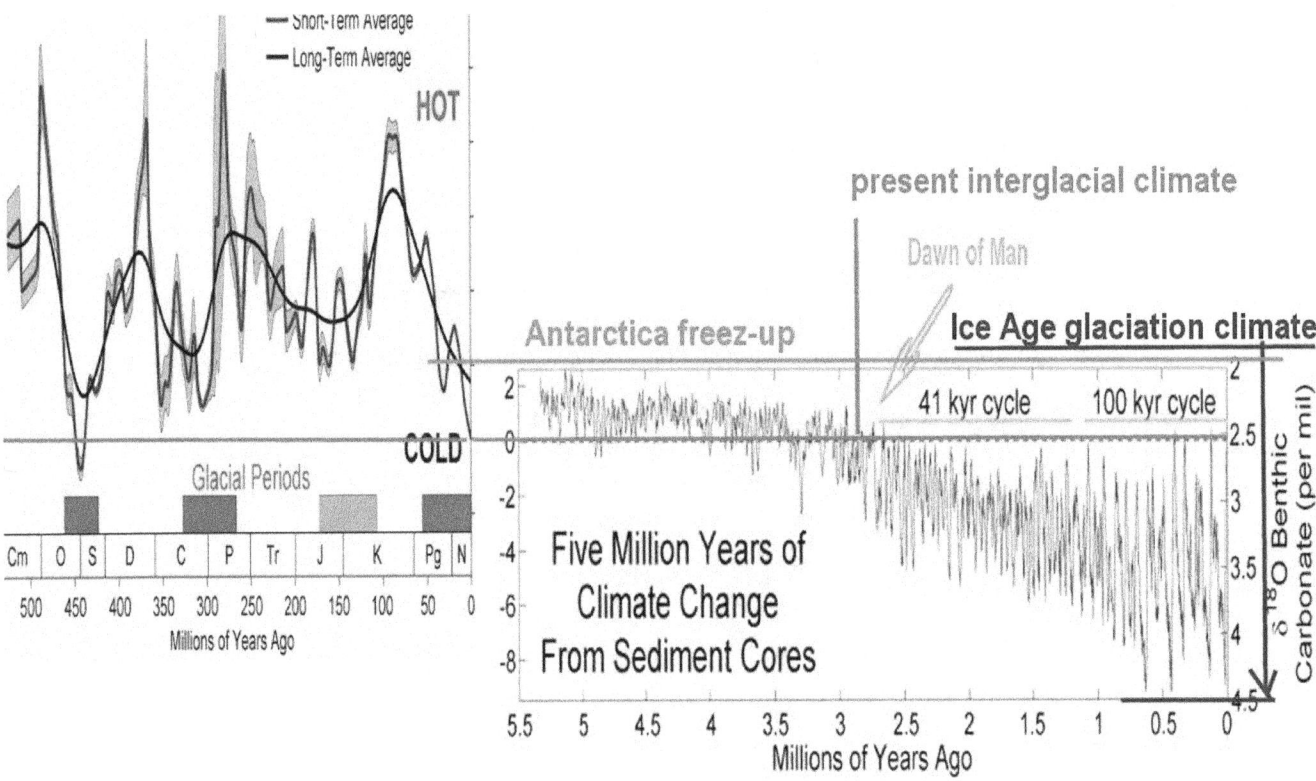

The available measurements that we gleamed from deep-sea sediments, tell us that Ice Age transitions are not gradual events, that they are threshold events, like falling off a cliff. That's what we see in the benthic records in deep-sea fossil sediments. When we drop below the level that supports our interglacial Sun, below the blue line, we fall off the cliff into glacial climate and extremely low CO2 levels, as the colder oceans absorb more CO2.

When we fall off a cliff everything becomes different

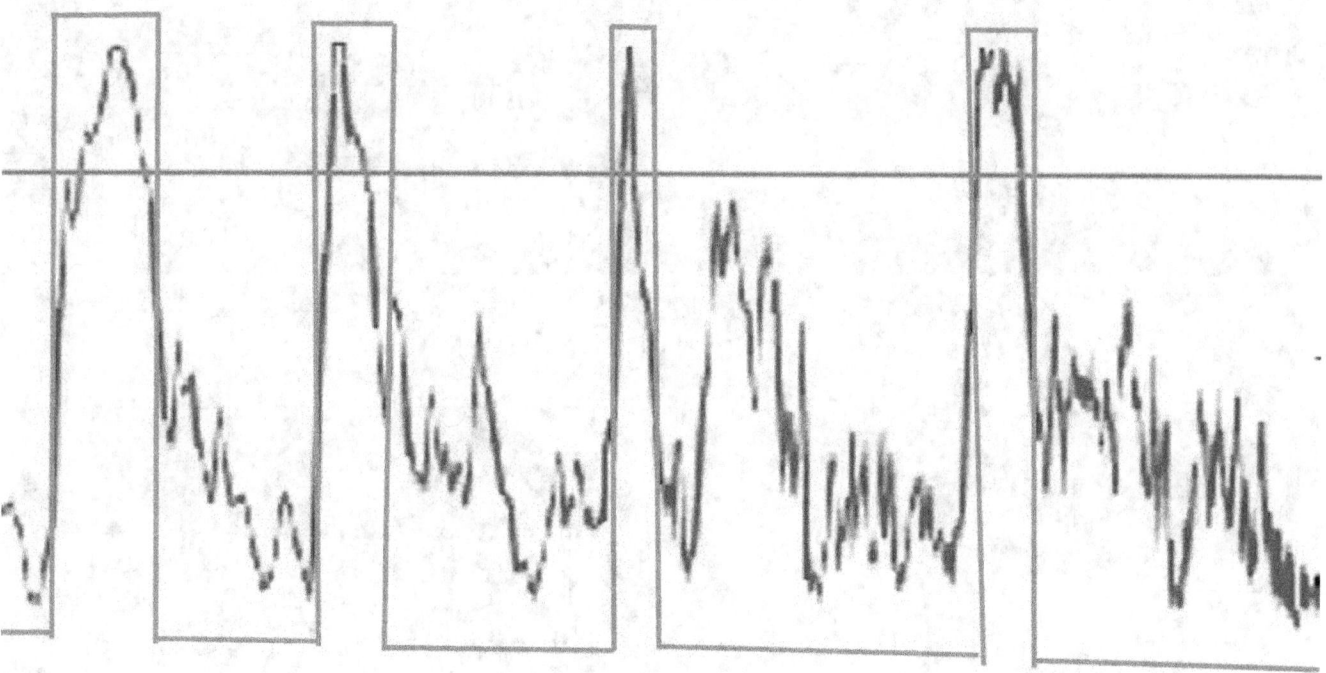

This means that Ice Ages are essentially digital events. When we fall off a cliff everything becomes different. A whole new world begins. Ice Ages are incomparable.

The Sun goes into a kind of hibernation mode

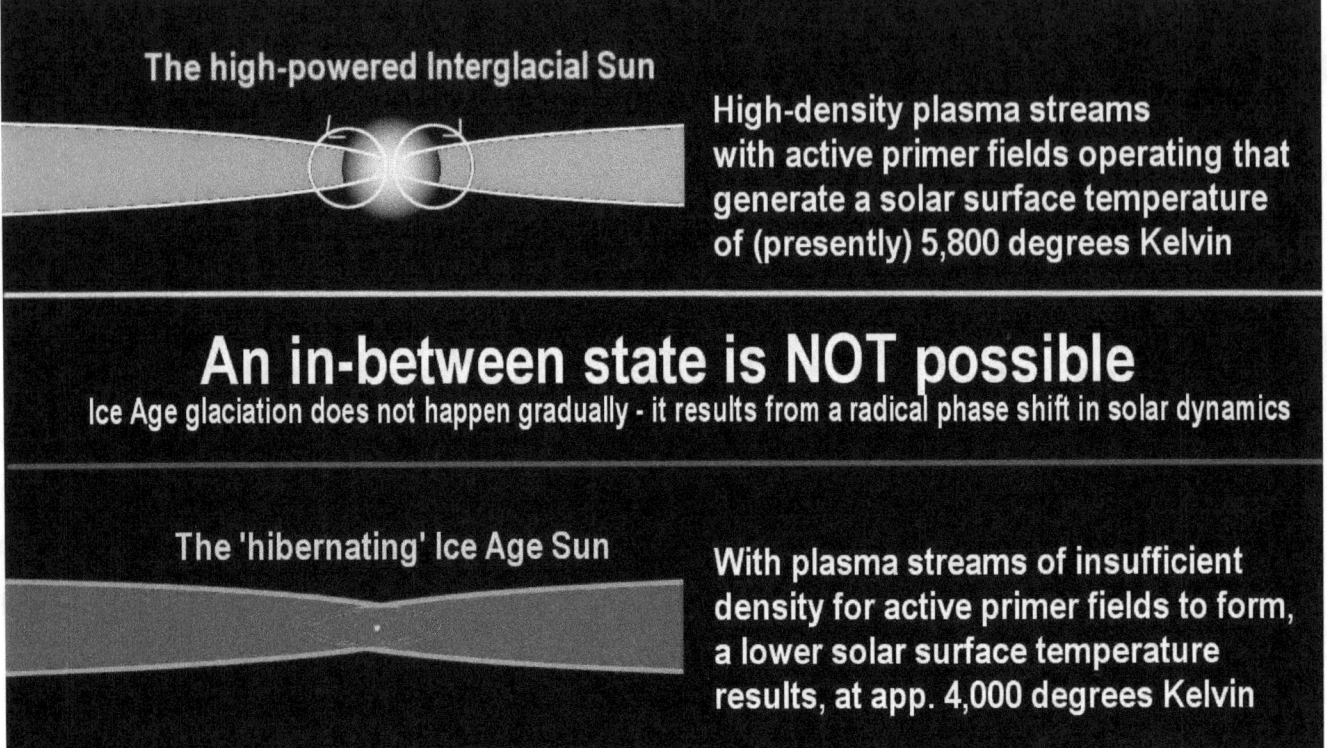

Ice ages happen when a feature of the solar dynamics, which presently focuses interstellar plasma unto the Sun, goes inactive. The Sun goes into a low-power mode when this happens, a kind of hibernation mode.

Ice Ages start and end in an on-off fashion

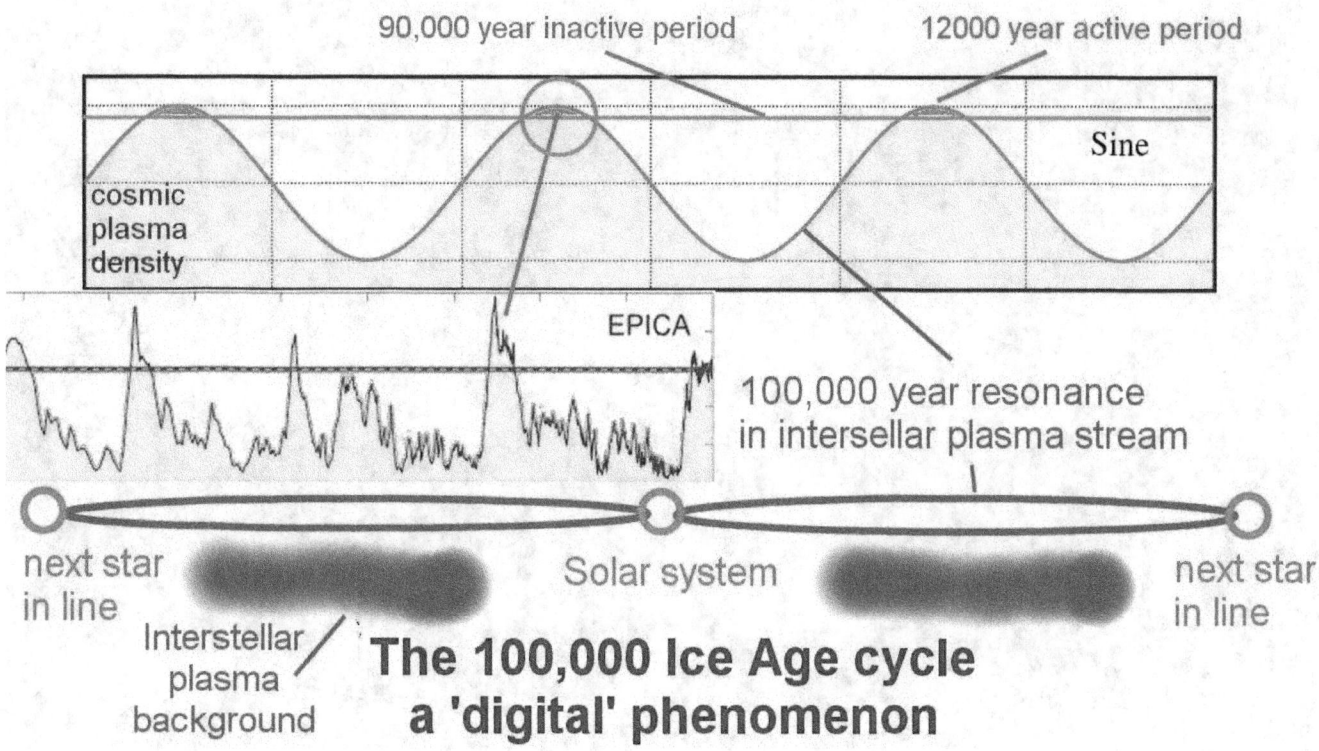

Ice Ages are therefore essentially threshold events. They start and end in an on-off fashion.

When the electromagnetic Primer Fields collapse

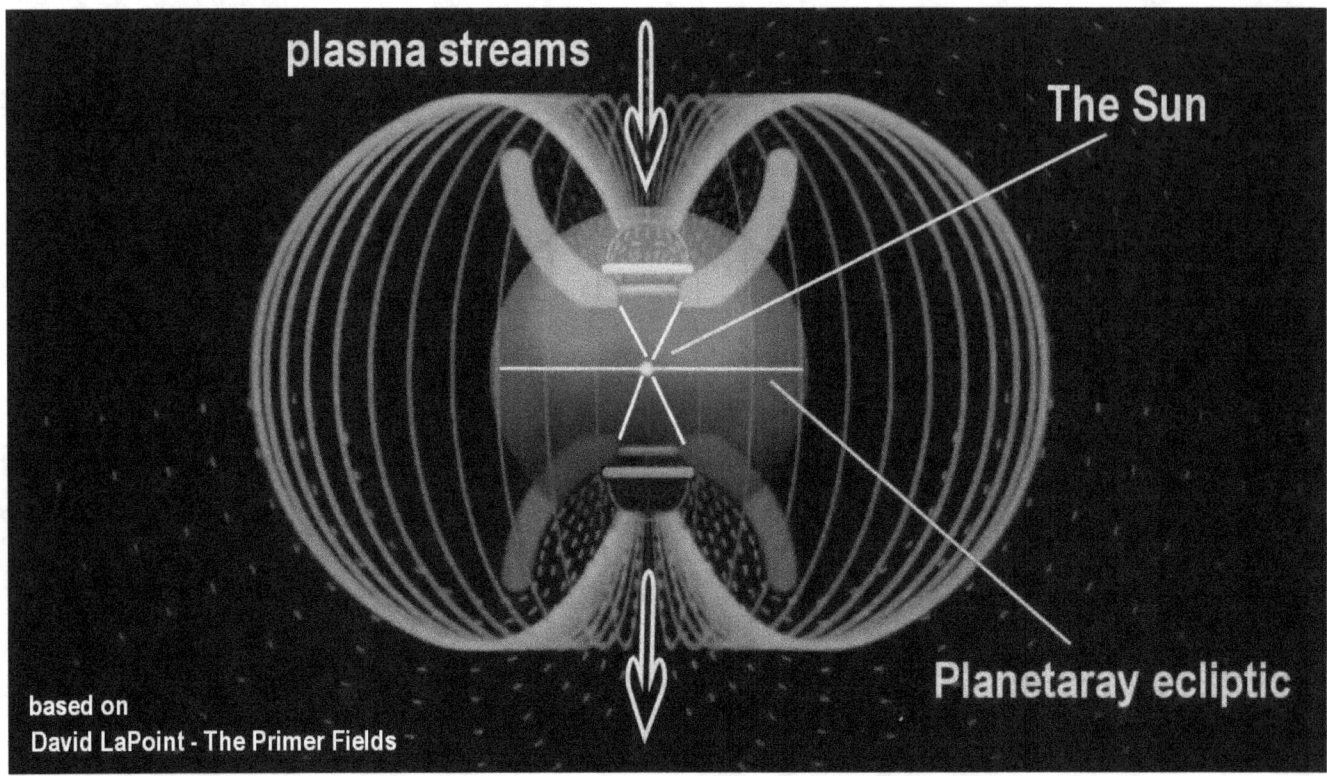

They start when the electromagnetic Primer Fields collapse that presently focus interstellar plasma streams onto our Sun, which the researcher David LaPoint had explored a few years ago, and has named the Primer Fields.

Most vividly apparent in the Red Square Nebula

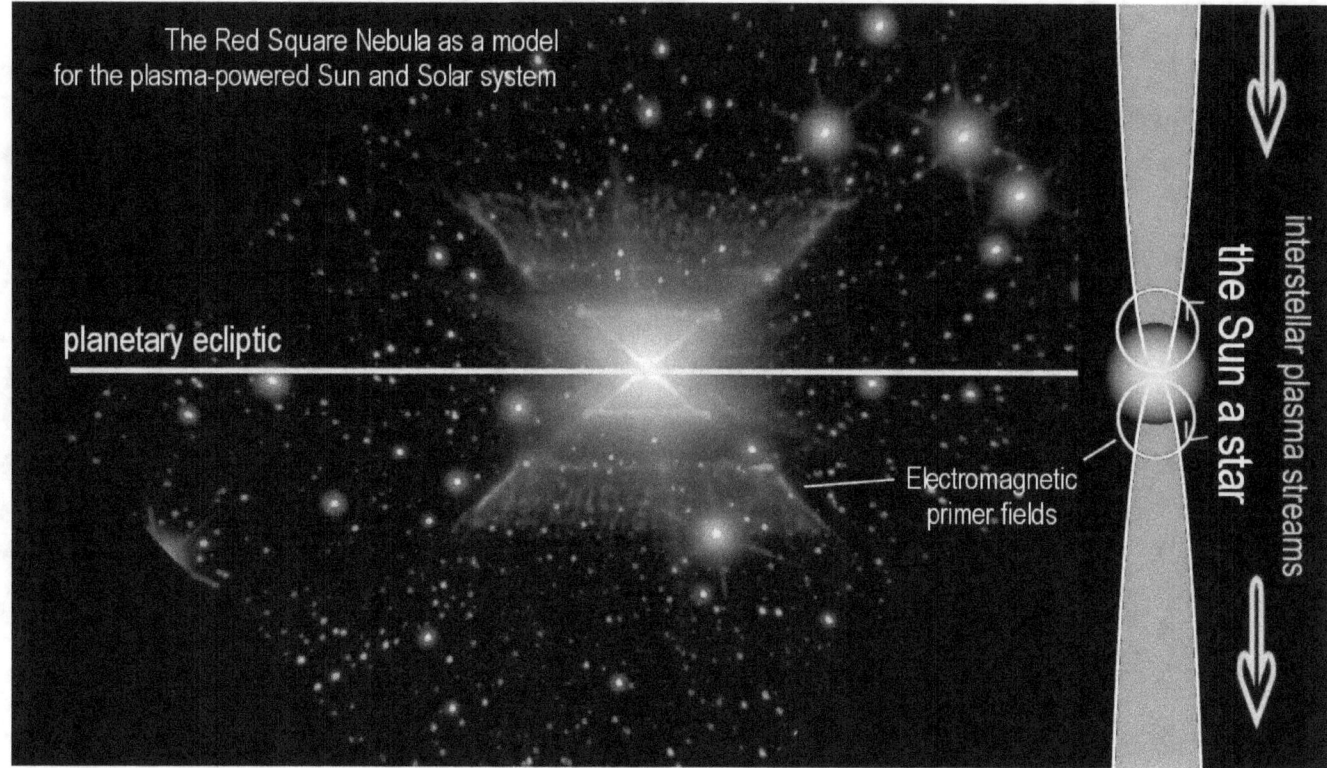

The plasma-focusing principle of the Primer Fields is most vividly apparent in space, in the Red Square Nebula. Normally, plasma is invisible, including the Primer Fields that focuses it onto a sun, Plasma doesn't emit light. However we can see its effects as it lights up atomic material in its path. By these effects, the operating principle becomes visible, including its focusing of interstellar plasma unto a Sun. The Sun is energized by it.

Every sun is a plasma star

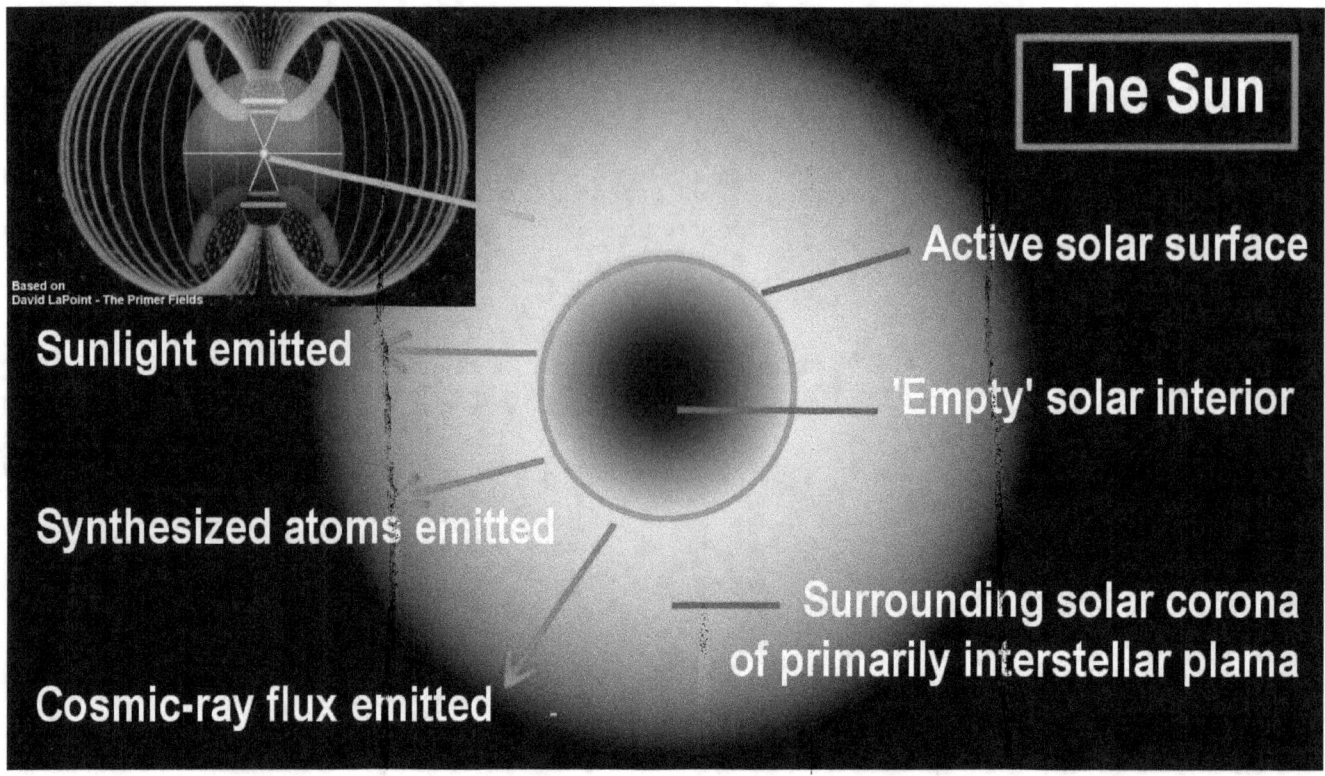

Every sun is a plasma star that interacts with interstellar plasma and is powered by it in surface reactions.

Red Square Nebula to illustrate the dynamics of our Sun

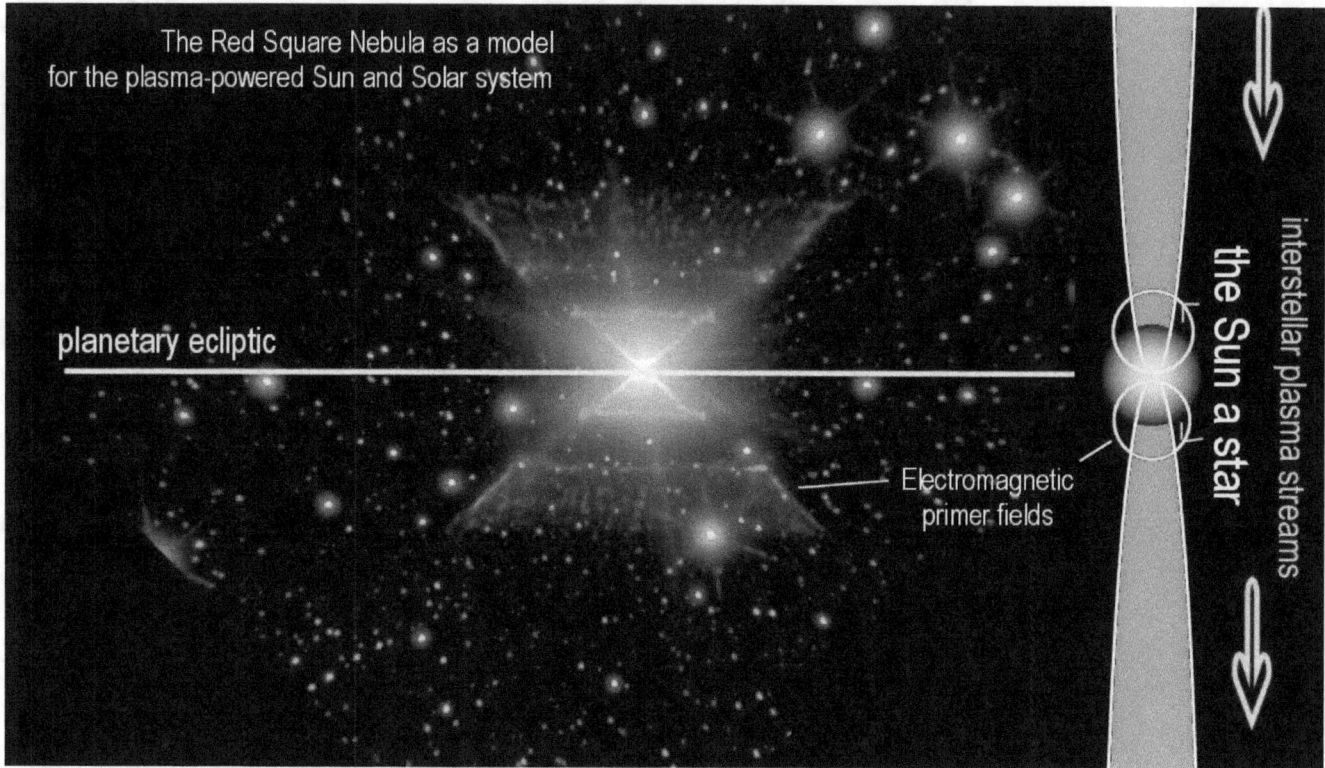

That's what we see being visible in the Red Square Nebula. When you see this image used in serious astrophysics as a example to illustrate the dynamics of our Sun, then celebrate, because you have hope on the horizon that your life won't end in 20 years or sooner. What you see is that critical.

Who Speaks for the Sun?

Who Speaks for the Sun?

Who Speaks for the Sun?

Designed to be counter-scientific in its effect

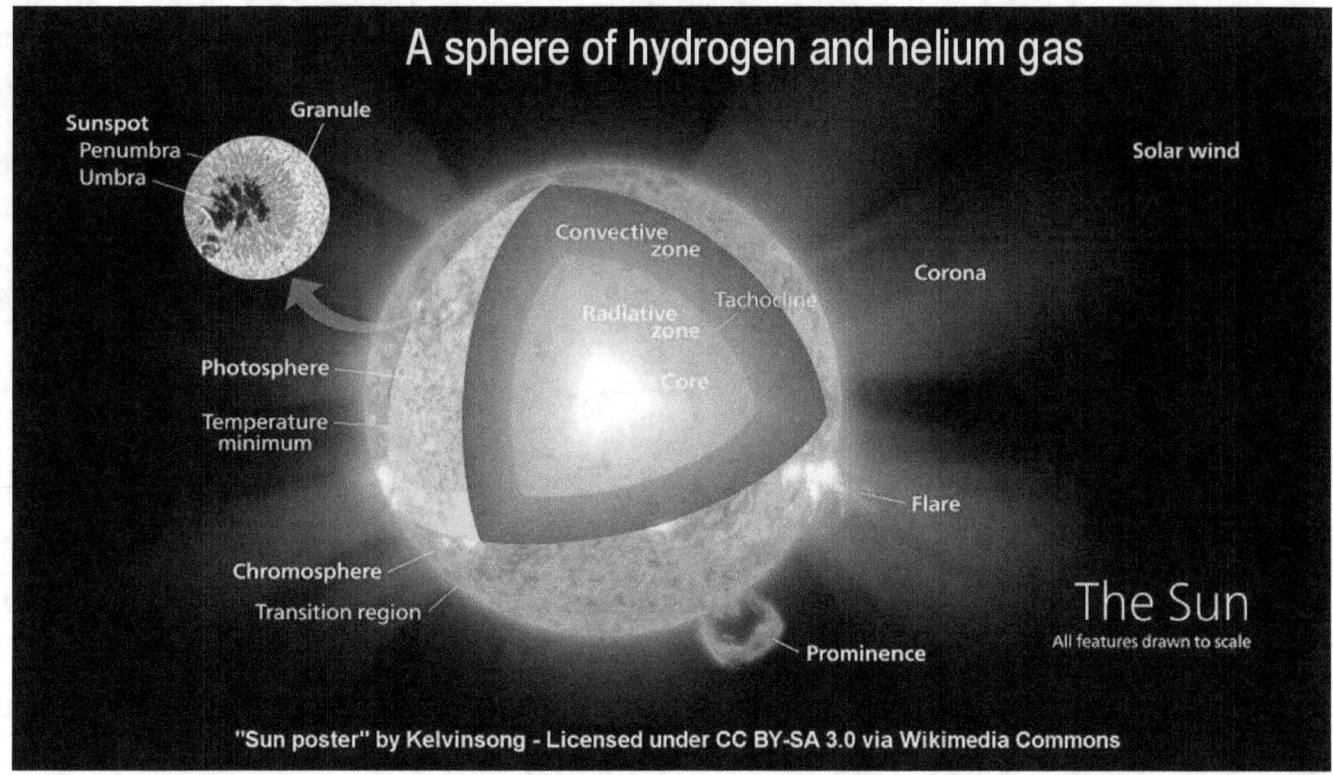

Society is far from being truthful with itself in the present world. The current model of the Sun, the internal-fusion gas-sun model, is so obviously false by it being physically impossible, that it was likely designed to be counter-scientific in its effect from the start, for political objectives.

The reason for counter-scientific objectives

The British writer HG Wells illustrated the reason for counter-scientific objectives in his novel, the Time Machine.

In the novel (The Time Machine)

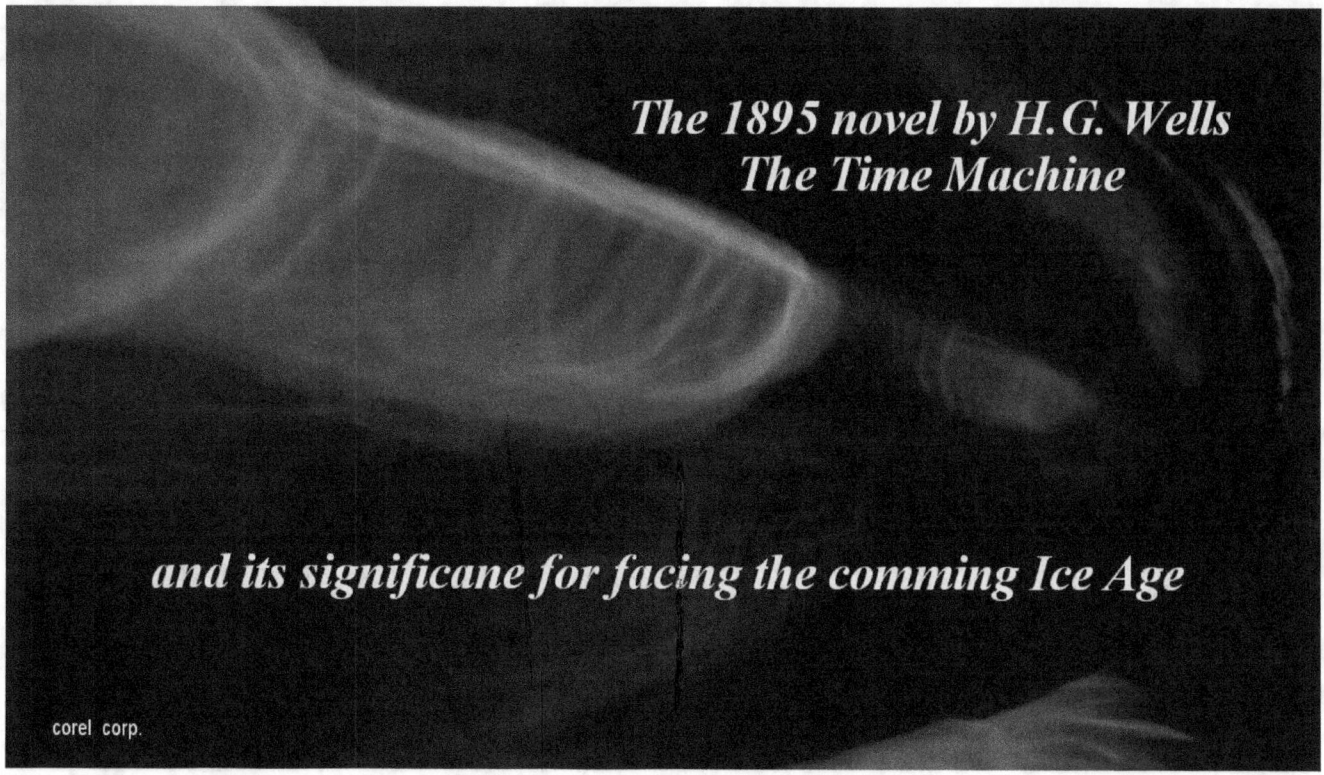

The 1895 novel by H.G. Wells
The Time Machine

and its significane for facing the comming Ice Age

corel corp.

In the novel (The Time Machine) the inventor of a time machine travels with it far into the future where he encounters a delicate, beautiful people who live serenely in a world rich in food, and without a care, who have no work to perform. He names them the Eloy, the elegantly lazy.

When the traveler's has his time machine stolen, he searches for it and discovers a second type of people. He discovers the Morlochs, the industrious science driven machine loving people who keep the place running. With it he also discovers the secret for the Eloys' idyllic existence. The Morelochs maintain them as livestock. They eat them for breakfast.

Wells was saying to the noble elite

Wells was saying to the noble elite of his time, the masters of empire, if you cannot find a way to constrain science, society will eat you for breakfast. Thus, science was changed. The debates of how to do it lingered on, into the 1920s. The gas-sun model may have been created as a deception.

The internal-fusion gas-sun model is so obviously fake

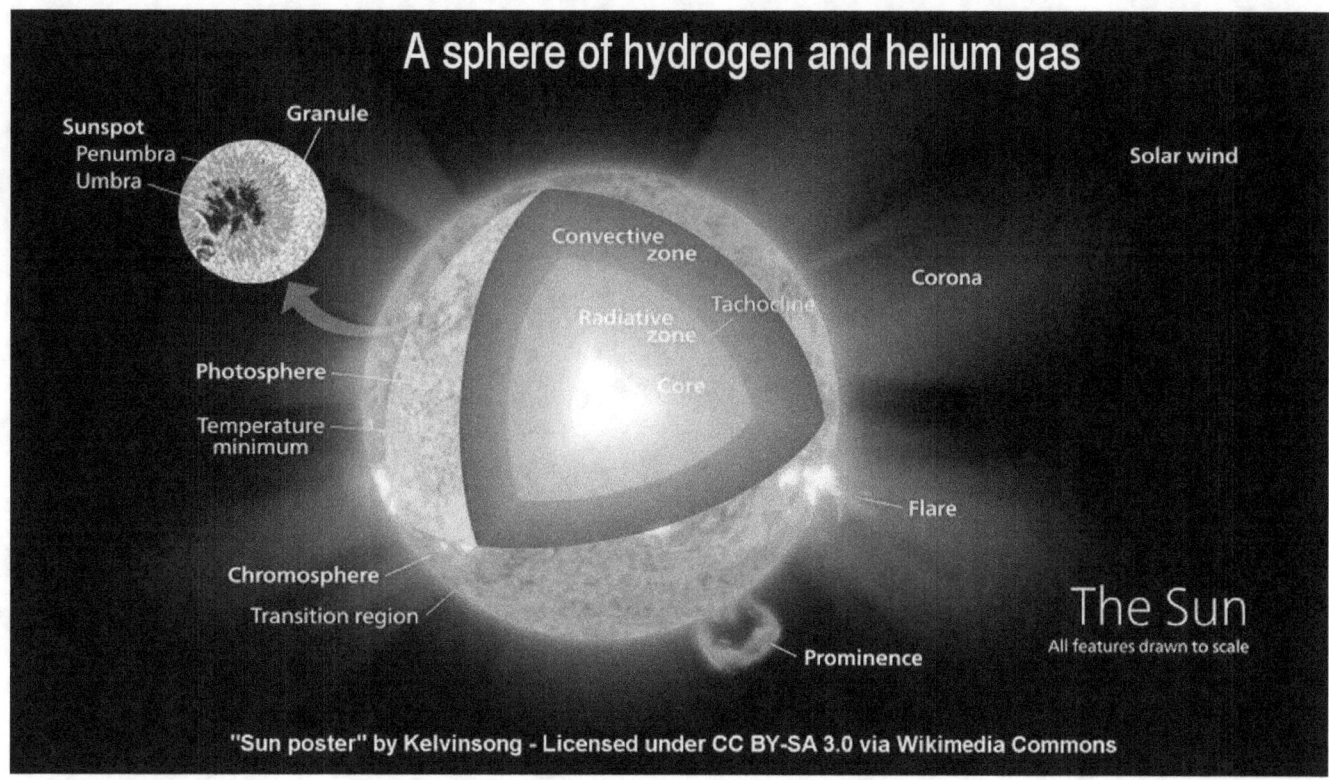

The internal-fusion gas-sun model is so obviously fake, as it violates so many basic principles of physics, that it is hard for a serious scientists to believe in the widely-taught official model.

Just look at the sunspots. The sunspots are dark.

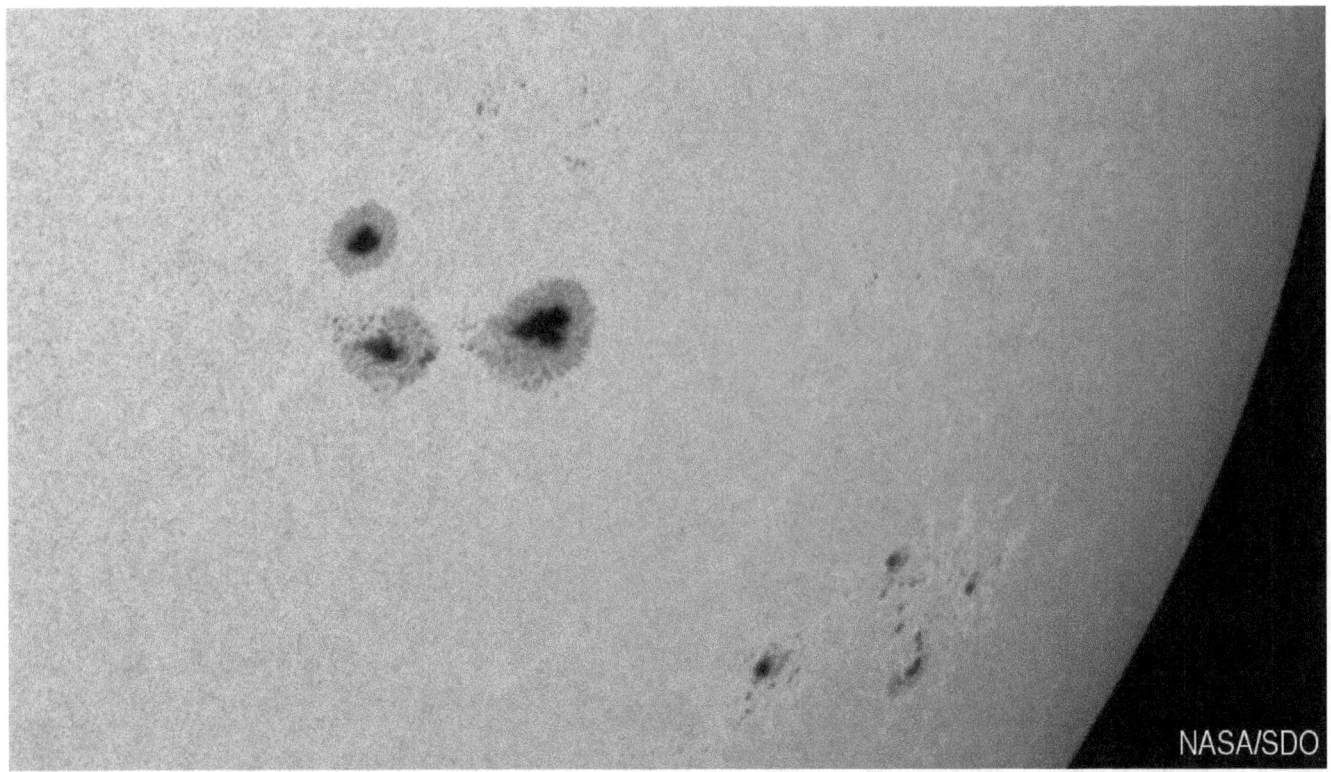

Just look at the sunspots. The sunspots are dark. They reveal a dark Sun under the shiny surface.. The sunspots should be brilliantly bright if the Sun was internally powered.

Dark energy streams through them that blocks light

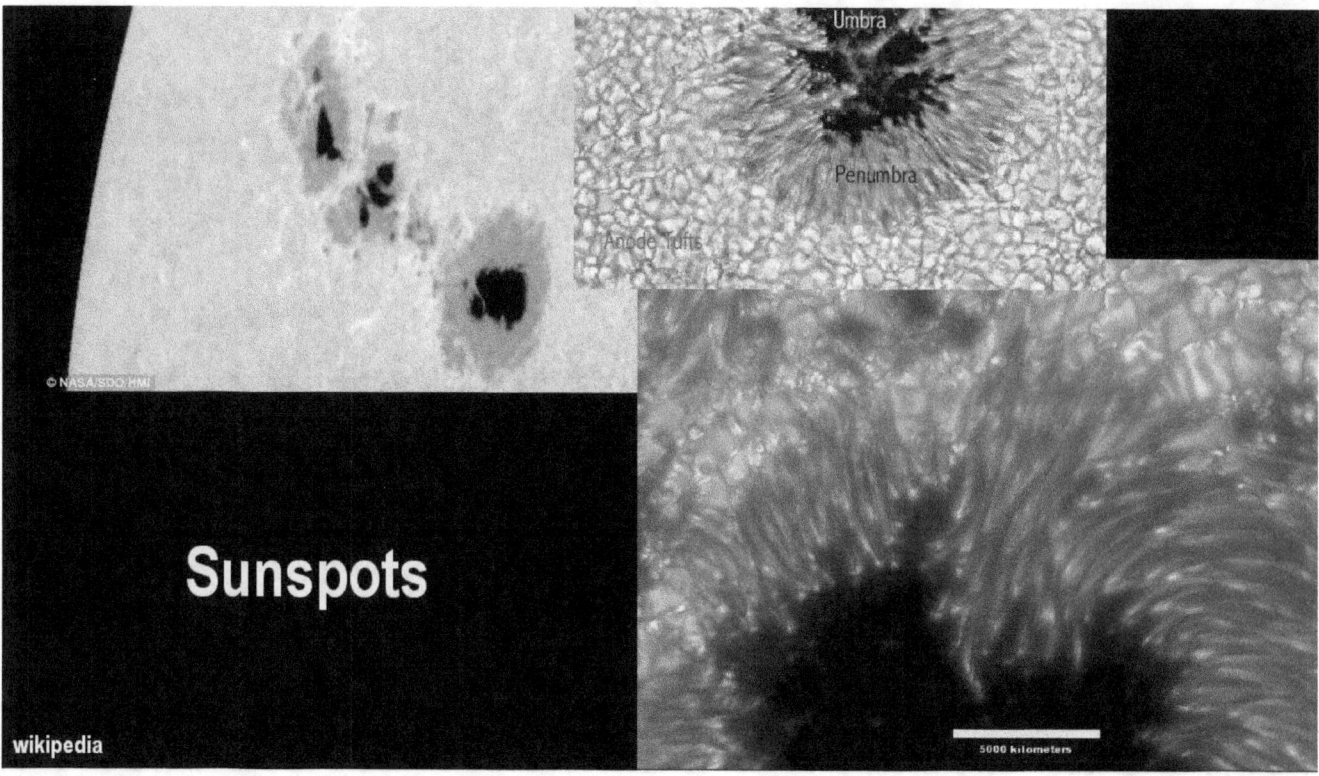

We are told that sunspots are dark, because dark energy streams through them that blocks light. With this, the fakery is excused. But with the Sun being a plasma star that is surface powered, so that nothing happens inside, the dark sunspots are expected.

Big stars make it plain that a sun cannot be a gas star

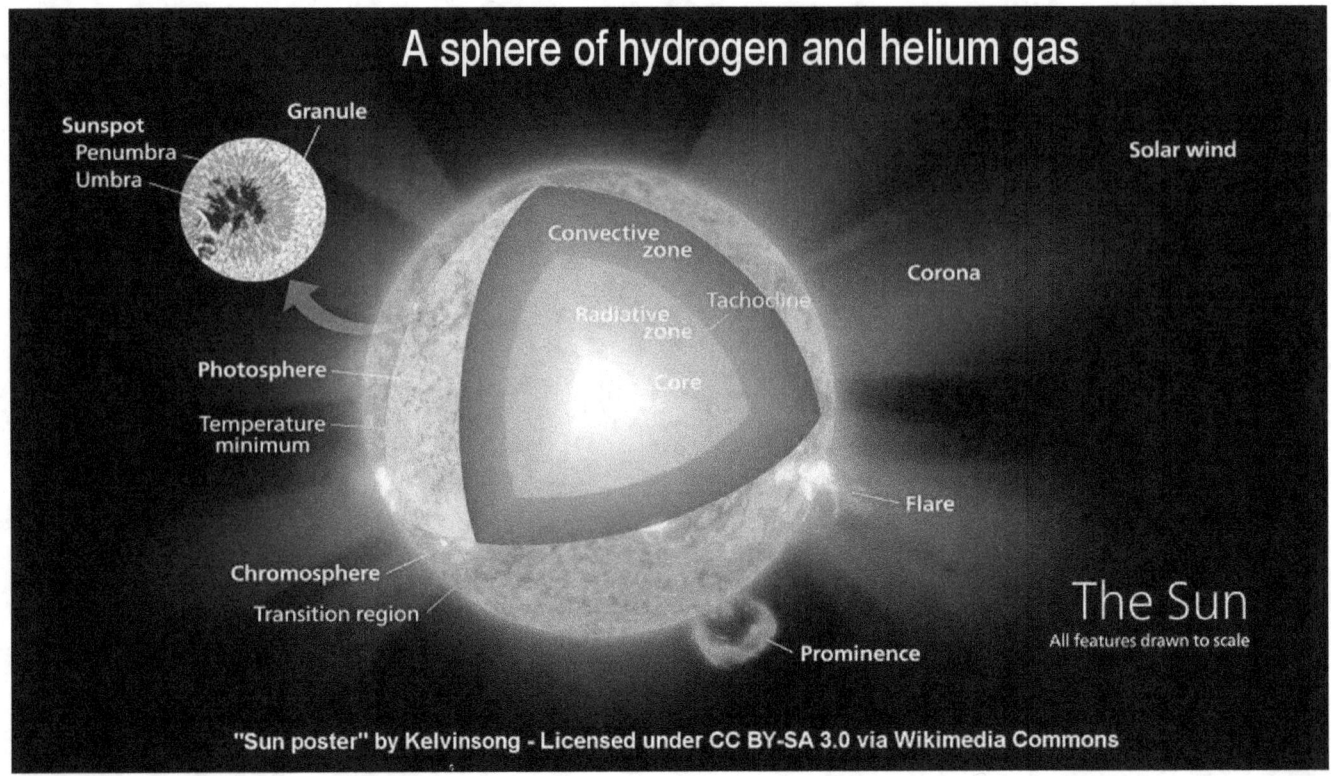

The big stars, too, make it rather plain that a sun cannot be a gas star.

UY Scuti is 5 billion times larger in volume

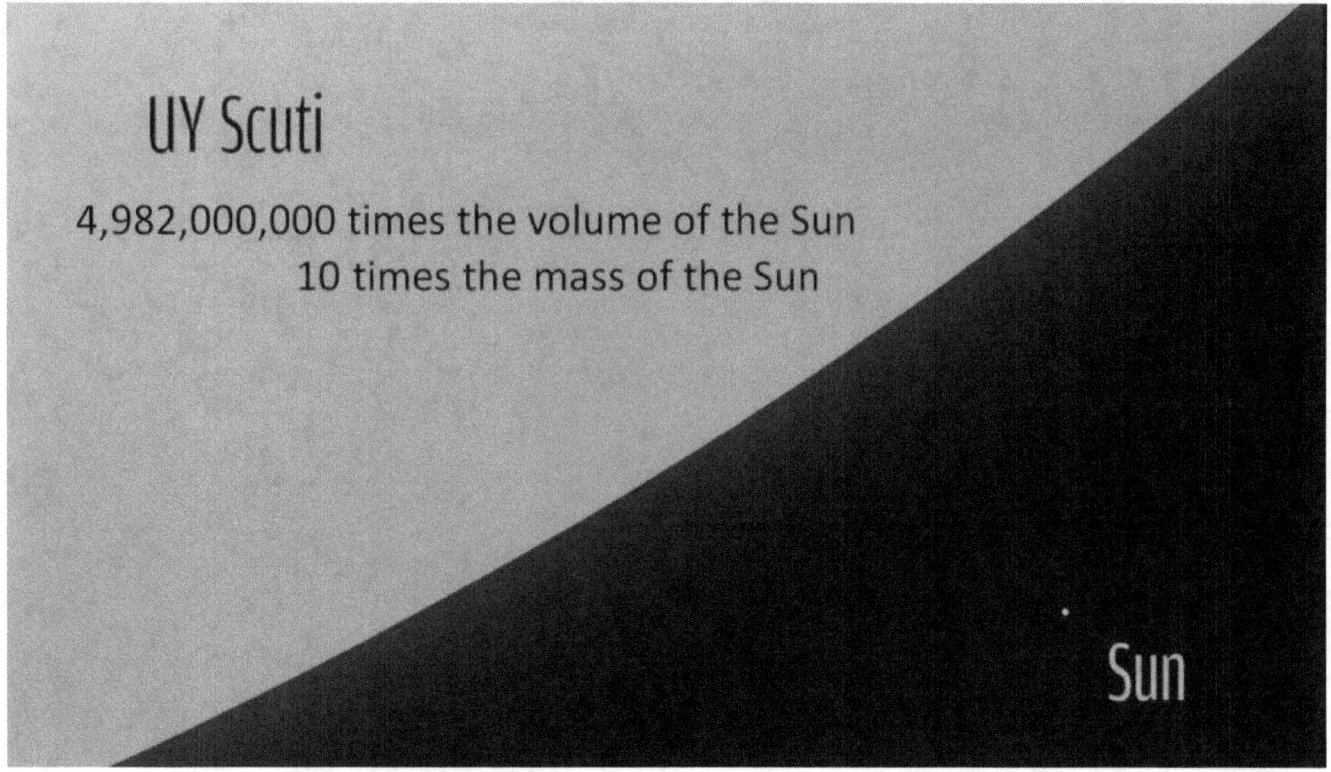

The giant star UY Scuti is 5 billion times larger in volume than our Sun, with only 10 solar masses to its credit. It takes a wild imagination to regard this giant empty star to be heated from within by gas-compression nuclear fusion. But as a plasma star that is externally powered, this giant largely empty star, makes sense.

The gas sun model only makes sense politically

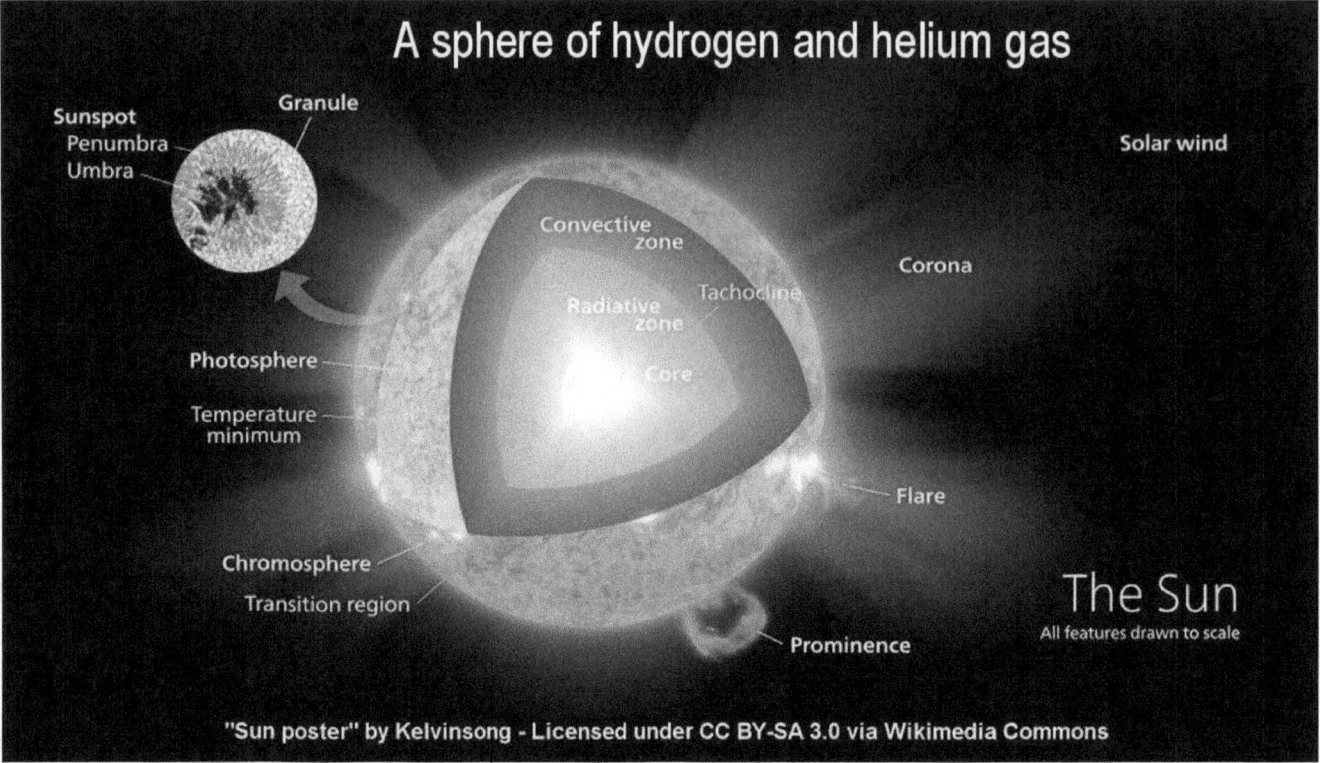

The gas sun model only makes sense politically, because the gas-sun model, defines our Sun as an invariable star. The masters of the plot tell us, that if the Sun doesn't change, all climate changes are manmade. So, please commit suicide and die to save the Earth.

So, please go back to sleep and don't burden yourself

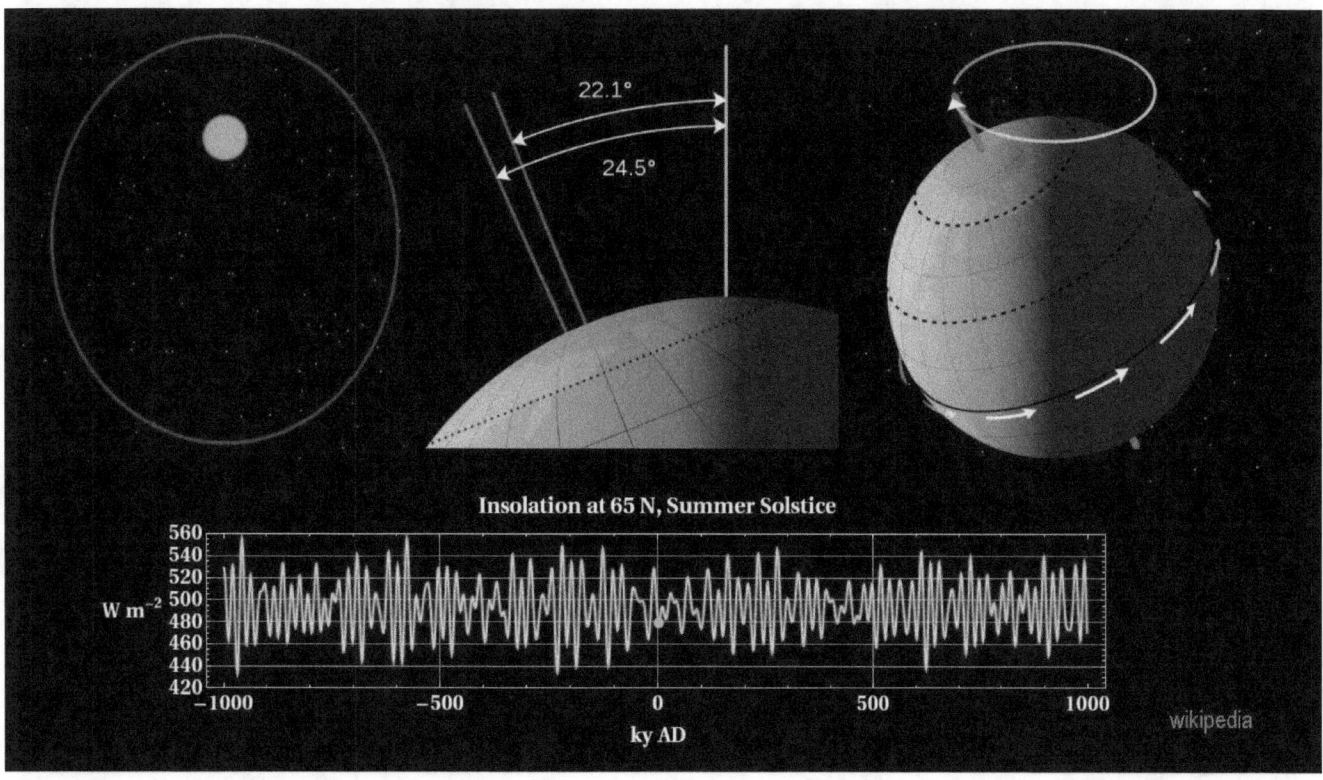

The masters also tell us that, because the Sun doesn't change, Ice Ages result as effects of long-term orbital variations with cycle times of ten's of thousands of years, and more. So, please go back to sleep and don't burden yourself, Ice Ages are far, far, distant.

If you listen to the masters you'll be dead in 20 years

(NASA) Beardmore glacier in Antarctica

The problem is, that if you listen to the masters you'll be dead in 20 years, because no one will then build the New World infrastructures for securing the world's food supply before the present agricultures collapse.

The depopulation of the planet will then happen, to less than a billion people, according to the imperial plan.

Should you step away from the master's song

Herbert George Wells in 1943
the man who changed
the course of science

wikipedia

Of course, should you choose to step away from the master's song of science pervasion, as you find plenty of evidence that what the masters have conjured-up is a big lie without substance or value or legitimacy, you will recognize that the fairy tales that are being taught are not really important, because nothing productive is achieved by contemplating errors laid upon errors as in the swamp of latent illusions.

When the principles of the universe are becoming recognized

The Red Square Nebula

The elevating recognition unfolds when the principles of the universe are becoming recognized, including, that we, as human beings, have the power within us to recognize the truth about the Sun,

To understand with it the real dynamics of the universe

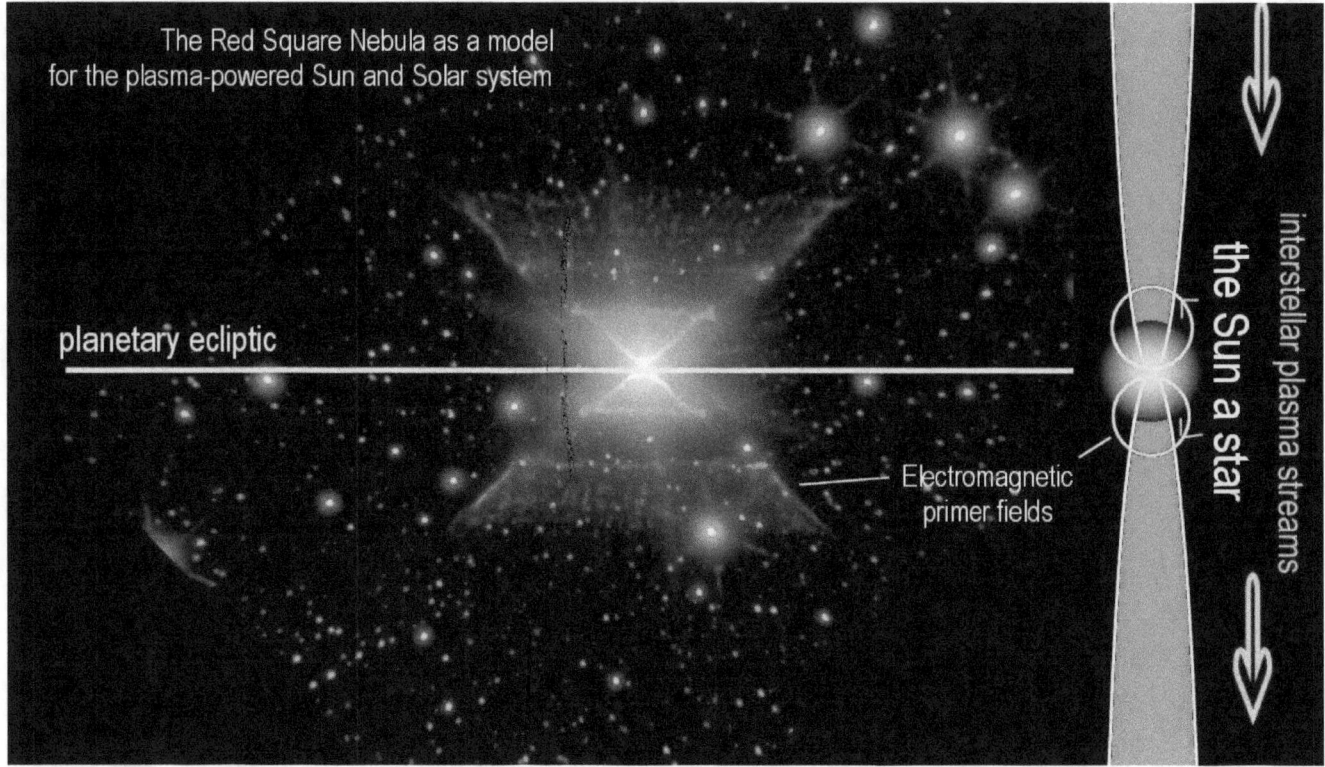

and to understand with it the real dynamics of the universe, which gives us the power to move with joy and act with confidence, as we see reality unfolding in the mind.

Reflected in the Red Square nebula

The structures that we see reflected in the Red Square nebula, are electromagnetic structures that focus interstellar plasma onto a Sun. The nebula is a rare case in which the dynamics become visible in the very large, which normally are invisible. Plasma is by its nature invisible, except in cases when its interaction with atomic material, such as in space, lights up the atomic material. In this way the principles become visually discernable.

David LaPoint replicated the plasma focusing process

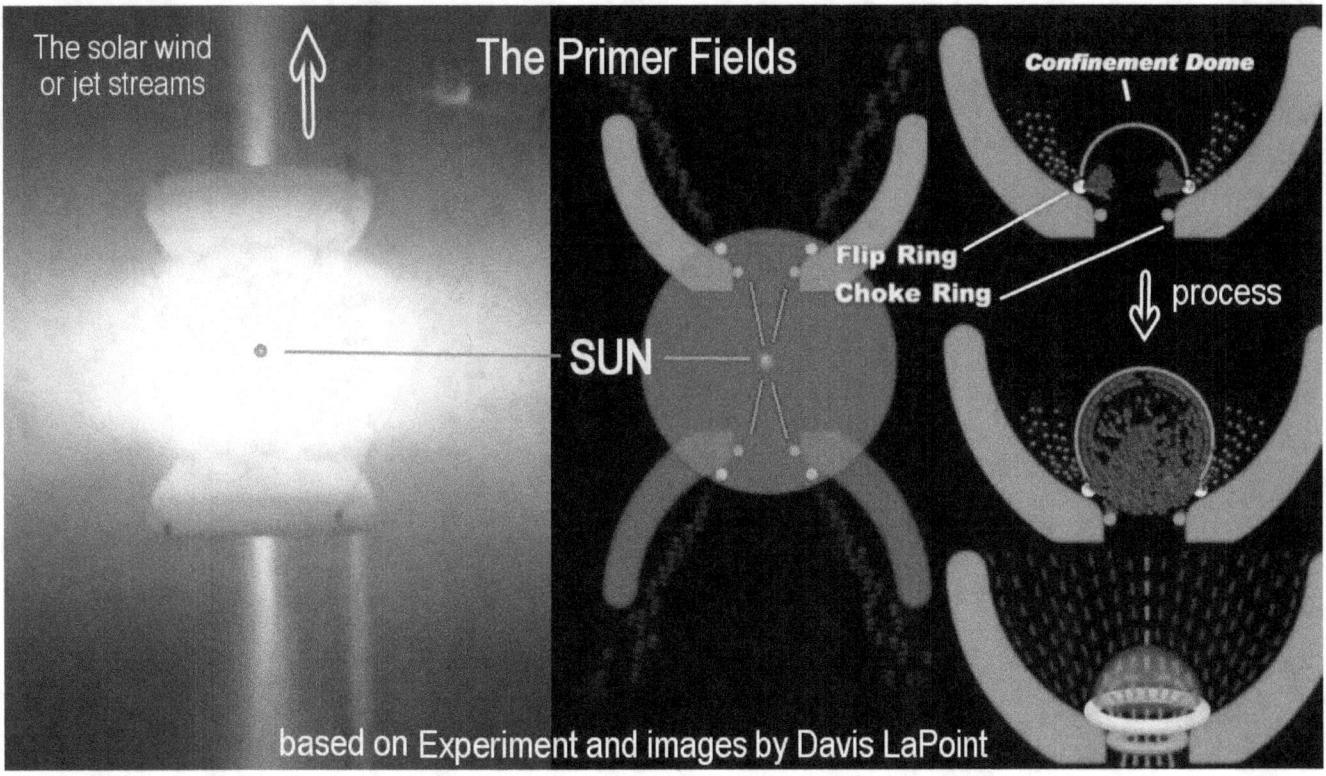

The researcher David LaPoint replicated the plasma focusing process in static laboratory experiments. He named the electromagnetic fields that form naturally in flowing streams of plasma, the Primer Fields.

The Primer-Fields' principle in high-energy experiments

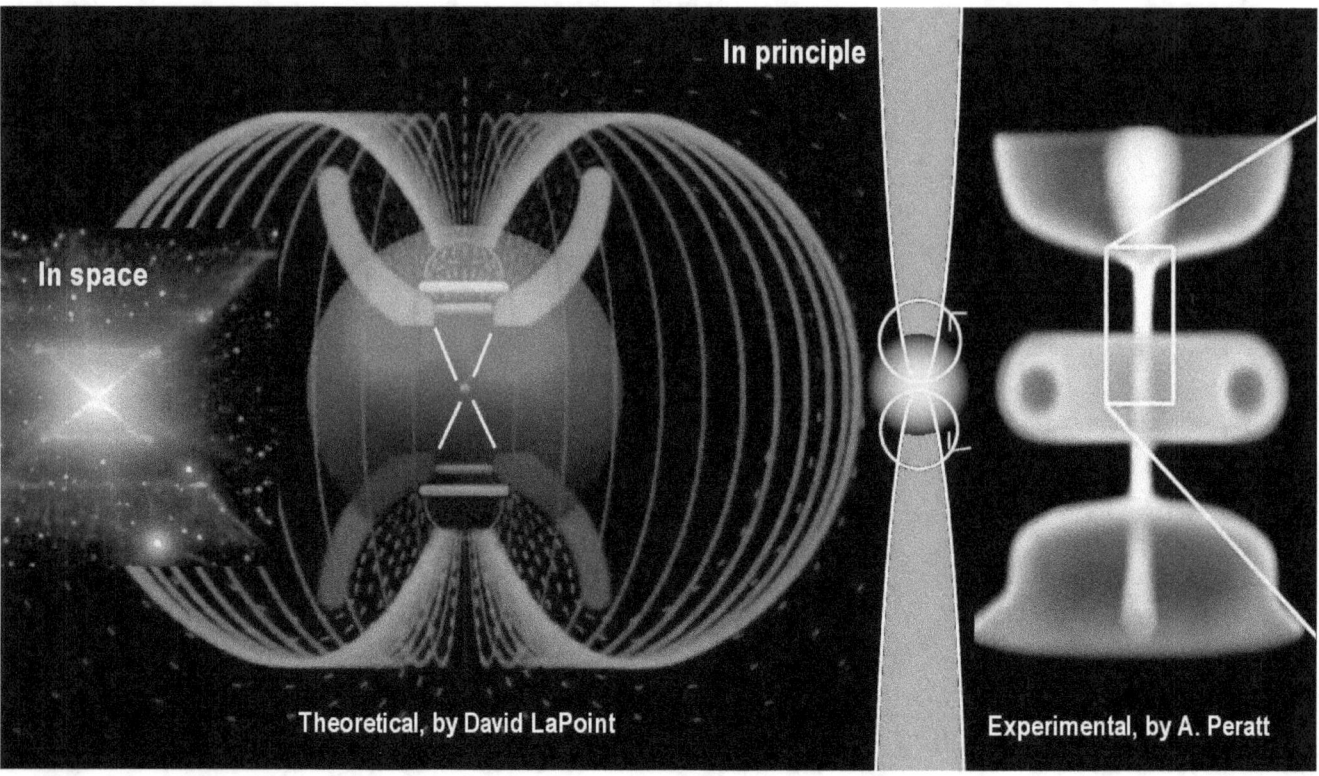

The Primer-Fields' principle has also been explored in high-energy dynamic experiments at the Los Alamos National Laboratory under the direction of Anthony Peratt, where a similar plasma-flow geometry was observed. The plasma that is focused onto a sun by these primer Fields, flows in interstellar space.

Plasma streams are self-concentrating

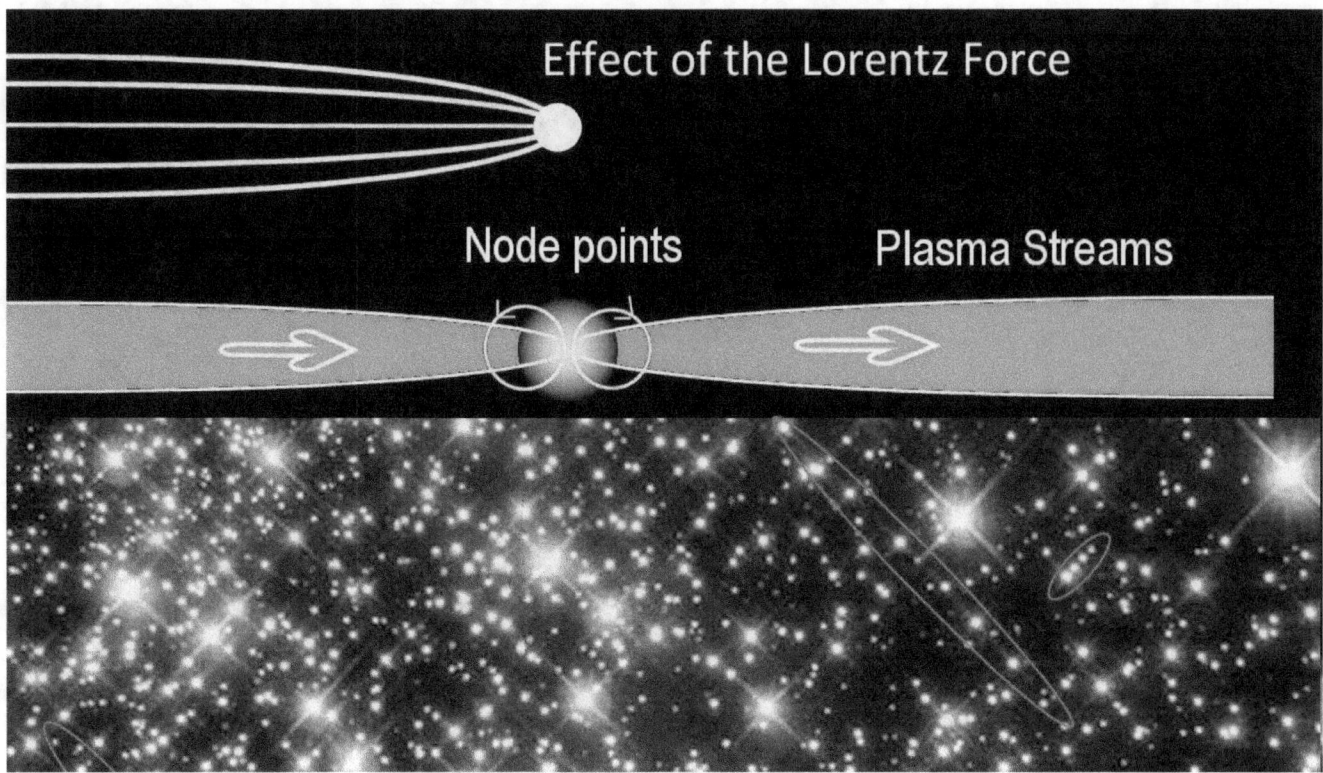

When an electric current flows in parallel wires in the same direction, the magnetic fields that the flowing electric particles generate, draw the wires towards each other, by what is called the Lorentz Force. The same happens in plasma flowing in space. The electrically charged plasma particles are drawn towards each other. Plasma streams are thereby self-concentrating. The more that they are pinched together, the stronger become the magnetic fields that increase the pinching.

When the pinching becomes extreme

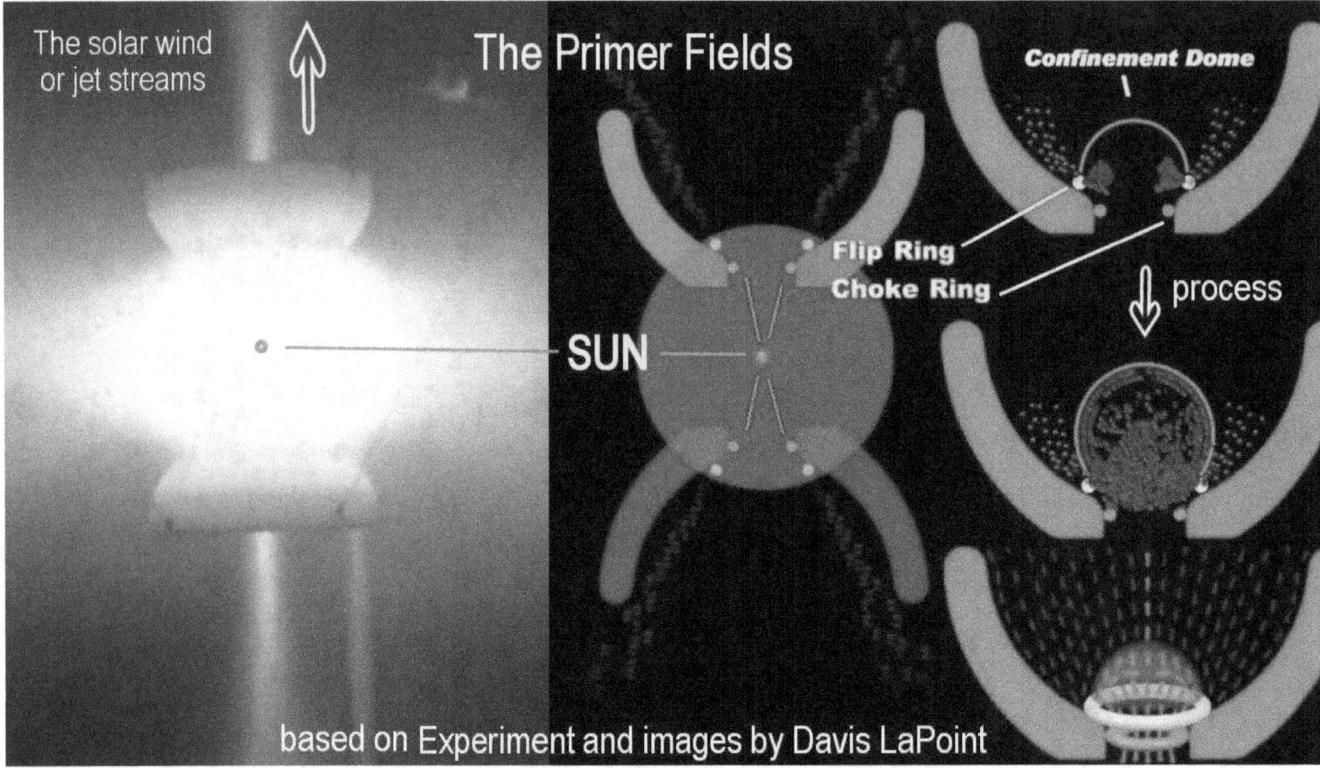

based on Experiment and images by Davis LaPoint

When the pinching becomes extreme the magnetic fields break down and form ring structures that flip the flowing plasma particles backwards under a magnetic confinement field, where the plasma becomes concentrated evermore. The highly concentrated plasma then becomes projected from under the dome onto a sun.

Atomic elements are synthesized, that light up the Sun

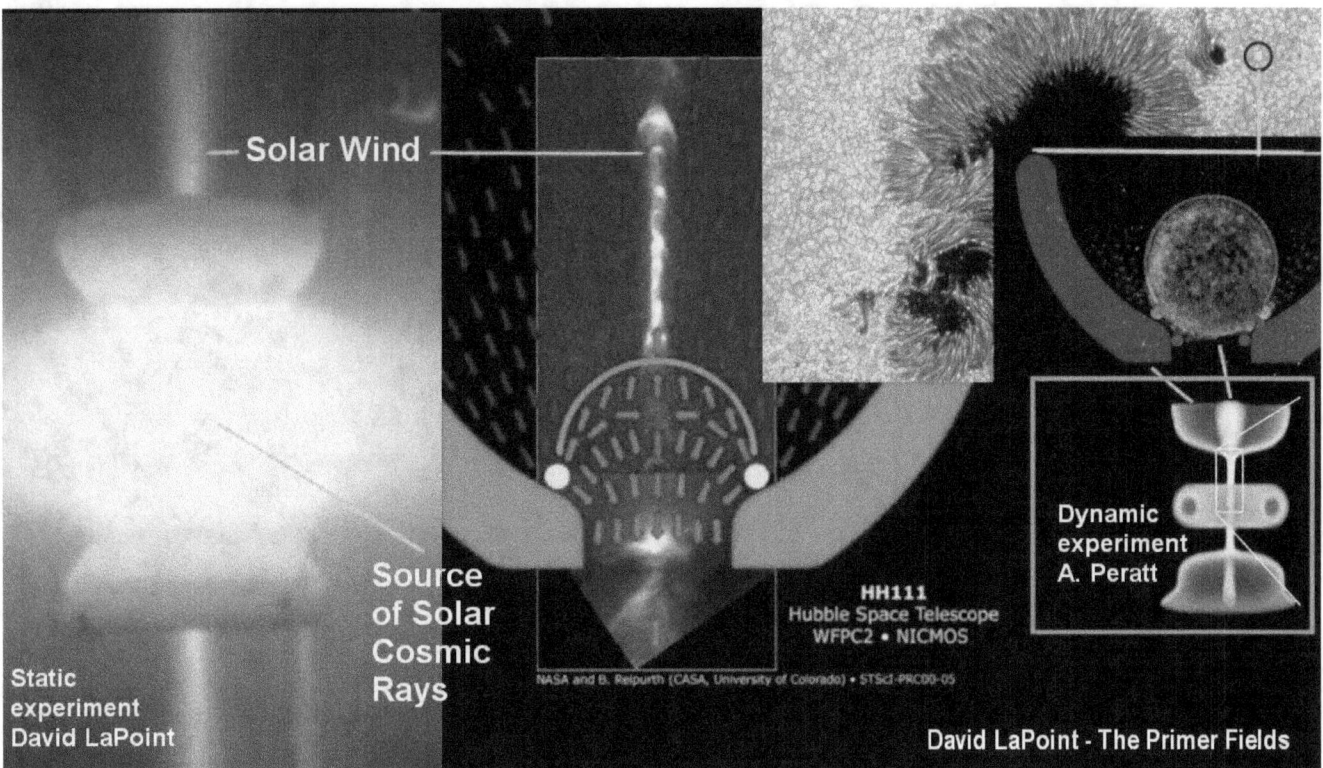

A sun is a plasma star. On its surface, by the force of extreme plasma interaction in similar primer fields, atomic elements are synthesized, that, by them being highly energized, light up the Sun. When the inflowing plasma pressure is greater than the magnetic confinement field can hold back, plasma escapes till the pressure drops below what the magnetic dome can contain. The escaping plasma becomes the solar wind. This means that for as long as the solar wind flows, there is enough plasma in the system to keep the Sun fully powered.

The Sun's venting off excess plasma pressure

Maximum temperature of liquid water at ambient pressure is 100 degrees Celsius: The Boiling Point

The Sun's venting off excess plasma pressure in the form of solar wind is comparable to a kettle venting off steam. When the energy input into a kettle is reduced, the steam diminishes and stops. On the Sun, when the solar wind diminishes and then stops, watch out, the Sun becomes dimmer thereafter.

The principles have been recognized in the Red Square nebula

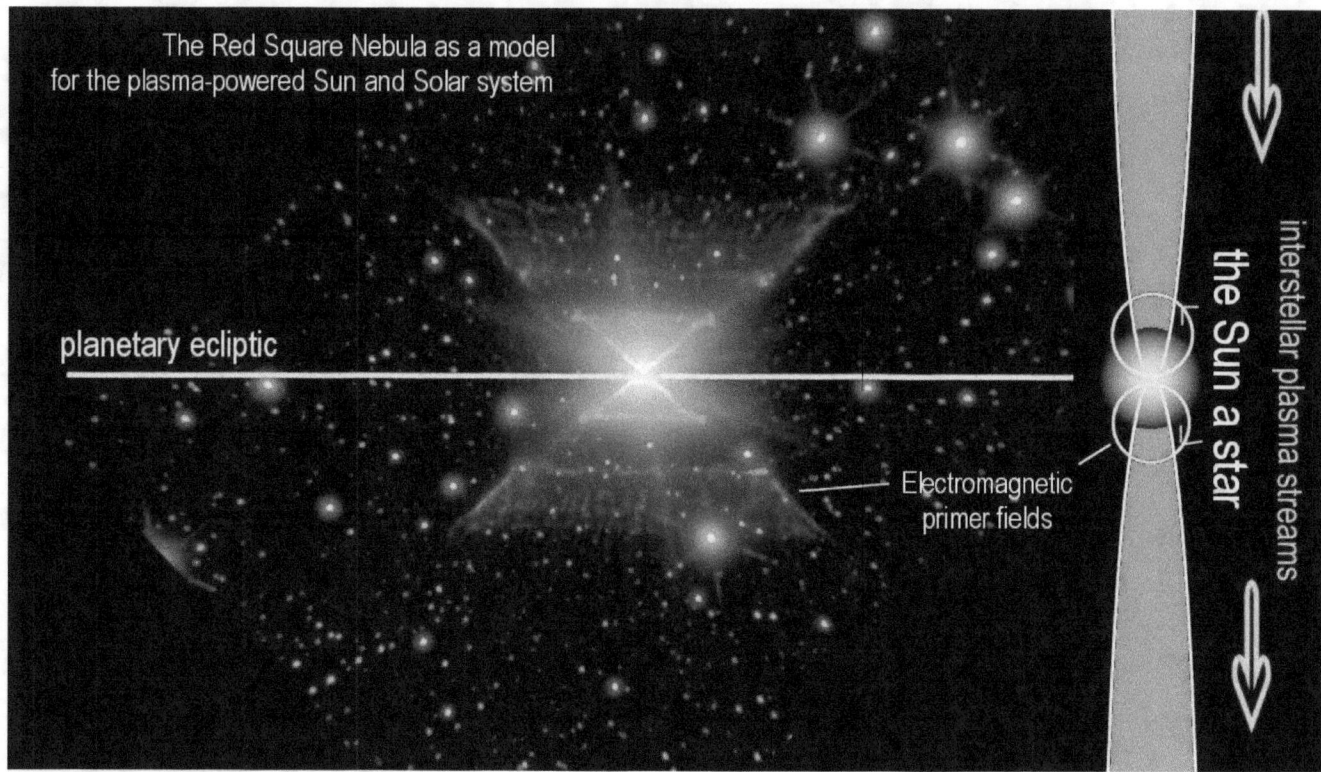

The Red Square Nebula as a model for the plasma-powered Sun and Solar system

planetary ecliptic

Electromagnetic primer fields

interstellar plasma streams

the Sun a star

The principles that produce the large electromagnetic structures in interstellar plasma streams that power a sun, have been recognize to exist in space. They have been recognized in the Red Square nebula.

The main features of the Primer Fields visible in the nebula

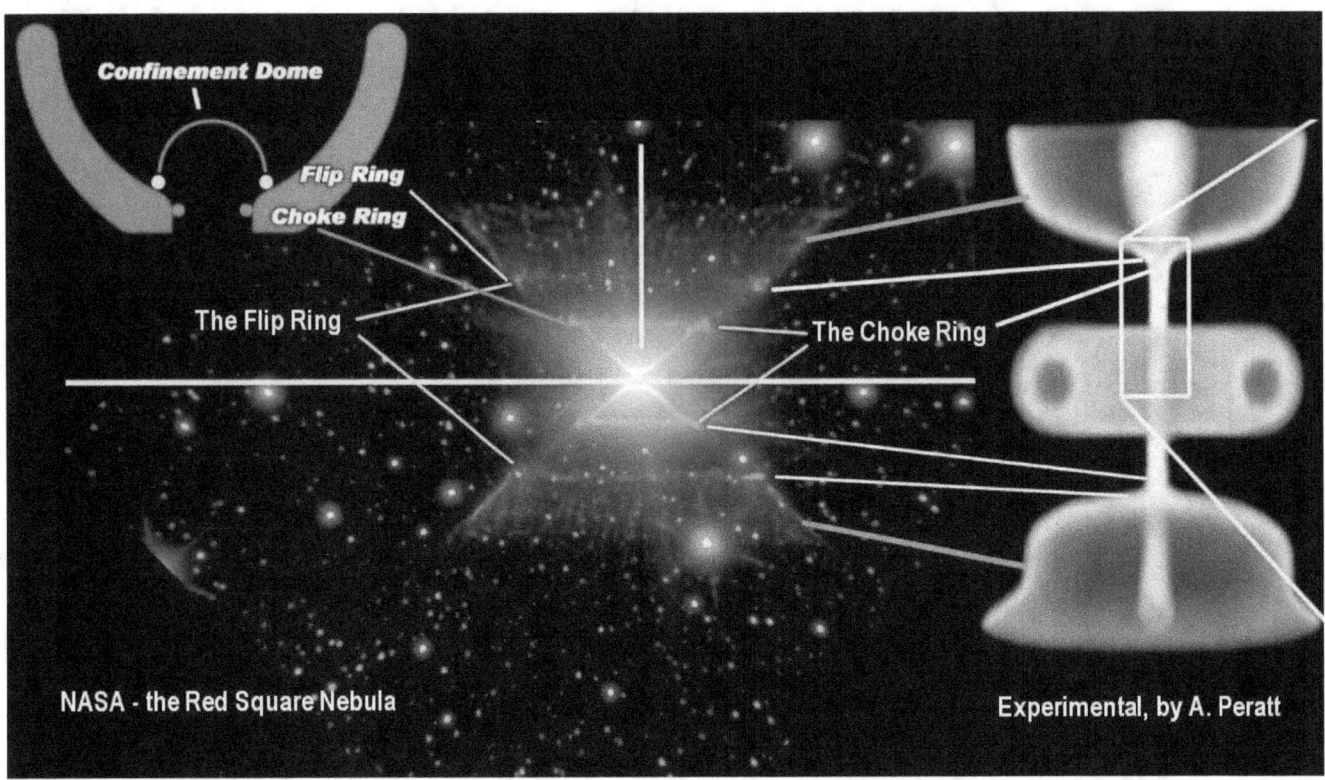

When one looks closely, one can actually see some of the main features of the Primer Fields visible in the nebula.

The Primer Fields for our Sun detected by Ulysses

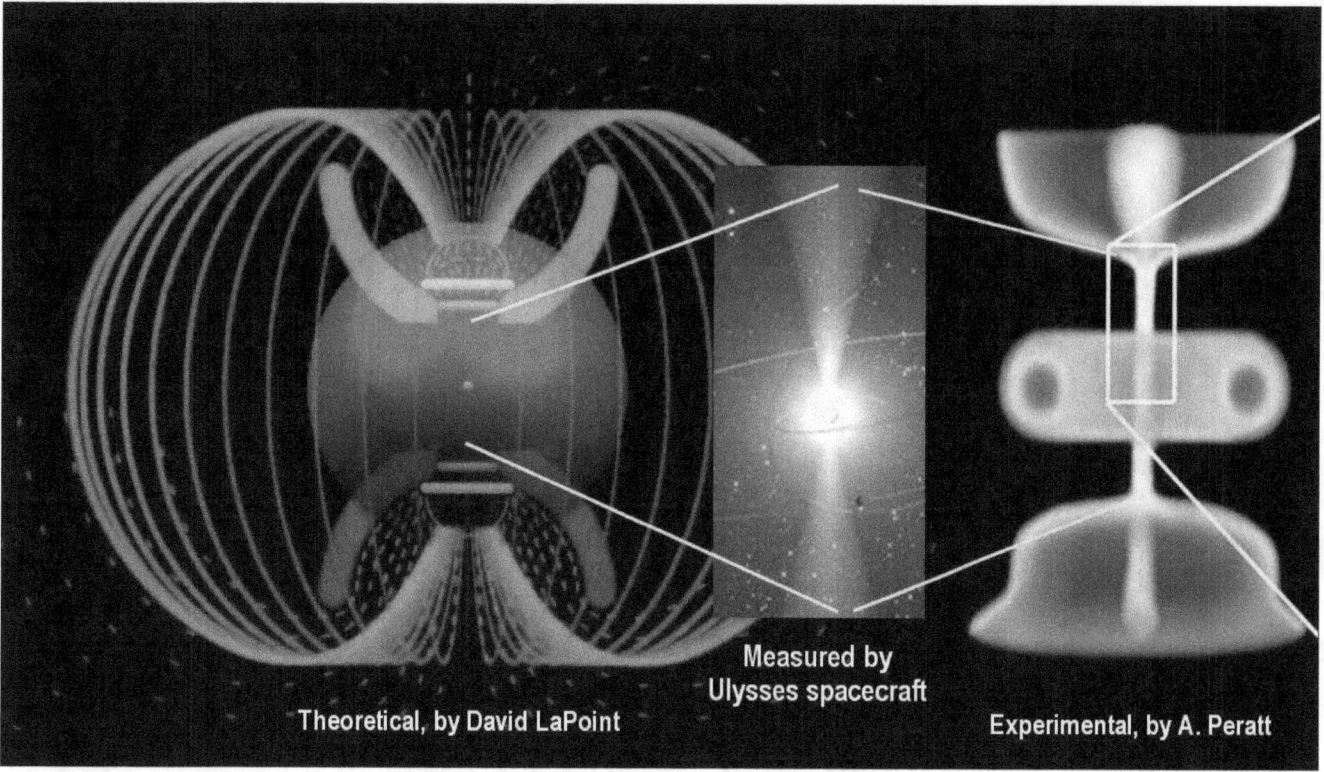

Theoretical, by David LaPoint

Measured by Ulysses spacecraft

Experimental, by A. Peratt

While the Primer Fields for our Sun are never visible, with the Sun being too weak for that, the plasma streams the feed into the Sun have nevertheless been 'seen' by their effects. They have been detected by the Ulysses spacecraft in the form of sharply defined voids in the measured solar-wind pattern over the Sun's poles. Of course they are not voids, but are instead dense plasma streams flowing onto our Sun, which the solar wind cannot penetrate.

NASA's proof that the Sun is a plasma star

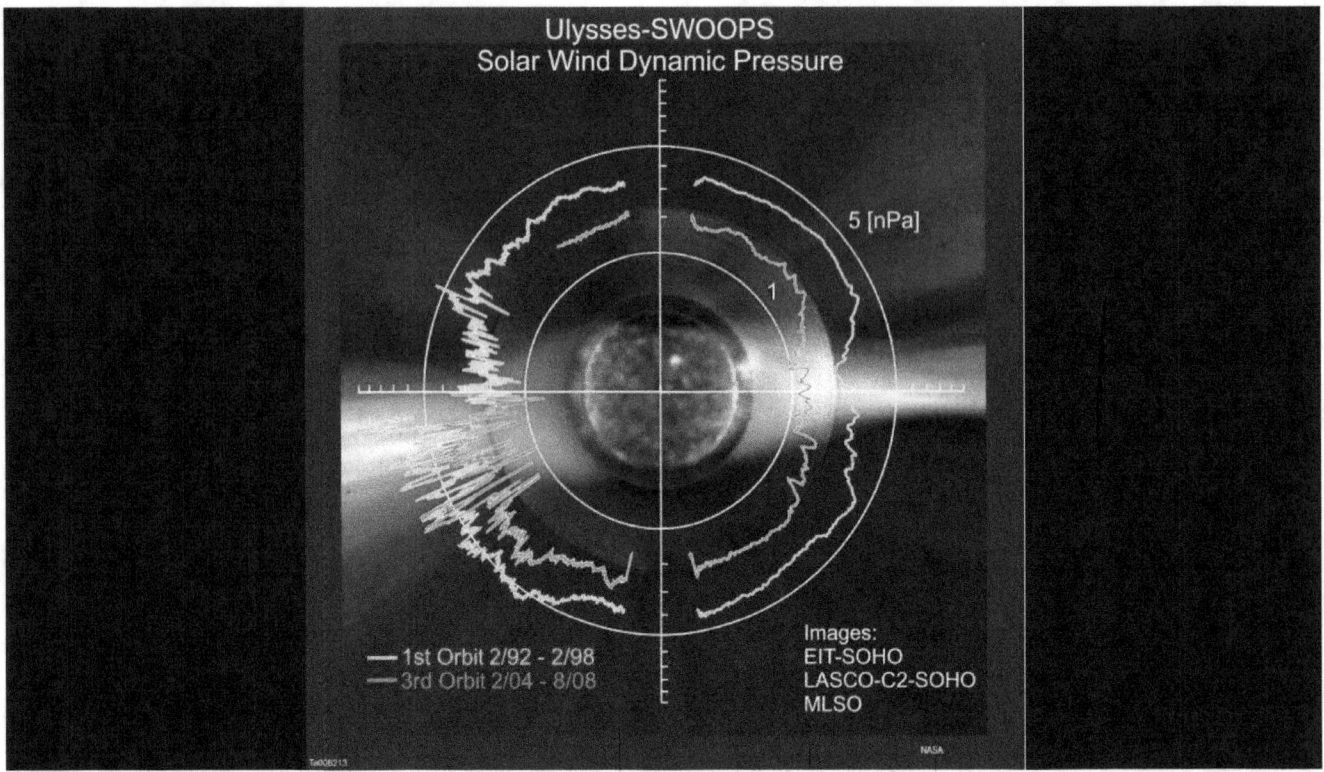

They only look like voids in in the solar wind measurements. With these voids, NASA's Ulysses space mission has delivered still another proof that the Sun is a plasma star. The Ulysses satellite orbited through the polar regions of the Sun for 12 years. Each time it passed across a polar region, it measured a sharply defined void in the solar wind pattern, right over the poles.

Plasma connection to the Sun from the Primer Fields

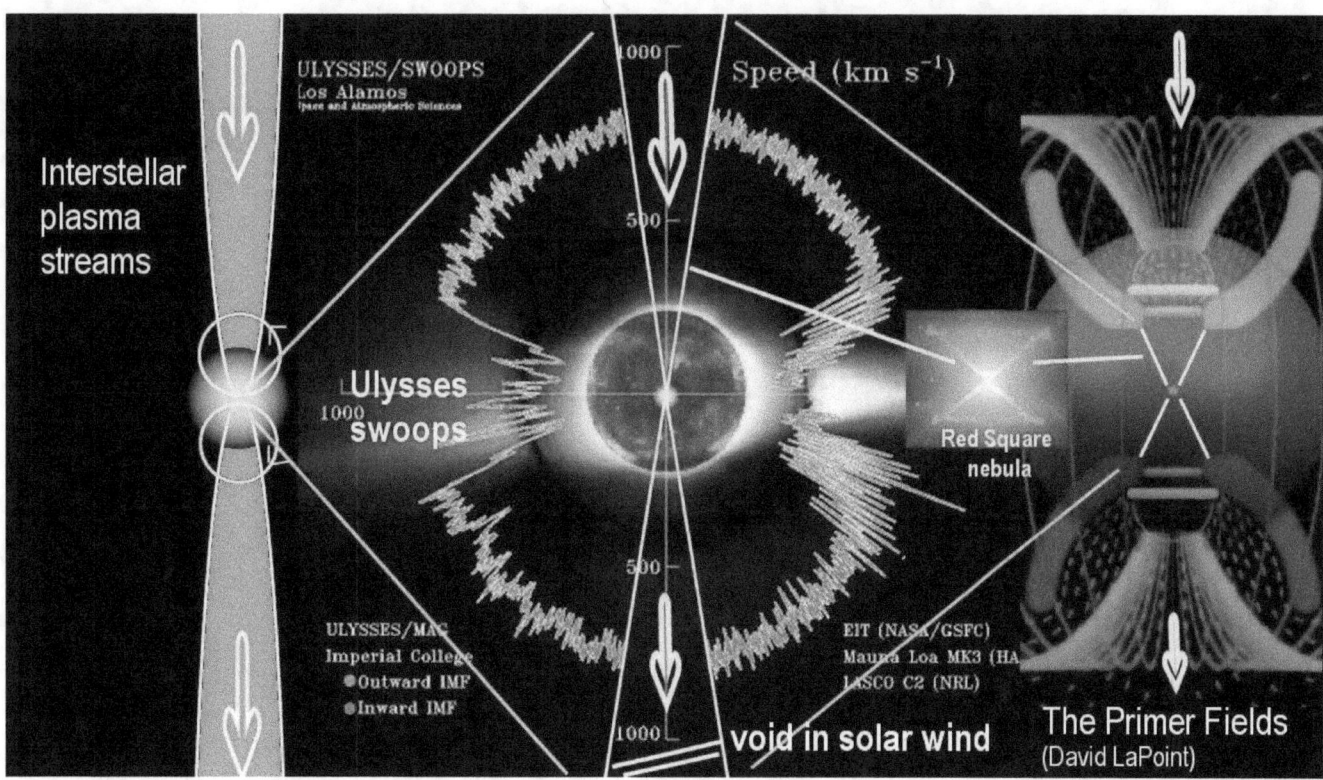

It is safe to say that these voids were caused by the plasma connection flowing to the Sun from the Primer Fields, just as we see similar structures converging onto a sun in the Red Square nebula. The two are the same. The proof of the principle of interstellar plasma streams flowing onto the Sun is important to us, because it renders our Sun as not being its own master, but being mastered by external conditions. The Sun becomes thereby a variable star that has its solar activity modulated by changing conditions in the interstellar plasma streams that flow into the Sun.

This is the critical feature that all the opposition movements against the the Manmade Global Warming doctrine fail to recognize, while it is the key feature that renders the Manmade Global Warming doctrine essentially obsolete. The doctrine assumes the Sun to be an invariable constant, whereby all climate changes are assumed to be manmade. No opposition movement in the sciences to date, counters the invariable Sun doctrine that the Manmade Global Warming doctrine is built on.

The 'Grand Solar Minimum' groups fail

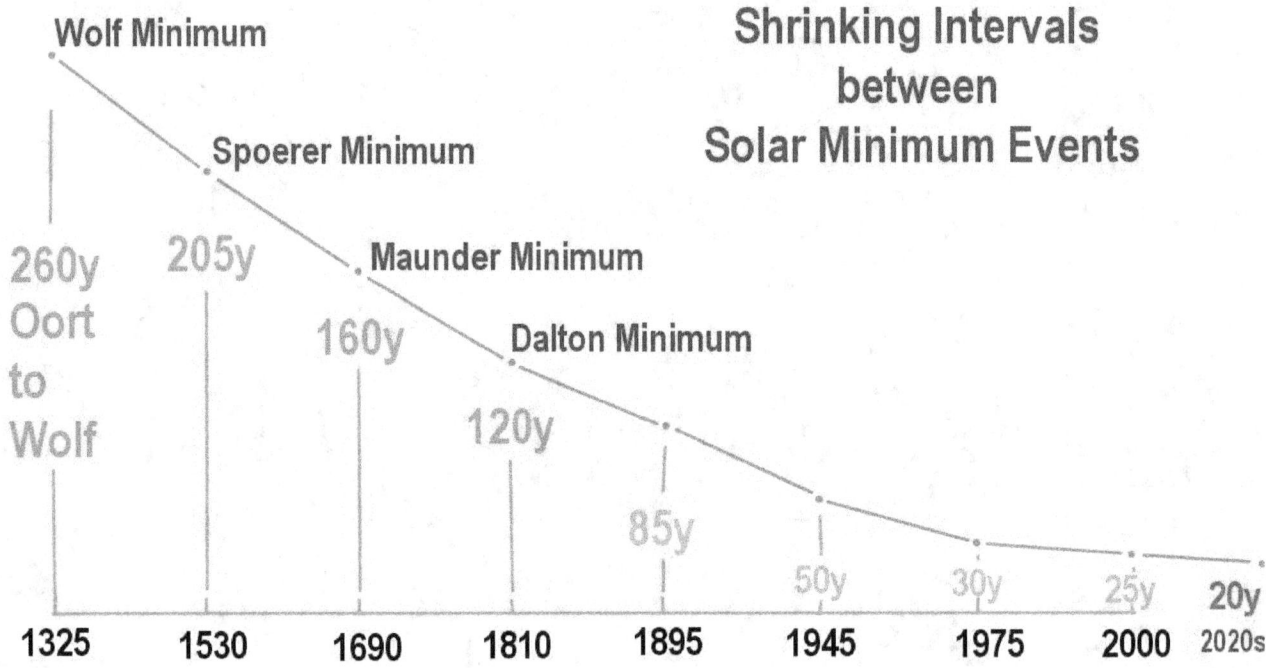

Even the 'Grand Solar Minimum' groups fail on this basis. While they acknowledge that the Sun goes through large cycles of changing solar activity, they assume that these cycles are mastered by the Sun itself, instead of them being imposed onto the Sun. Thus they fail to recognize that the historic cycles have all diminished and are no longer valid as climate factors. By this failure they block the recognition of the Ice Age dynamics, which has tragic consequences for humanity, just as the Manmade Global Warming doctrine blocks the recognition of the Ice Age dynamics for the same reason, except that the failure is intended in this case.

Not a single climate science group has recognized

NASA

To date, not a single climate science group has recognized that Ice Ages result when the Sun's Primer Fields collapse as the interstellar plasma streams diminish below the cut-off threshold for the Primer Fields. This is why no preparations have been made anywhere in the world for the consequences of the Ice Age phase shift in the 2050s that all scientific measurements point to.

The principle of the Primer Fields of critical importance

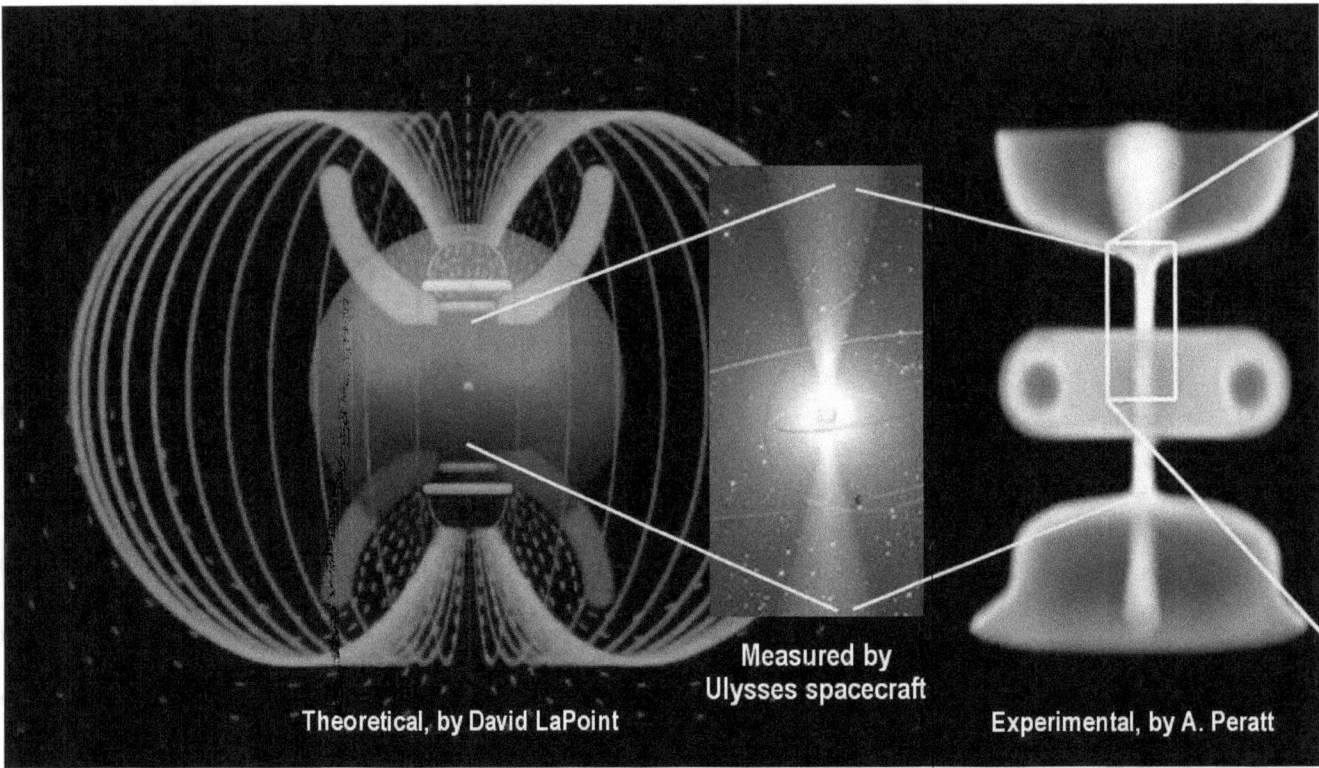

Measured by
Ulysses spacecraft

Theoretical, by David LaPoint

Experimental, by A. Peratt

The principle of the Primer Fields is therefore of critical importance for us, because the Primer Fields are formed by the magnetic effects of flowing electrically charged particles. This means that a minimal rate of flow and plasma density is required for the fields to form and function. This also means, that when the interstellar flow-rate drops below the minimal threshold needed for the Primer Fields to be maintained, the operating Primer Fields collapse. In this case, when the fields collapse that focus concentrated plasma onto the Sun, the Sun becomes less powered and an Ice Age begins on Earth.

Built on this false model of the Sun

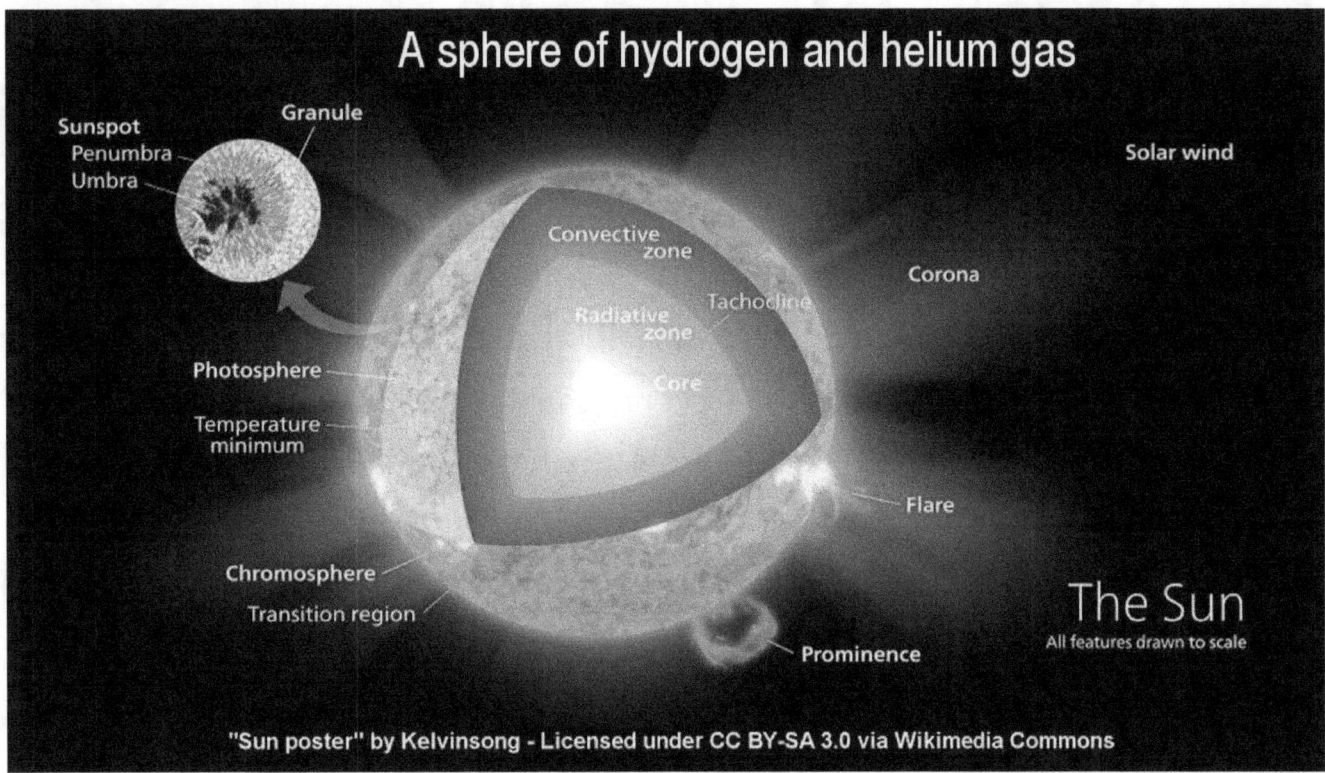

This fact is totally obscured by the false model of the Sun as an internally powered gas star, which renders the Sun an invariable star. The Manmade Global Warming doctrine is built on this false model of the Sun. No opposition movement against the Global Warming doctrine has yet countered this model of the invariable Sun, and recognized our Sun correctly, to be a plasma star, a variable star, and Ice Ages to be digital phenomena.

Ice Ages are Digital Events

Ice Ages are Digital Events

They are cosmic On-Off events that affect our Sun.

This means get ready! Forget the fur coats. Think Big.

Ice Ages are Digital Events

They are cosmic On-Off events that affect our Sun. This means get ready! Forget the fur coats. Think Big.

The Sun reverts to a low-power default mode

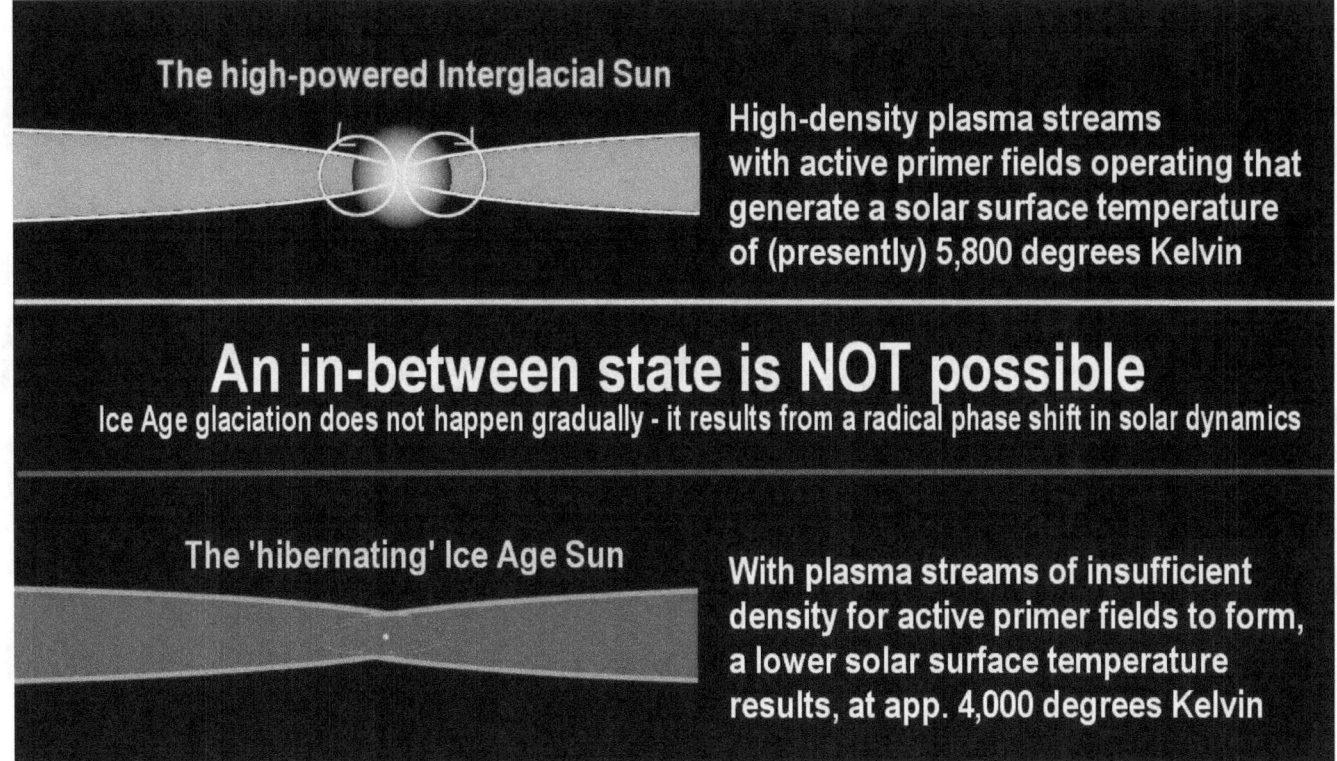

The high-powered Interglacial Sun

High-density plasma streams with active primer fields operating that generate a solar surface temperature of (presently) 5,800 degrees Kelvin

An in-between state is NOT possible

Ice Age glaciation does not happen gradually - it results from a radical phase shift in solar dynamics

The 'hibernating' Ice Age Sun

With plasma streams of insufficient density for active primer fields to form, a lower solar surface temperature results, at app. 4,000 degrees Kelvin

As I said before, when the Primer Fields collapse, the interstellar plasma stream is no longer focused onto the Sun but flows loosely around it. At this point the Sun reverts to a low-power default mode, a type of hibernation mode. That's when the climate on Earth goes cold. The glacial period begins. We call it the Ice Age. And so we should. The Earth becomes largely a planet of desserts and ice, when the Sun hibernates.

But how do we know that Ice Ages are caused by the Sun going into hibernation?

Proof of the Hibernating Sun

Proof of the Hibernating Sun

Proof of the Hibernating Sun

The proof is located in historic Berillim-10 ratios

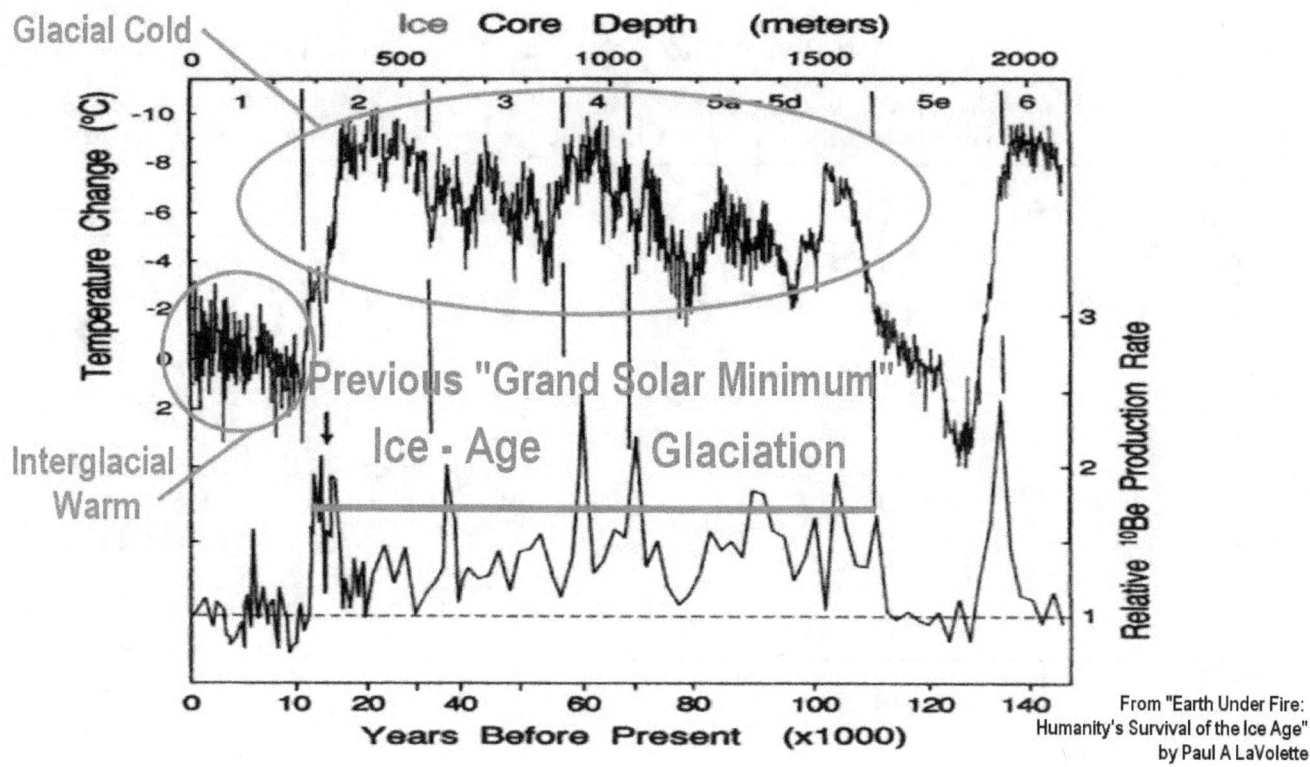

From "Earth Under Fire:
Humanity's Survival of the Ice Age"
by Paul A LaVolette

The proof is located in historic Berillim-10 ratios. Berillium-10 is a radioisotope that is produced exclusively by cosmic-ray collisions in the atmosphere. When the Sun is weak, it has almost no plasma corona surrounding it. The means that the Earth is hit with the full volume of solar cosmic-ray flux. The Berillium-10 ratio is therefore correspondingly high.

Note, that during the entire span of the glaciation period, the Berillium-10 ratio was extremely high, shown in the lower graph. A weaker Sun that emits such great volumes of cosmic-ray flux, in spite of its weakness, can only be a hibernating Sun that has almost no plasma corona surrounding it.

The high Berillium-10 ratios during the glacial period proof conclusively that Ice Age glaciation is caused by the Sun operating in low-powered mode, and that interglacial periods are caused by the Sun operating in high-powered mode.

Also note that the start and termination of the last glaciation period happened sharply. Cyclical orbital variations cannot cause such sharp transitions as have been measured. Only plasma-electric effects can cause this by the Sun's Primer Field's becoming active or inactive.

One might argue here that the high volumes of cosmic-ray flux that produced the high Berillium-10 ratios, were in part galactic in origin, because a hibernating Sun, without Primer Fields on operation, would Not have a plasma heliosphere surrounding it that attenuates galactic flux, so that the Earth would be exposed to the full volume of the galactic cosmic-ray flux.

While this is true, it should be noted that the attenuation that the heliosphere provides is rather minuscule.

Voyager 1 measured only a 35% increase in cosmic-ray flux

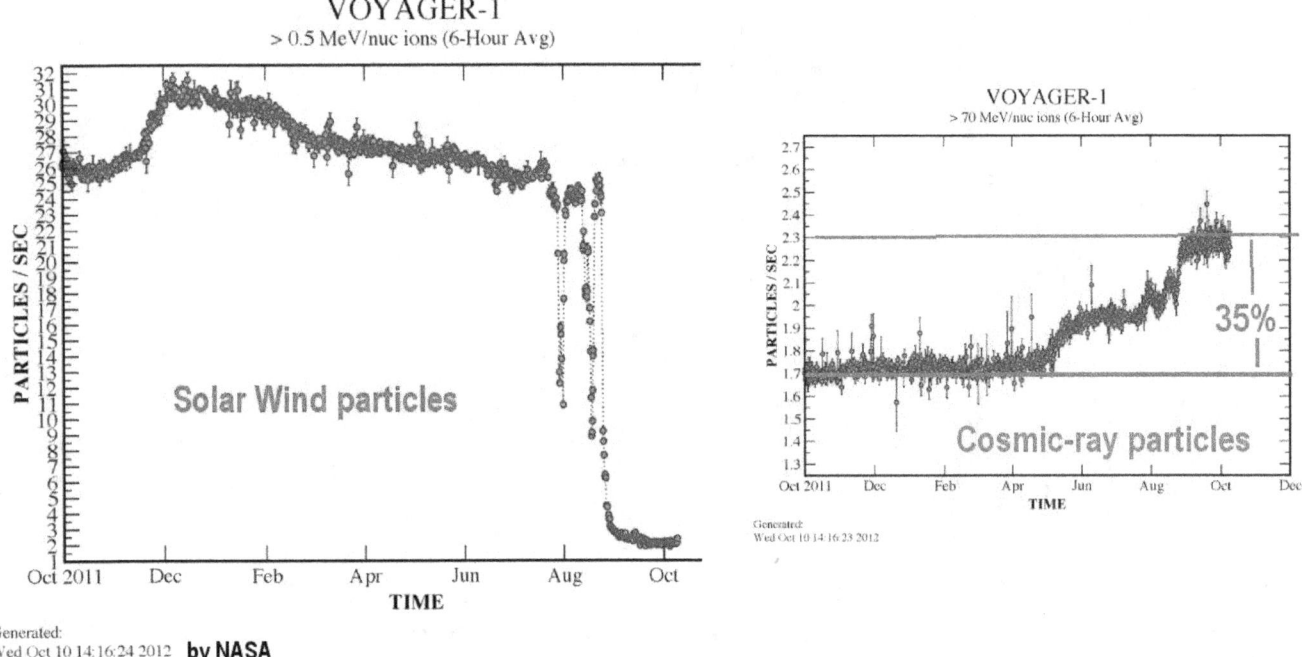

When the Voyager 1 spacecraft penetrated through the shell of the heliosphere into interstellar space, it measured only a 35% increase in cosmic-ray flux density that is itself minuscule in comparison with the solar cosmic-ray density that the Earth encounters by its close proximity to the Sun.

During the hibernation phase of the Sun

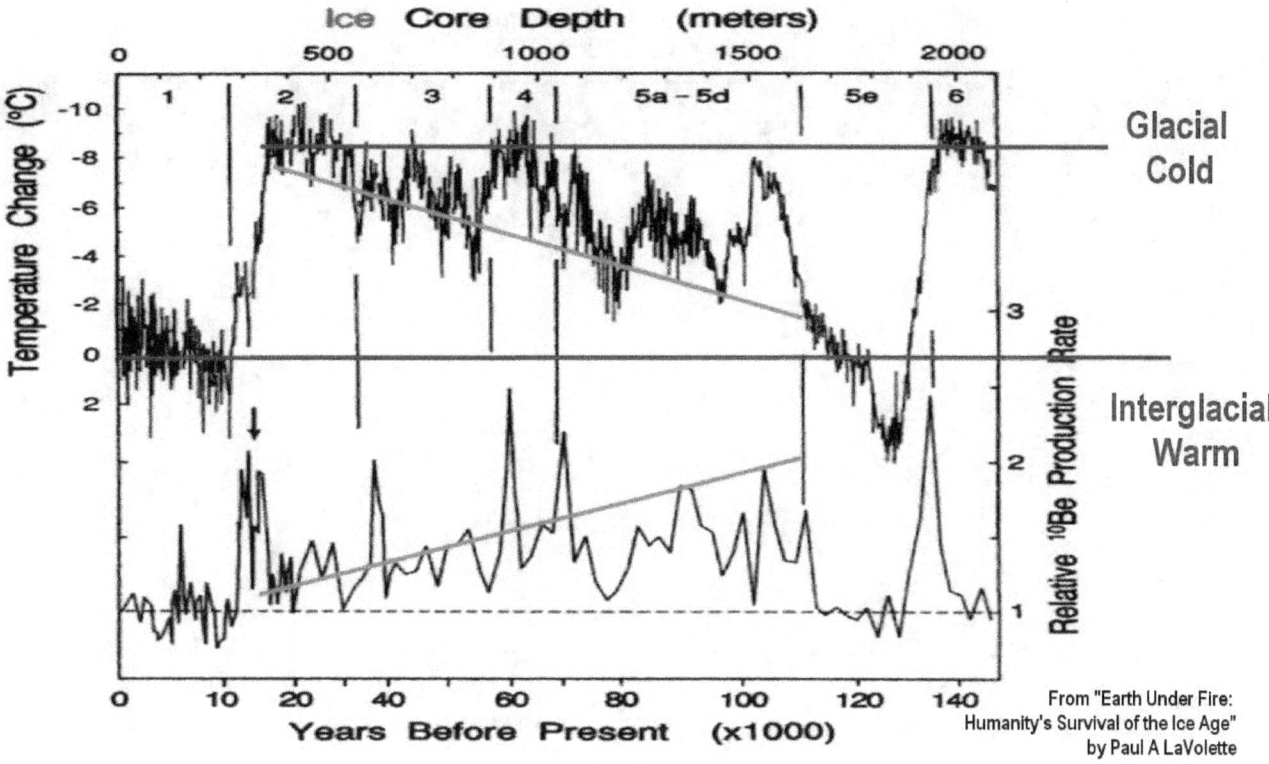

From "Earth Under Fire: Humanity's Survival of the Ice Age" by Paul A LaVolette

The bottom line is that even during the glacial period, during the hibernation phase of the Sun, solar activity varies dramatically and affects the climate on Earth.

When the last glaciation began, roughly 110,000 years ago, the Sun cooled down rapidly, but the ocean-temperature change lagged behind significantly. This tells us that we might get away with open-air agriculture in the tropics in the immediate period after the Ice Age phase shift. The Berillium-10 ratios also tell us that the Sun becomes progressively colder during the glaciation period, which is reflected in corresponding climate cooling, so that the initial cooling may be less harsh, and may be comparable to the Younger Dryas period prior to the interglacial startup.

This much climatic cooling is hard to imagine

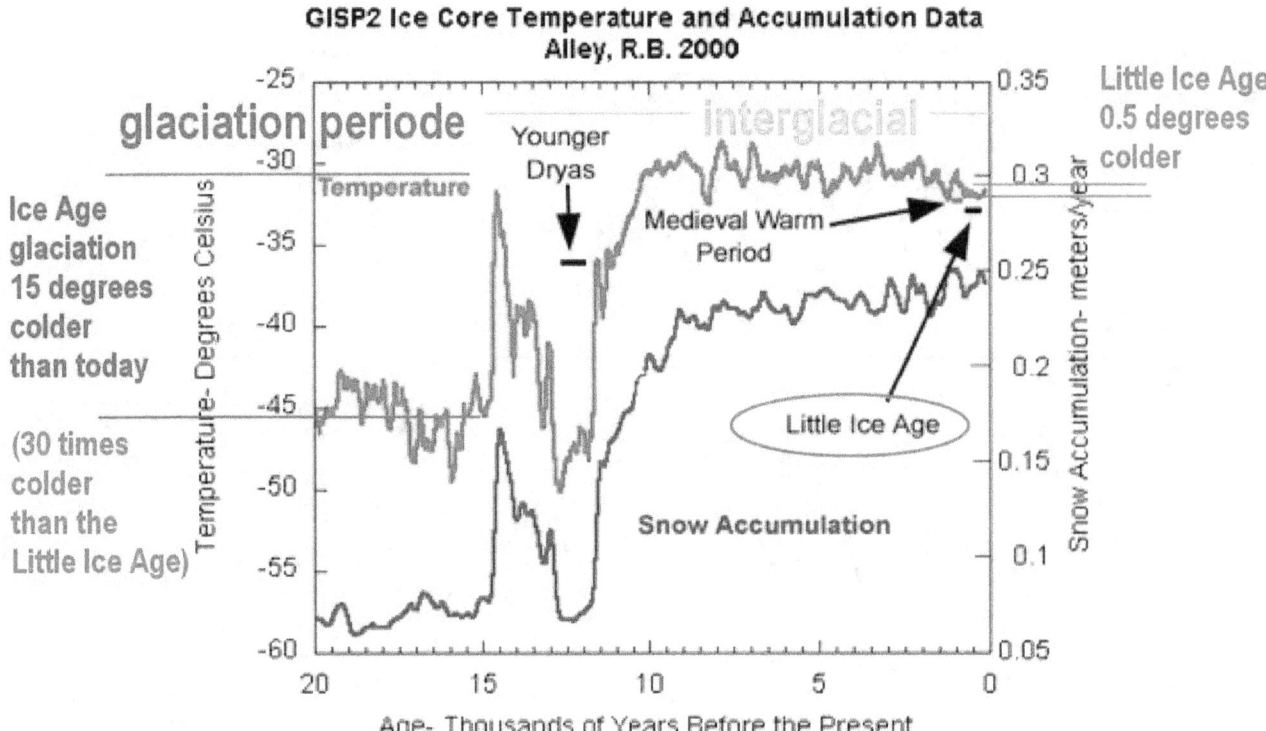

The Younger Dryas period was roughly 30 times 'colder' than the Little Ice cooling had been. The Little Ice Age had resulted in a half a degree of average cooling recorded in the Greenland ice sheet, below today's average. The Younger Dryas was on average 15 degrees below today's level. This much climatic cooling is hard to imagine.

Even harder to imagine

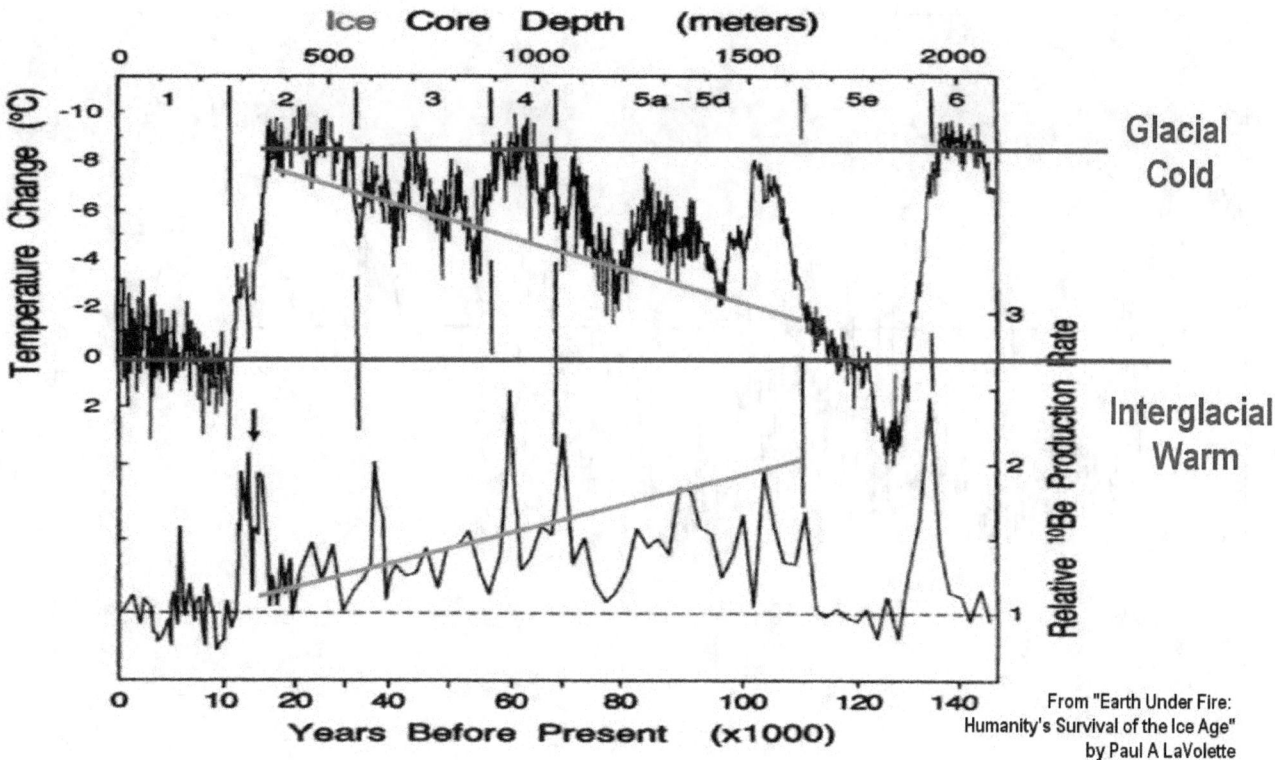

From "Earth Under Fire:
Humanity's Survival of the Ice Age"
by Paul A LaVolette

It is even harder to imagine the full Ice Age that was significantly colder than the Younger Dryas event which doesn't show up well in the ice cores from Antarctica.

The initial Ice Age cooling at a slightly higher level

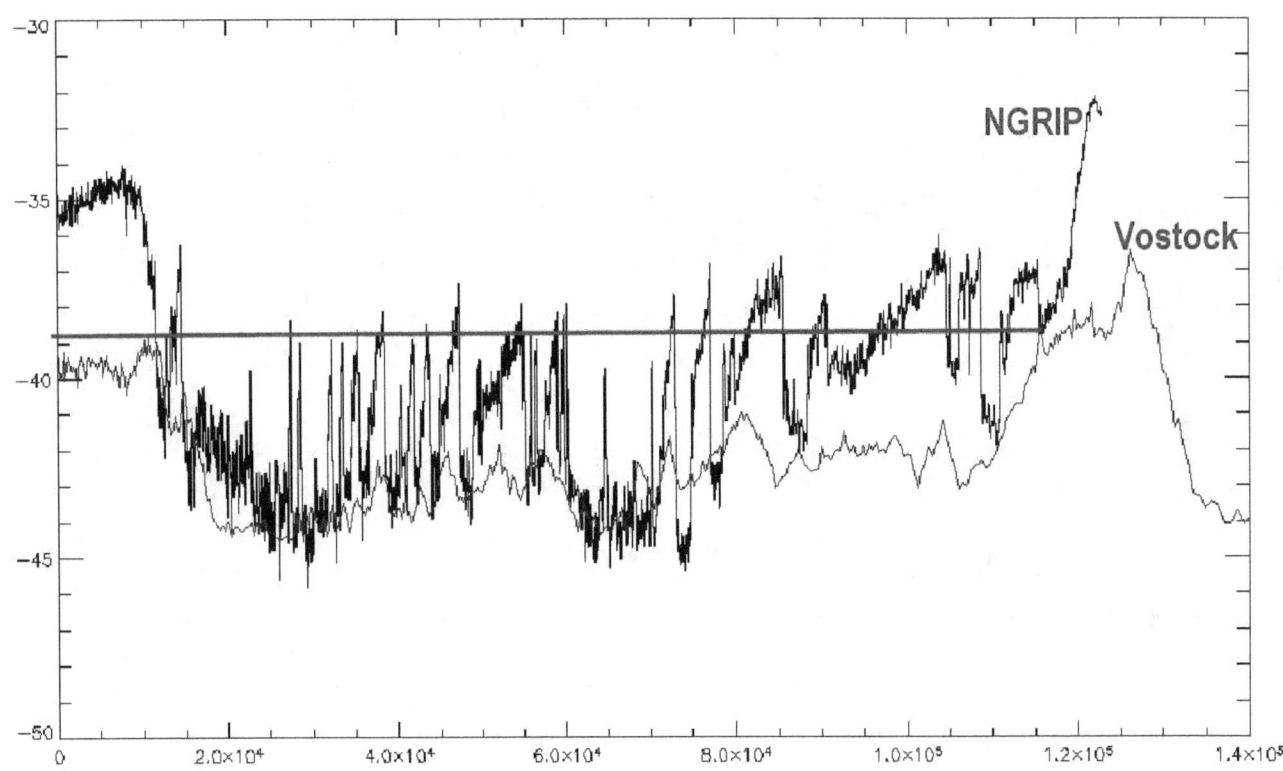

The ice core records from North Greenland indicate that the initial Ice Age cooling ended at a slightly higher level, comparable to the mid-point of the Dryas cooling.

246

A 20-times deeper cooling implies extinction

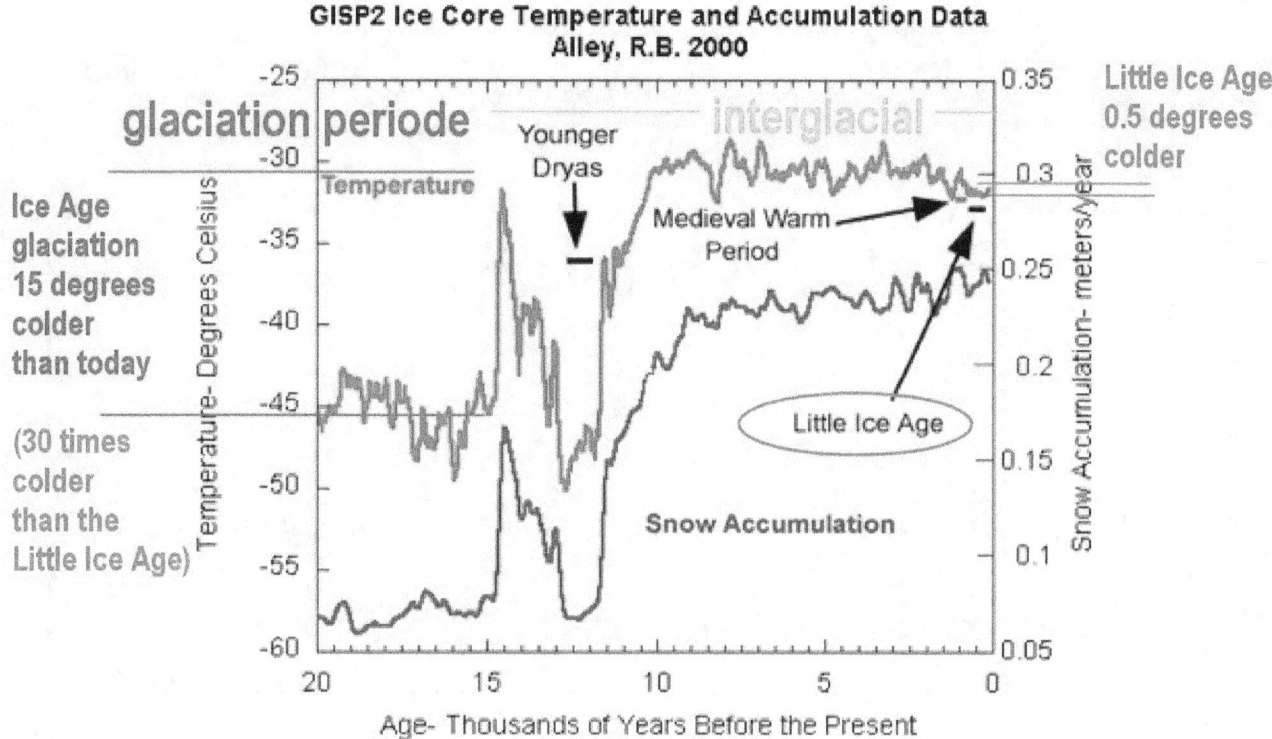

In this case, the initial cooling would have been only 20 times larger than the cooling that caused the Little Ice Age, which of course is likewise unimaginable in consequences, since the minuscule cooling that caused the Little Ice Age had depressed agriculture already past the starvation level to the point that some areas of Europe suffered population losses by starvation upwards to 30% in some regions. A 20-times deeper cooling implies extinction in these regions. This is what we face when the Ice Age phase shift happens. This is what we have to built technological infrastructures for to protect the future of humanity.

We should not ignore

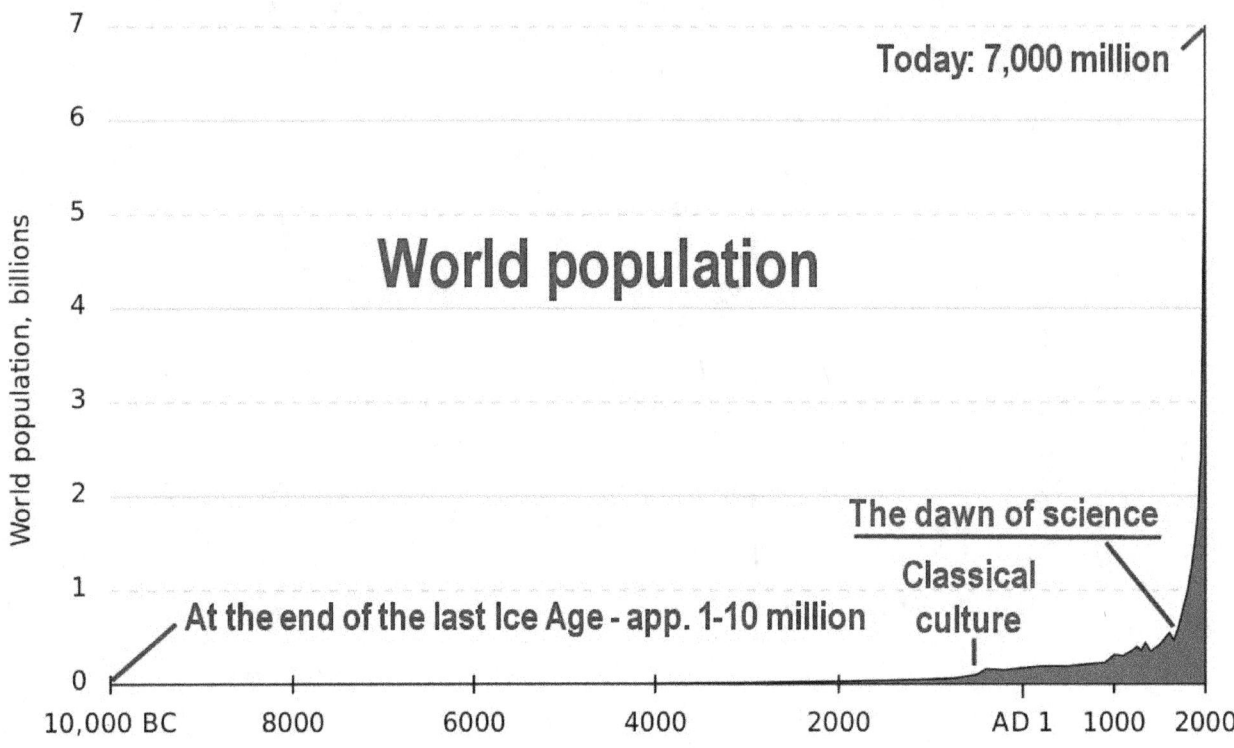

We should not ignore that according to the best estimates in archeology, the world population was as low 1 to 10 million people who were probably living largely of the sea, since during an Ice Age the land areas are largely desert. This means that humanity's transition to the next glacial period with a potentially 7,000 times larger population, can only be achieved with technological resources, such as indoors agriculture and worldwide water distribution.

Ice Age phase shift is potentially as close as the 2050s

And, because the coming Ice Age phase shift is potentially as close as the 2050s, we better start the infrastructure-building soon. Ideally, it should have already started.

We better build a New World to have a future

This means we better wake up fast, scrap the political divisions and insanity, join hands across the world, and build ourselves a New World to have a future. What we have operating today doesn't measure up by a long way. It is already collapsing.

When the hibernation of the Sun happens

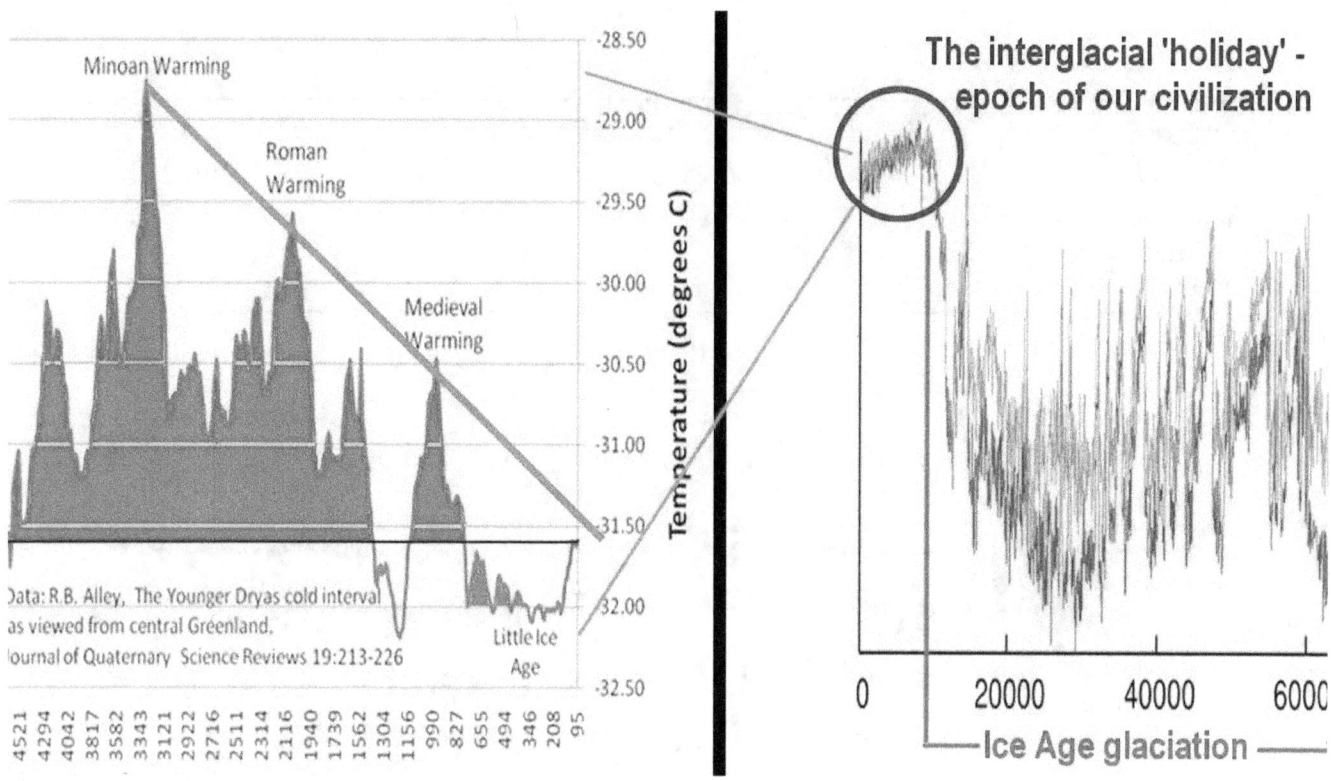

When the hibernation of the Sun happens, a totally different world begins for us on Earth. The world becomes incomparable with what we experience today or have any knowledge of from the past. We have only the ice core records to guide us, in terms of what to expect.

Just look at where our wonderfully warm interglacial climate of the last 12,000 years is located. You find it encircled in blue. Our entire civilization with all its ups and downs, including its warm spells and little ice ages, developed within the blue circle. The interglacial world that we have lived in, and still do, is a brilliant anomaly in the larger bleak landscape.

Interglacial anomaly is created by the peak period

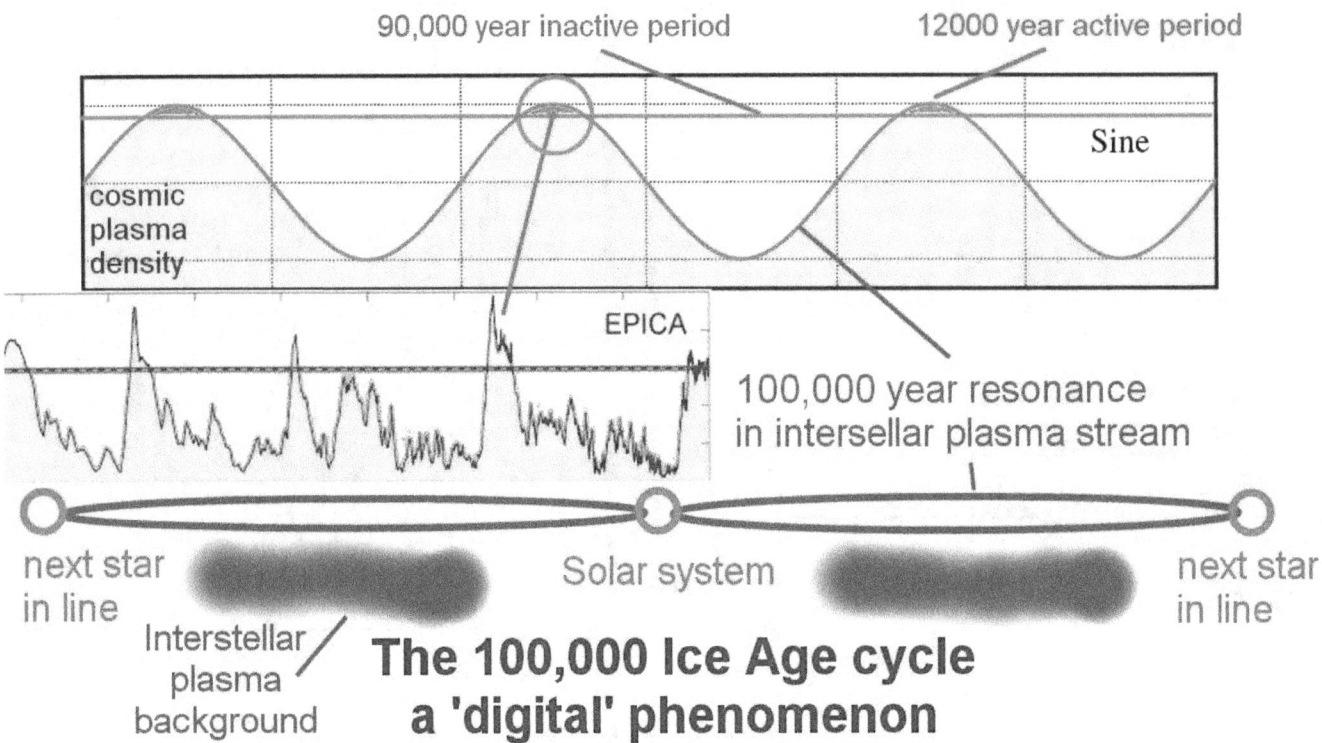

The interglacial anomaly is created by the peak period of the resonance effect in the interstellar plasma streams that are associated with our solar system, which power our Sun. We wouldn't exist if it wasn't for the peak of the resonance pulse that takes us past the threshold where Primer Fields form that focus plasma onto our Sun.

When Primer Fields form

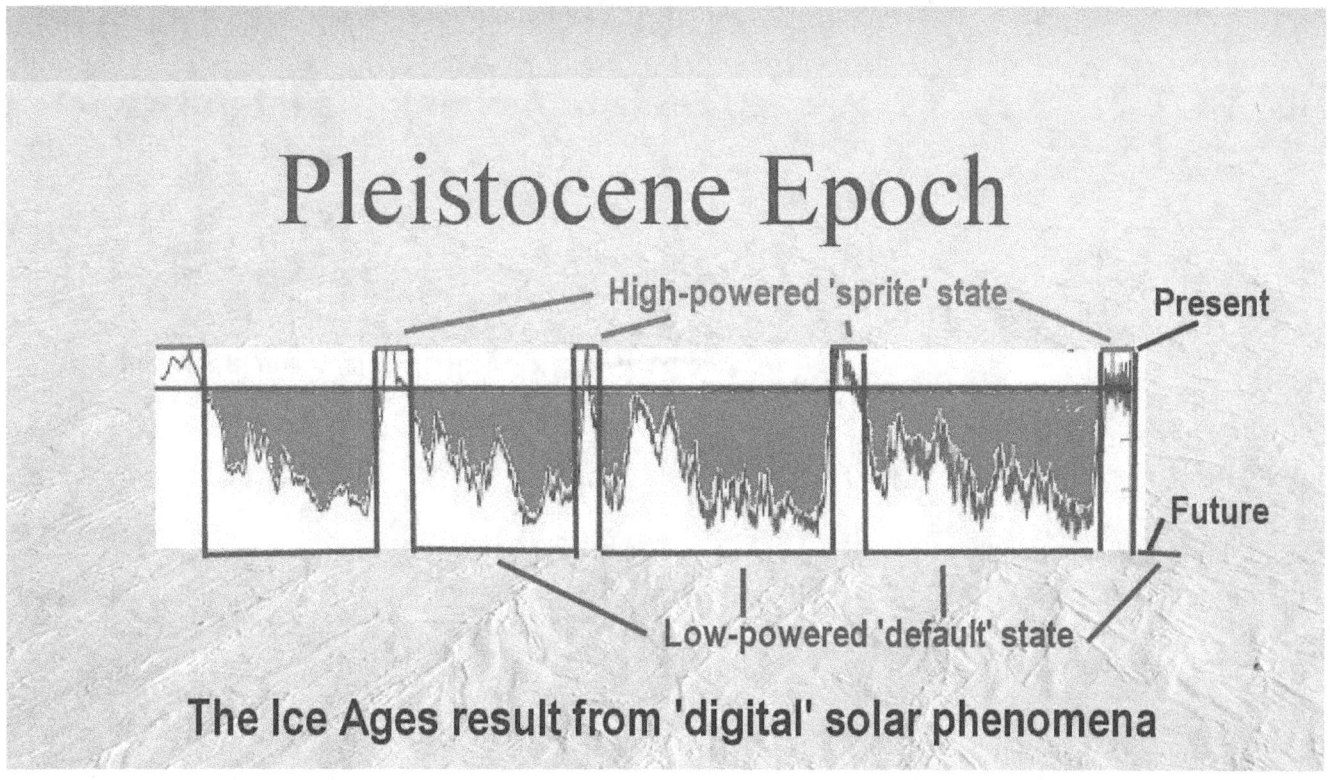

When Primer Fields form, the Sun is 2.5 times more energetic, which creates the warm climates that we enjoy today. Without the Primer Fields the Earth is cold and the survival-rate low. This means that the on-off timing is critical for us.

The Primer Fields imbalance creates an asymmetry

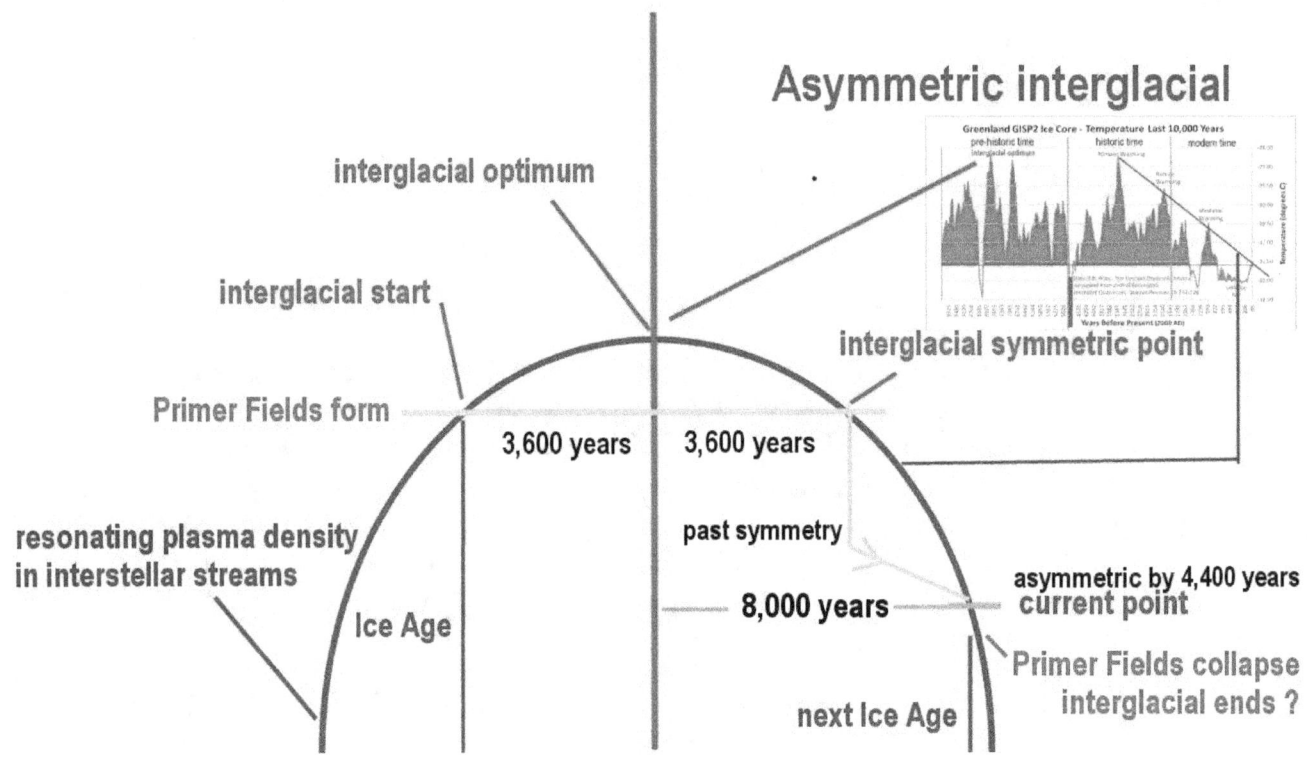

Since the Primer Fields, when they form, increase the rate of flow of the plasma stream that creates them, they require a higher plasma density to start up than is required to maintain them. This imbalance creates an asymmetry.

When the Primer Fields formed roughly 12,600 years ago, with which the last Ice Age ended, the climate warmed up for 3,600 years to its interglacial maximum. We are presently 8,000 years past this maximum, or 4,400 years past the symmetry point. This means that the Primer Fields are barely hanging on. And it also means that the slope for the rate of change is getting steeper as the resonance pulse in the interstellar plasma stream is getting weaker. That we are getting near the cut-off threshold for the Primer Fields, which is now accelerating, large climate instabilities are being experienced that break evermore historic records.

An entire 26-car freight train was blown off a railway bridge

A train was blown off the tracks in northern New Mexico. Damage to roofing and power lines was reported across eastern New Mexico, including in Clovis and Las Vegas, earlier on March 13. Winds gusted to 104 mph on San Augustin Pass and 100 mph at Cloudcroft.

NMSP
@NMStatePolice

State Police on scene of a #trainderailment on SR 469 near Logan, NM involving 26 rail cars. No injuries reported. Wind was contributing factor in crash.

703 2:17 AM - Mar 14, 2019

Adapt 2030 - Winds of Change Blow in Bombogenisis Blizzard Ulema (802)

For example, when was the last time that an entire 26-car freight train was blown off a railway bridge by strong winds?

We experience extremes now in ever increasing numbers

We experience these types of extremes now in ever increasing numbers, like snow storms in March with winds up to 100 mile an hour that pile up the snow into huge drifts.

But as we experience these extreme conditions, let us not forget that the cause is rooted in the phenomenon by which we ourselves exist.

The cause that has enabled us to exist

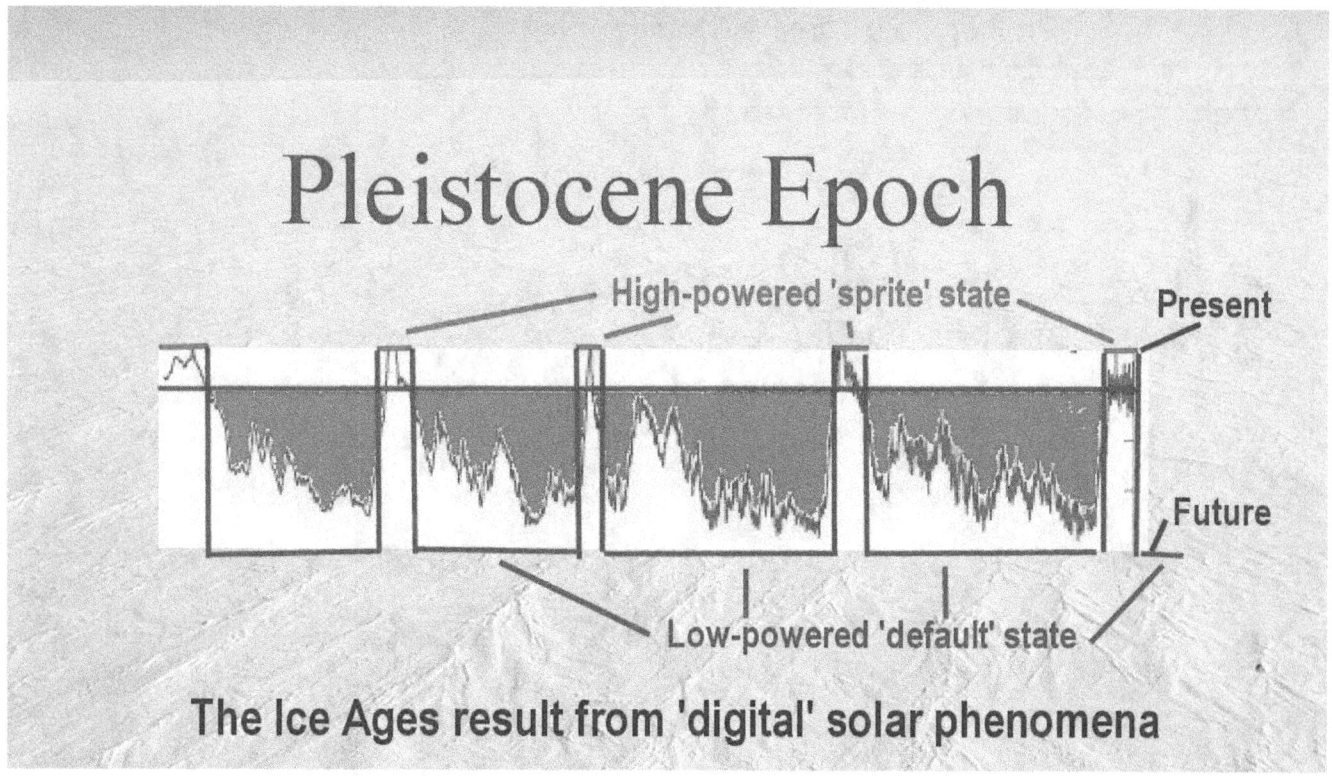

The cause that has enabled us to exist, is the resonance effect in the plasma streams that enables interglacial climate recoveries to happen. If it wasn't for the resonance effect that enabled the interglacial recoveries that gave humanity a chance to rebuild itself, we would likely have become extinct long ago.

Galaxy is presently at its weakest state in 440 million years

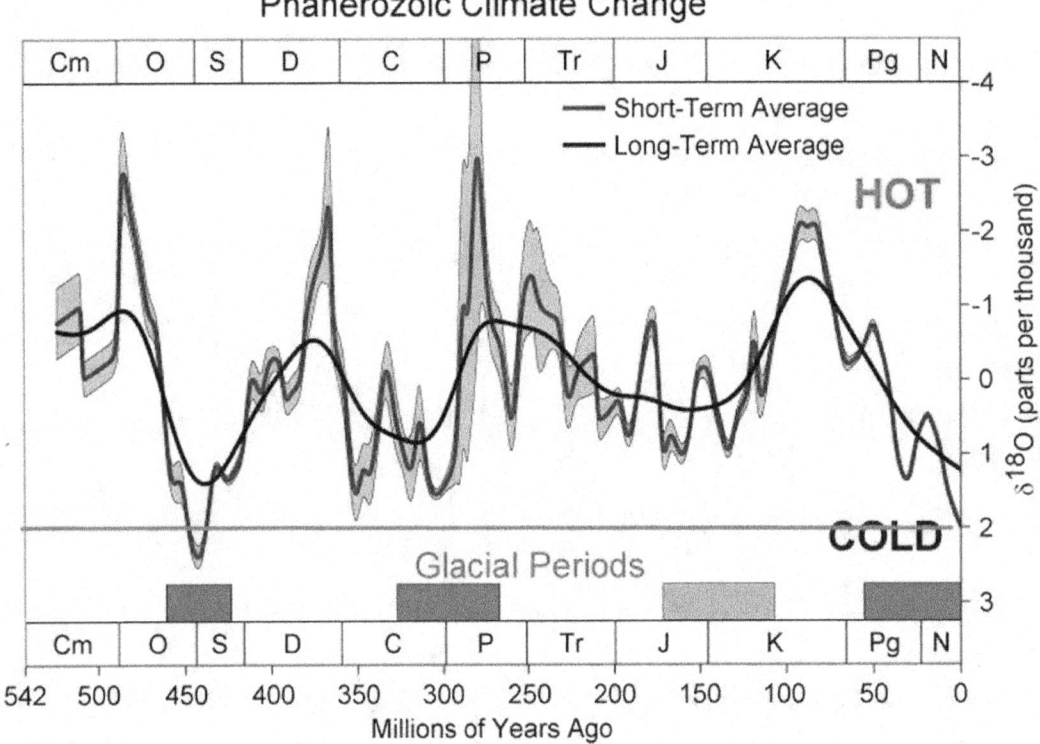

We should also not forget that we are in the current critical situation, because the entire galaxy is presently at its weakest state in 440 million years. If it wasn't for this extreme weakness in the galaxy, we wouldn't be in an Ice Age Epoch at all.

The reason why the galaxy has become extremely weak

The reason why the galaxy has become extremely weak in plasma density, is the result of the resonance effects in the intergalactic plasma streams in which our entire galaxy is a node point.

Large distances in intergalactic space result in long resonance effects

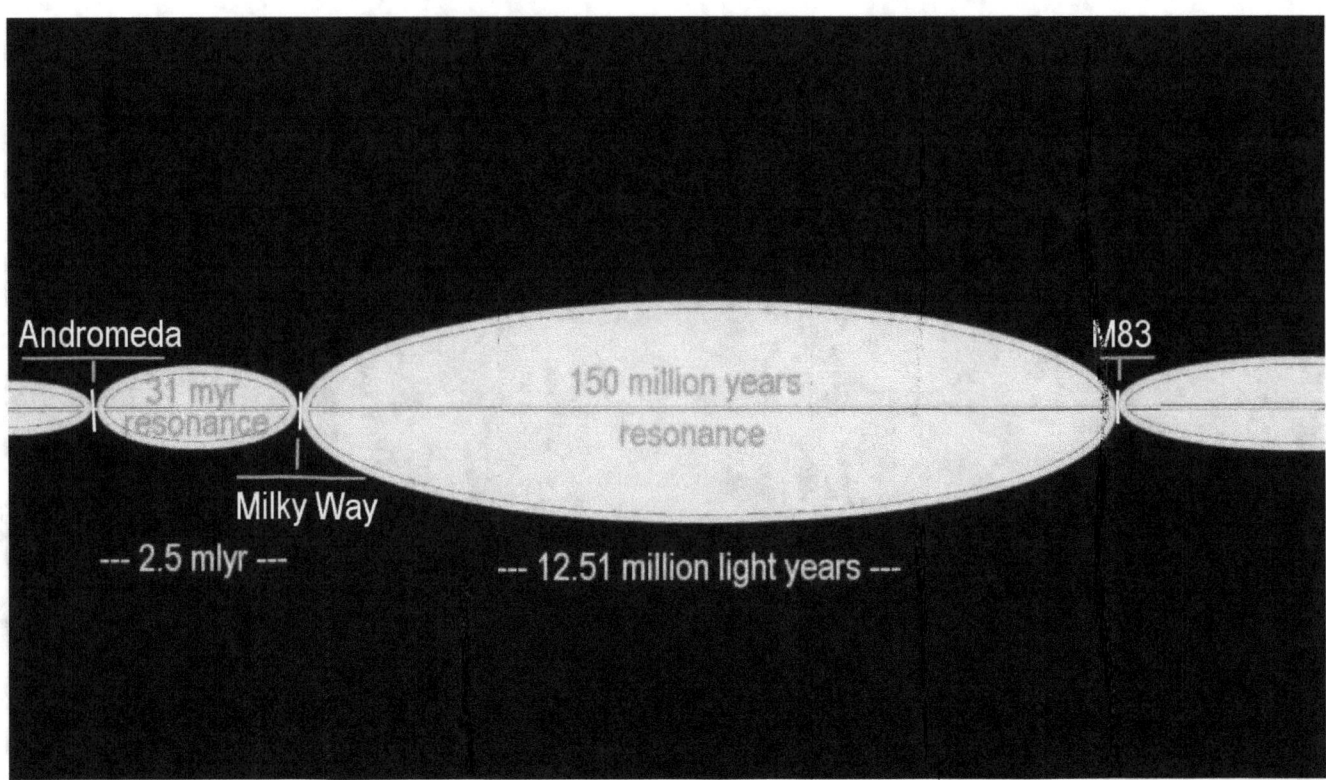

The extremely large distances in intergalactic space result in long resonance effects measured as 31 million year cycles, and 150 million year cycles, which are overlaid on each other.

Overlaid effects created a roller-coaster ride of climate conditions

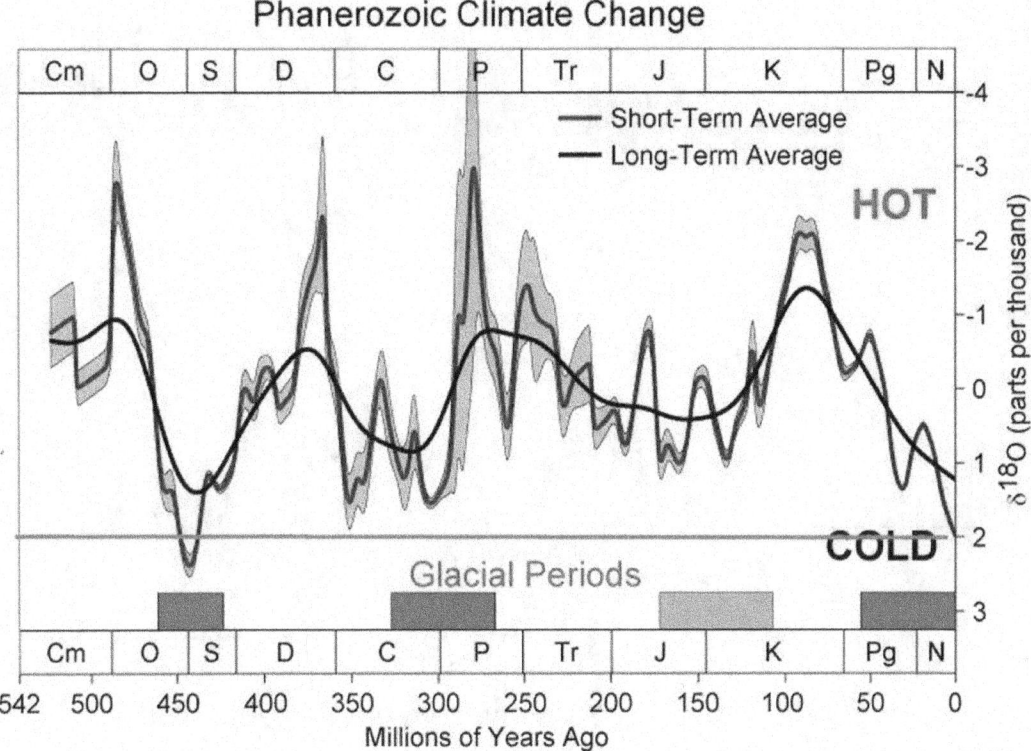

Their overlaid effects created a roller-coaster ride of hugely changing climate conditions on Earth, including the deep cold of the epoch of the ice ages in the last 2 million years.

Since these effects are caused far away in intergalactic space, millions of light years distant, and the effects are enormous in scale, there is nothing we can do on Earth to affect any facet of them. However, we can affect our reactions to them. We can built us a technological New World where the cosmic effects won't affect us, no matter how large they promise to become.

Projecting forward the startup of the last Ice Age

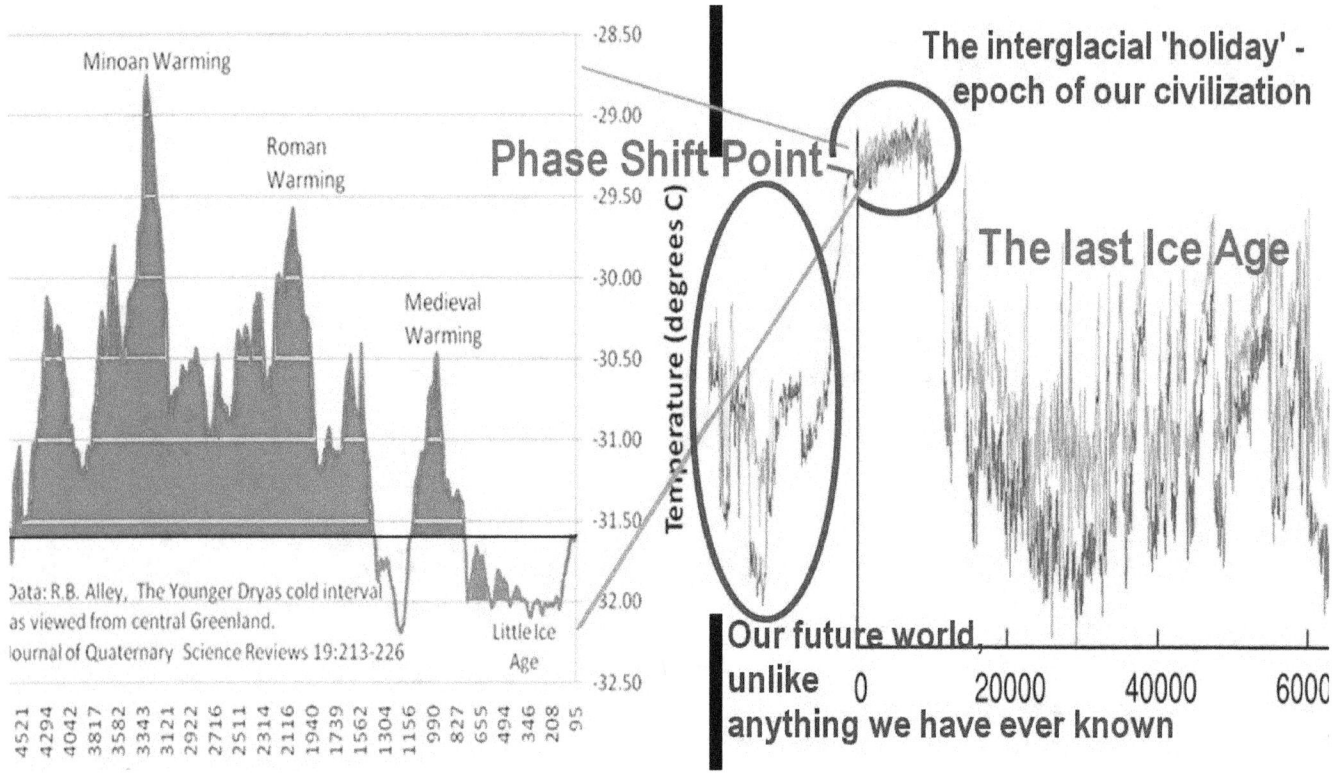

We can gleam to some degree the extent of the climate change that the cosmic system has in store for us, by simply projecting forward into our time the measured data from the startup of the last Ice Age.

The forward projection tells us that we are about to enter into a type of climate that we cannot imagine, as we have no historic experience as a reference for it, but which we must prepare ourselves for without fail.

That's what we are up against. But this isn't scary, is it? It is something that we can deal with when we decide to do so. In fact we will come out richer by it when the New World has been built, even by the process itself, of building the New World.

Segment 4 - To Create a New World

Segment 4 - To Create a New World

Part 1	Challenged to Create a New World
Part 2	Who Speaks for Draining the Swamp?
Part 3	Real History that we Cannot Step Away From
Part 4	World Development Project with Forgiveness
Part 5	Climate is Not a Factor in the unfolding history of love
Part 6	Who Speaks for Humanity?
Part 7	Speaking the Truth is Liberating

Segment 4 - To Create a New World

Part 1 Challenged to Create a New World

Part 2 Who Speaks for Draining the Swamp?

Part 3 Real History that we Cannot Step Away From

Part 4 World Development Project with Forgiveness.

Part 5 Climate is Not a Factor in the unfolding history of love

Part 6 Who Speaks for Humanity?

Part 7 Speaking the Truth is Liberating

Challenged to Create a New World

Challenged to Create a New World

Challenged to Create a New World

A World-Bridge of infrastructures afloat on the equatorial seas

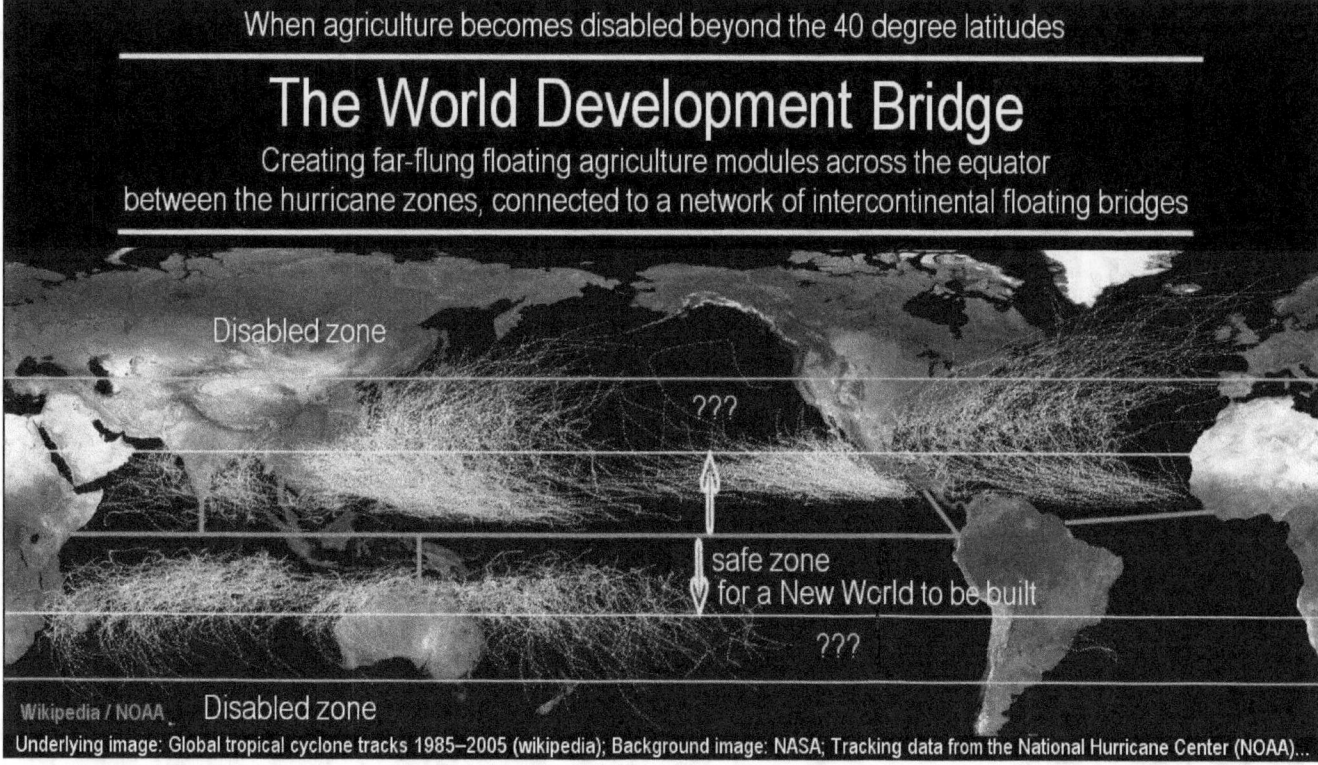

We can step away from the already unfolding great climate collapse by us building us a World-Bridge of infrastructures afloat on the equatorial seas, far from the ice and cold. And we can have this newly created world fully operating when the Ice Age phase shift happens. In fact we need to have much of it already built and in operation as we move deeper into the boundary time zone before the big Ice Age phase shift occurs.

When the Ice Age phase shift occurs

When the Ice Age phase shift occurs, our current climate will collapse as if a dimmer switch has been flicked. The Sun's radiated energy becomes rapidly reduced at this point, by 70%. That's huge. But that's what we see in ice core records. And it affects the whole world. Still, working together globally, we can prepare ourselves for what lays ahead, without missing a beat in the process.

Under the dimmer Sun, less water is being evaporated

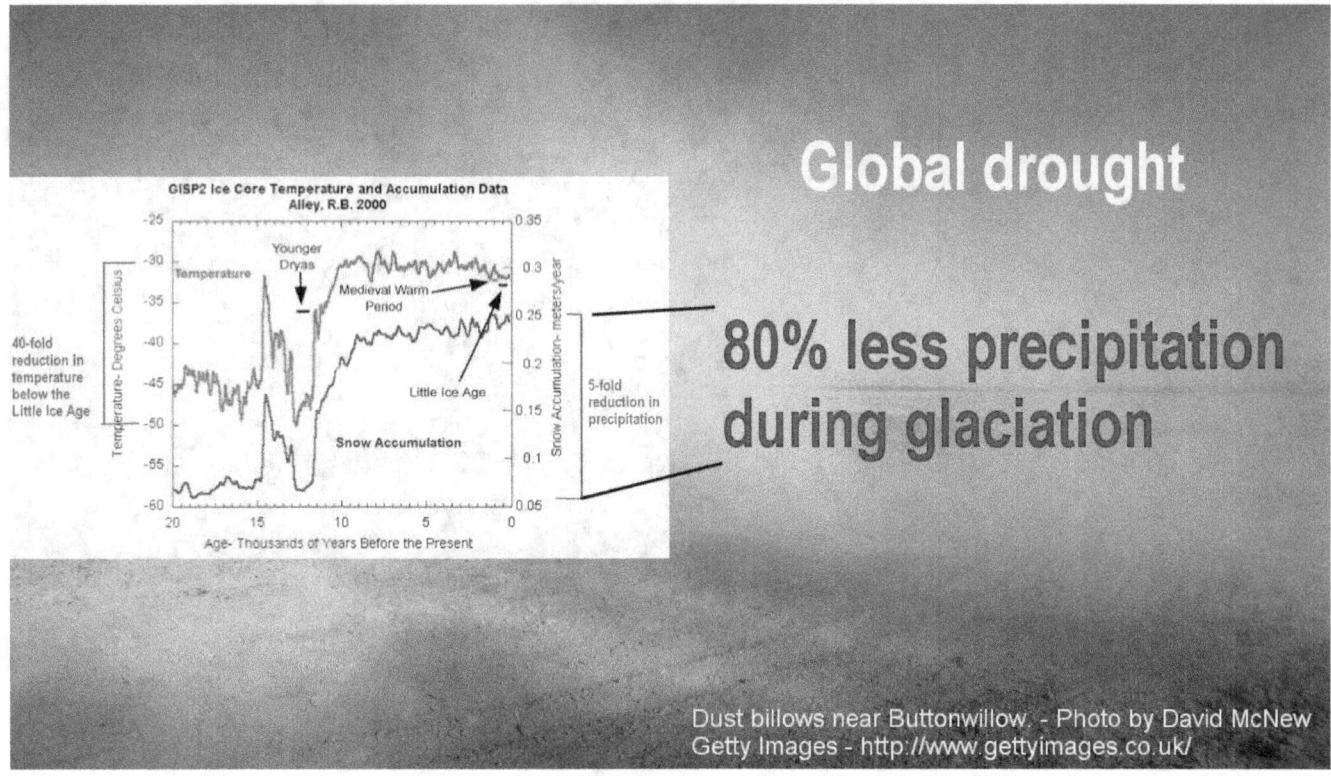

Also, under the dimmer Sun, less water is being evaporated, whereby rainfall diminishes by 80%. This too, is what we have gleamed from the ice core records.

We have to cope with that also, and we can deal with it easily by us stepping away from the swamp of latent errors. By us recognizing us as human beings, we recognize that we are not impotent, even in the face of such impossible-seeming challenges.

Diverting the out-flow of the world's biggest tropical rivers

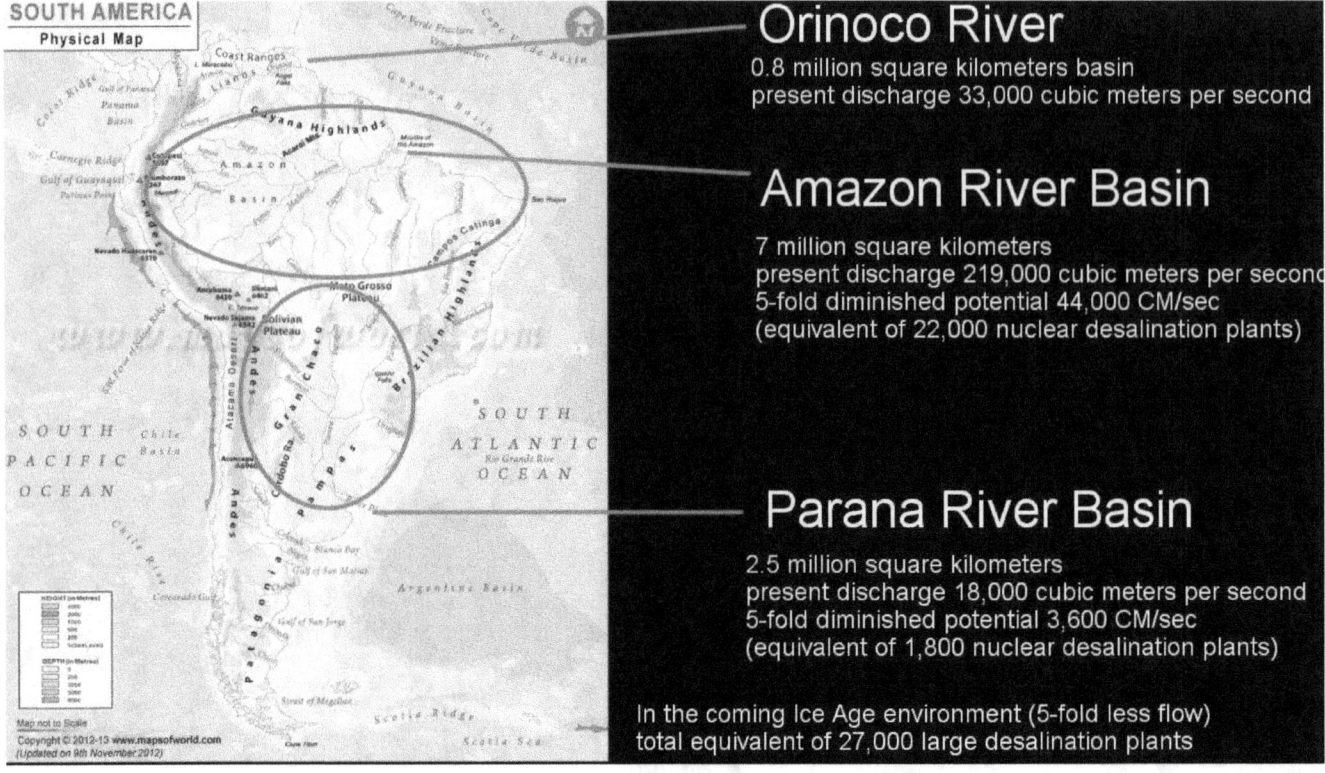

We have the capacity with our creativity to supplement the little rainfall that we will likely still get in the tropics, by diverting the out-flow of the world's biggest tropical rivers, like the Amazon and the Congo rivers, which won't completely dry up. We can divert their outflow, from flowing into the oceans to flow into the World Bridge system instead, and into continental areas that may still remain in operation during Ice Age conditions.

Large populations, with large industries and agricultures, require large freshwater resources. Desalination will some day be sufficiently developed to carry the load. Until then, a worldwide water distribution network will be needed.

The infrastructures that we must urgently build

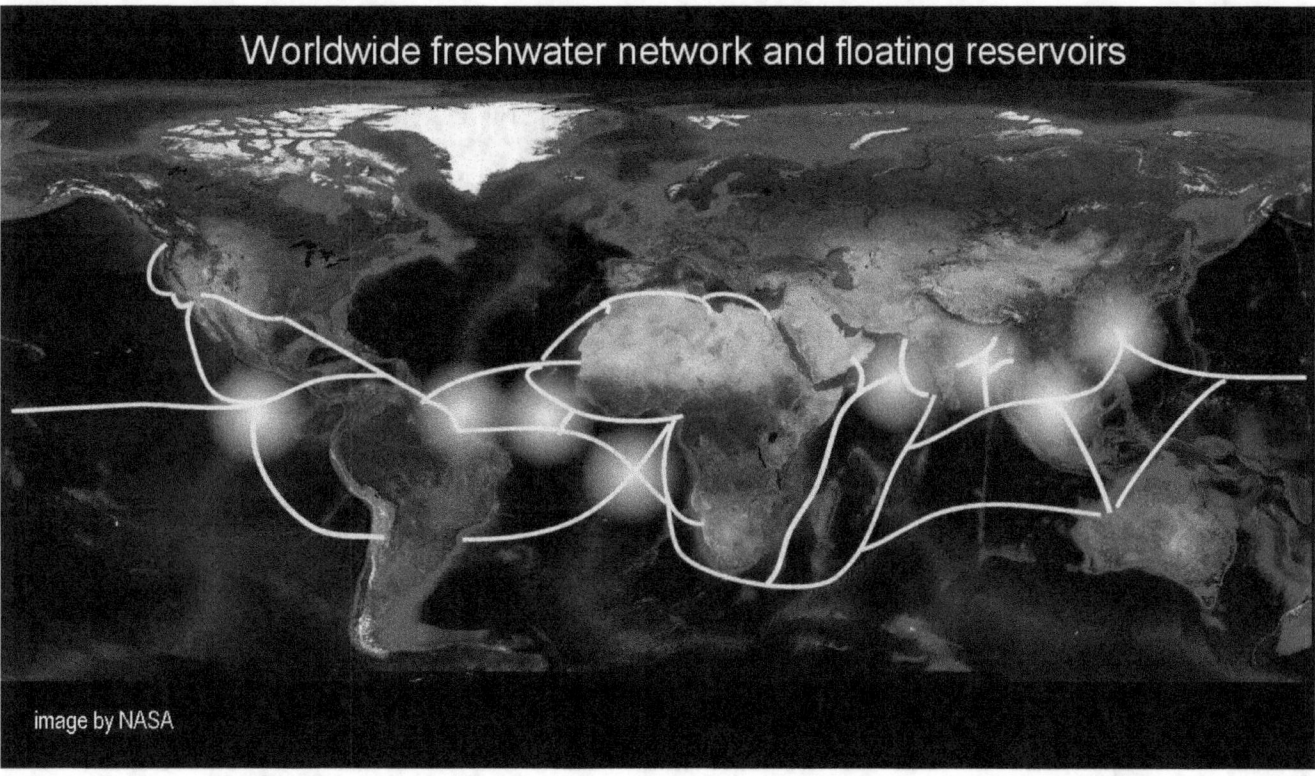

The infrastructures that we must urgently build to protect our food supply at the present stage in the boundary zone, must be designed to meet the known, critical, extreme requirements of the full Ice Age. While the requirements pose a significant technological challenge, the big challenge for today is to get the construction process started. If we don't start, we won't get anything built.

As human beings, we have the capacity on hand

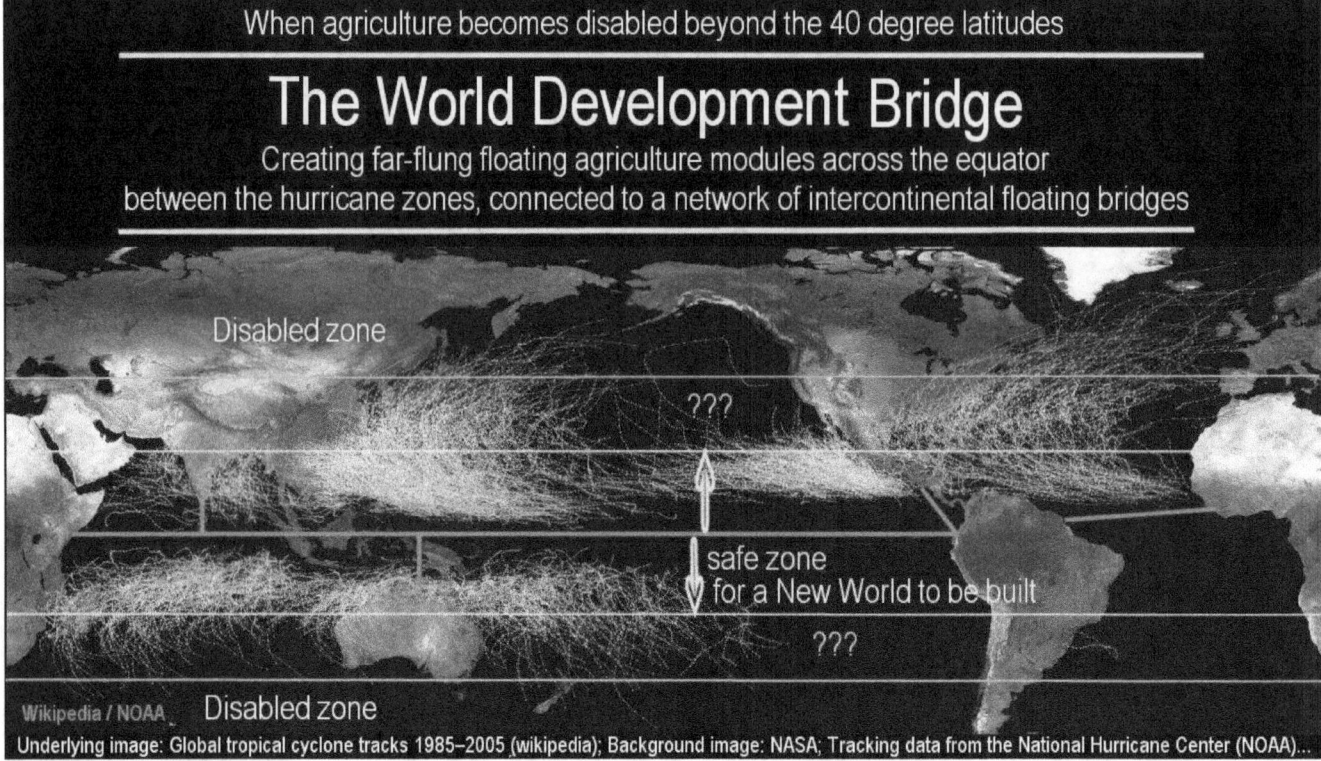

As human beings, we have the capacity on hand to build us a new world out of the reach of the collapsing climate. Floating agriculture along the Equator can provide us the vitally needed new platform for continued living on this planet in an Ice Age environment.

If this option becomes implemented, the whole of humanity will have a future without fail. If it isn't implemented, the near total collapse of humanity will result by default as a consequence, and this too, without fail. This much is certain.

It is also certain that no nation can do this alone, and that no other viable option does exist. This means that we have no choice really, but to make this one option that we have, implemented reality. That's today's highest priority.

Who Speaks for Draining the Swamp?

Who Speaks for Draining the Swamp?

Who Speaks for Draining the Swamp?

Draining the swamp is the greatest challenge of our time

Draining the swamp is the greatest challenge of our time

But in the real world, the task is easy

Draining the swamp is the greatest challenge of our time. But in the real world, the task is easy.

Draining the swamp simply means, for society to let it go, to walk away from it. The swamp of latent errors has no real value, no validity, no substance. Errors never had substance, validity, nor value.

Without society draining its life into the swamp

Without society draining its life into the swamp, the swamp dries up like so many dead leaves that litter the garden in spring and blow away with the wind.

When one steps outside the grasp of the swamp of ages-old latent errors

When one steps outside the grasp of the swamp of ages-old latent errors, the world becomes accordingly brighter and more truthful.

Thus, when one takes these steps, one begins to realize that there exists no actual need for the swamp to be drained.

When society stops pouring its life away into the swamp

When society steps away from the influence of the swamp, no matter how daring this may appear, that is, when society stops pouring its life away into it, the swamp vanishes on its own as if it had never existed. The collapse of the swamp happens thereby naturally, because the swamp of latent errors never had any real substance in itself to begin with. Whatever the swamp became was pored into it by society.

When we let the swamp dry up in the mind

PARIS2015
UN CLIMATE CHANGE CONFERENCE
COP21·CMP11

COP 21: Heads of delegations by GUSTAVO-CAMACHO-GONZALEZ - Licensed under CC BY 2.0 via Commons by Presidencia de la República Mexicana -delegates

Poster of the Climate Conference.
Licensed under Fair use via Wikipedia

The swamp itself has no real history, with which to grab us from its murky waters of latent illusions. When we let the swamp dry up in the mind, as we stop pouring our life into it, whereby its imagined history is gone; its hold on us is gone likewise.

With society becoming truthful with itself

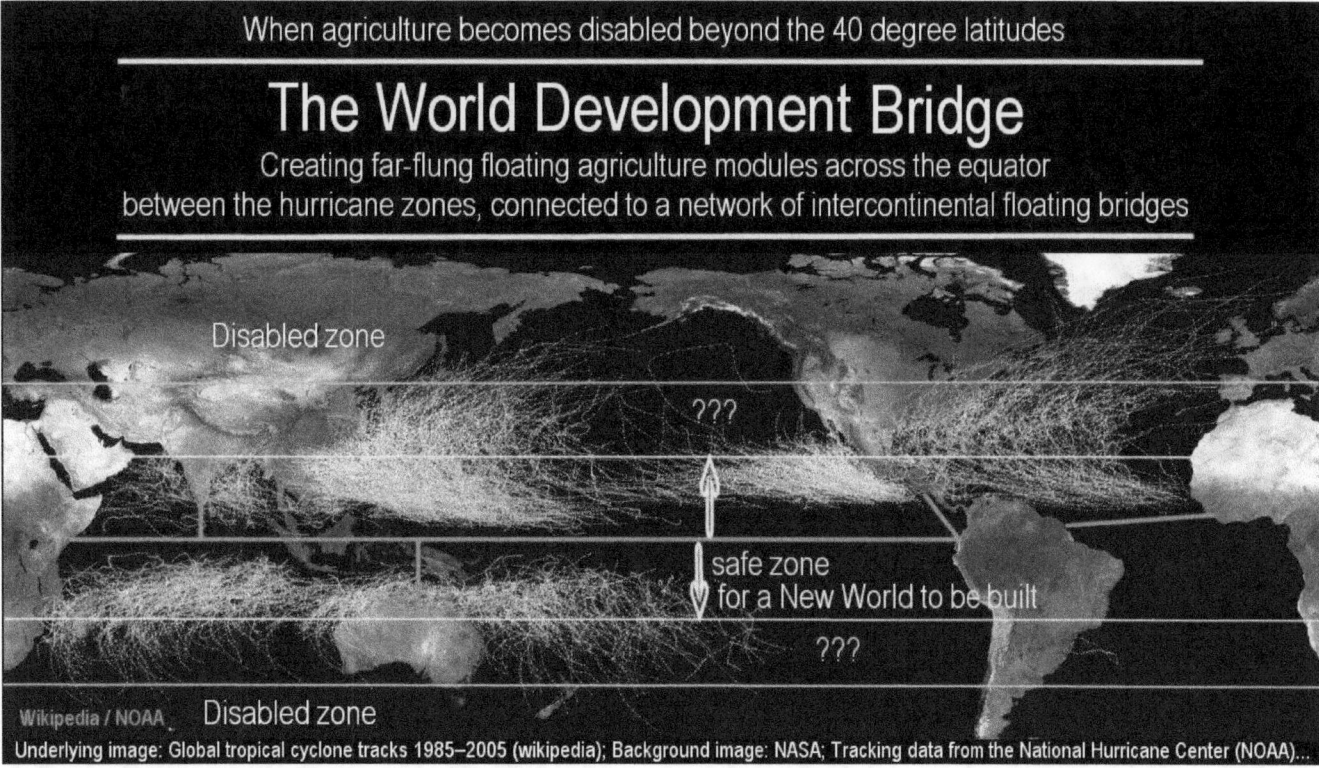

Then, with society becoming truthful with itself, it becomes easy for it to commit itself to building the World-Bridge infrastructures with floating agricultures and cities for its future living in a radically cooling world as we are moving ever closer towards the Ice Age phase shift in the 2050s.

Real History that we Cannot Step Away From

Real History that we Cannot Step Away From

Real History that we Cannot Step Away From

Real history, that is our spiritual history

Real history, that is our spiritual history, is a factor that we ultimately cannot step away from, no matter how intensely we try. A powerful example is the history of love. This history is rooted in our humanity. It is real. Poets have written about it, seemingly forever, and still do. Musicians sing of it. We live it, as we cherish one-another, and traverse worlds upon worlds in the name of love.

A line of separation between scientific humanity and imperial depravity

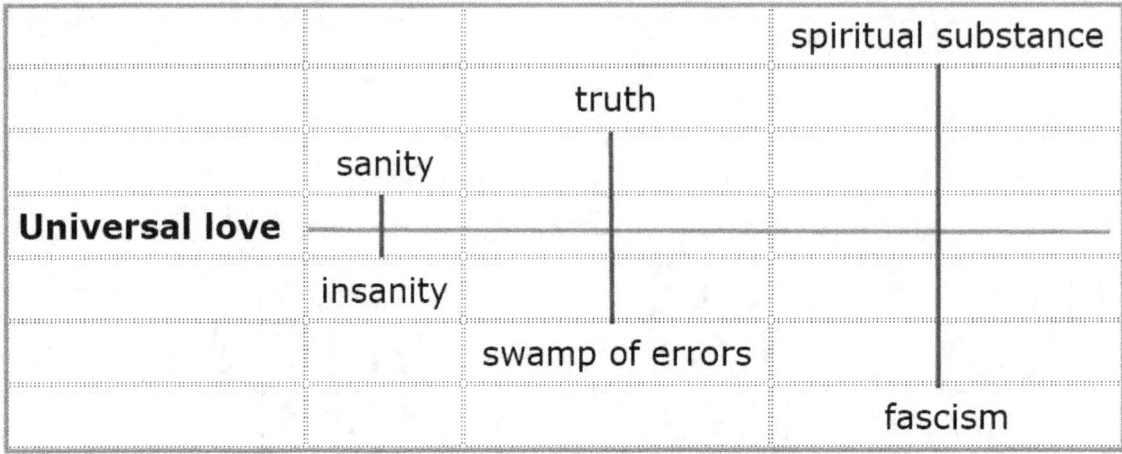

Love furnishes a line of separation between scientific humanity and imperial depravity

In the larger world, love furnishes a line of separation between sanity and insanity, between truth and the swamp of latent errors, and between spiritual substance and fascism, and so on.

A clear line of separation is needed between sanity and insanity, truth and the swamp, and the substance of civilization and fascism, because without love these opposites tend to mingle and society becomes never free. Universal love stands as a standard for reference thereby. If a concept uplifts the whole of humanity and impels one to take action to promote it, then the love for our common humanity separates the chaff from the wheat, or the swamp from the truth, or fascism from the value of humanity. In this case the opposites can never mingle and the false drops off into never-land.

During the Peace of Westphalia conferences in 1648

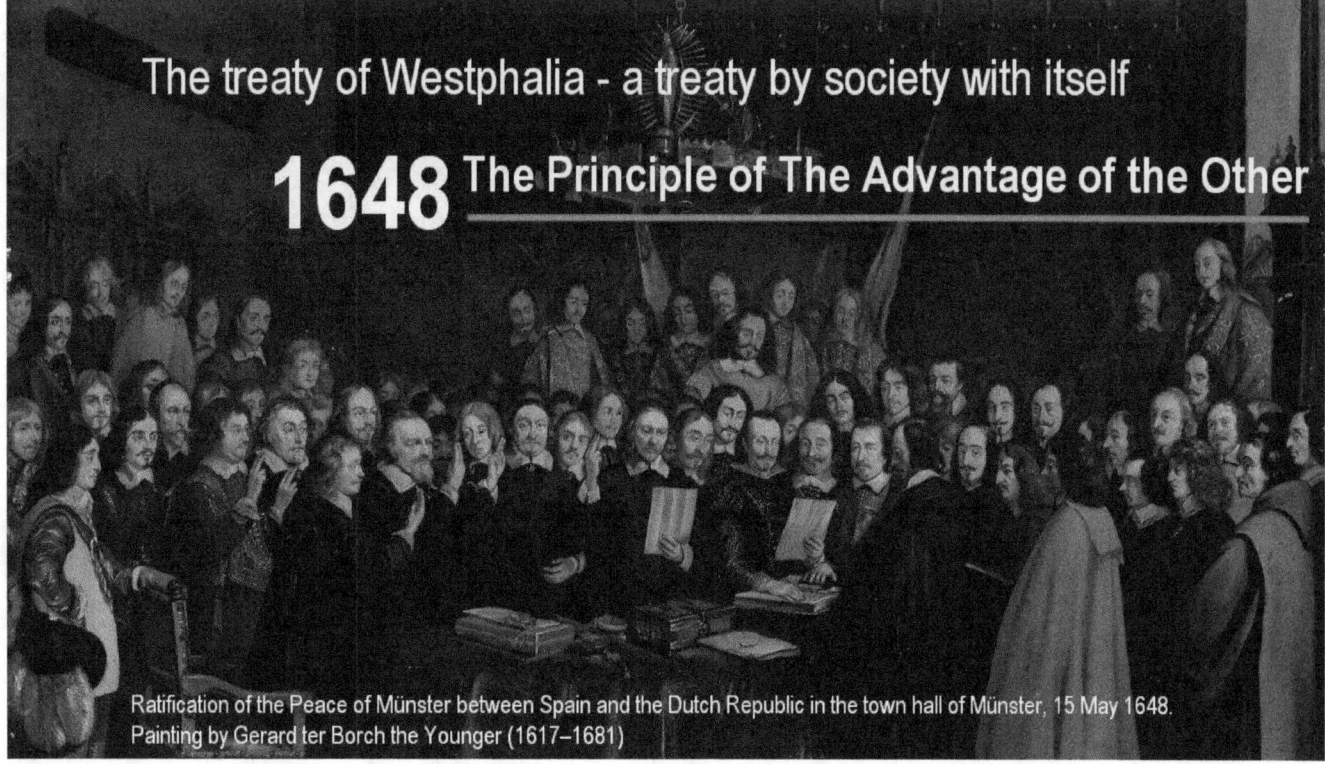

The treaty of Westphalia - a treaty by society with itself

1648 The Principle of The Advantage of the Other

Ratification of the Peace of Münster between Spain and the Dutch Republic in the town hall of Münster, 15 May 1648. Painting by Gerard ter Borch the Younger (1617–1681)

During the Peace of Westphalia conferences in 1648, this type of focus enabled peace to become realized after almost a hundred years of feuds and war. It became possible to set up a new foundation for civilization and its redevelopment.

The question may have been asked in those days what is worth to be identified as intrinsically human and is rooted in the heart? On this basis a remarkably tall type of world constitution was created that still stands in principle. On this tall constitutional platform all the wrong was forgiven and small-minded notions were laid aside for the price of peace. In today's world the price is to have a future that society must win.

No actions will be taken until the digital nature of the Ice Age phenomenon is understood

No actions will be taken be taken to secure the future of humanity, until the digital nature of the Ice Age phenomenon is understood and acknowledged, which gives us two opposite and incomparable climates on Earth, by the flipping of the Sun between its high and low powered states.

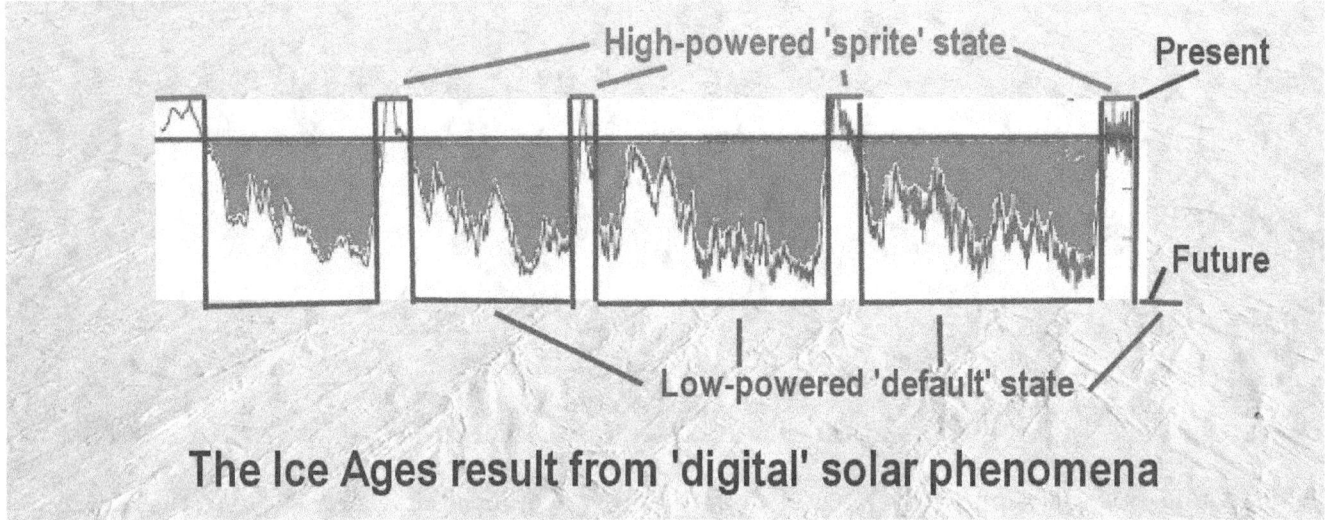

The Ice Ages result from 'digital' solar phenomena

This means that we need to lay aside all the small-minded notions that are entertained about the galactic and solar systems and their effect on our climate, because no actions will be taken to secure the future of humanity until the digital nature of the Ice Age phenomenon is understood and acknowledged that gives us two opposite and incomparable climates on Earth by flipping the Sun between its high and low powered states.

Without this understanding no infrastructures will be created for the future of humanity, even in response to the current climate collapse while we are still the boundary zone to the near Ice Age phase shift.

It takes a major upwards leap in the self-perception of humanity to raise itself out of the trap of small-minded notions, the kind of leap that requires a deep love for humanity. This love must be such that the Ice Age infrastructures will be built, and be constructed fast, even if there existed but the most minute chance that the Ice Age will unfold as the leading edge scientific measurements indicate, because to fail would mean the end of civilization and humanity with it. Love is a force that can prevent us from gambling with our future existence.

World Development Project with Forgiveness

World Development Project with Forgiveness

World Development Project with Forgiveness

Much of it was paid in forgiveness in 1648

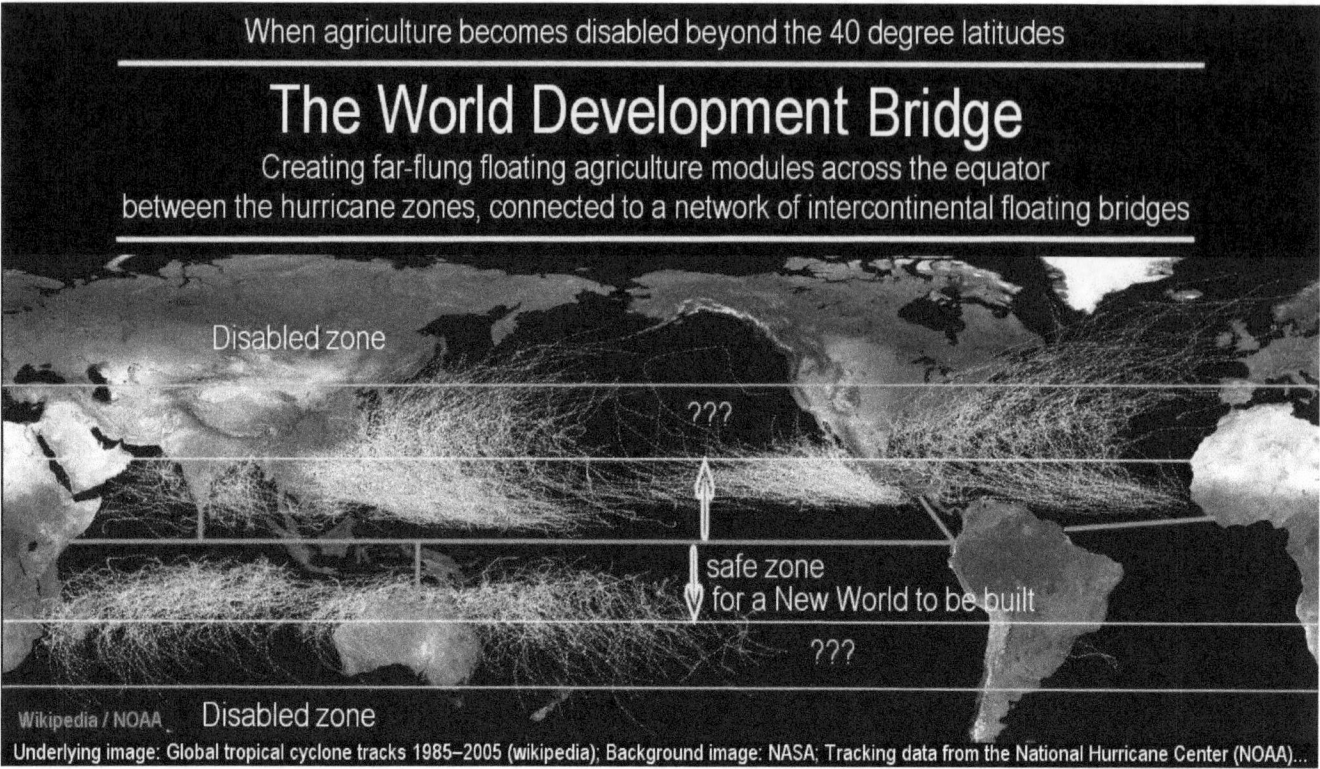

A appears that with this kind of powerful incentive furnished by universal love for our humanity, we have a good chance that we will build the World Bridge infrastructures, especially in considering our spiritual history, the history of universal love that we have experienced in the past in 1648 and in other periods of building a renaissance.

Of course there is always a price to pay for the separation of humanity from its swamp of latent errors to become possible. The price is not paid in dollars. Much of it was paid in forgiveness in 1648.

Without forgiveness, the forgiveness of its small-minded notions and their consequences, humanity cannot be free from its swamp, but remains attached to it by the remaining unbroken links. And without society becoming free to act for its humanity, the World Bridge infrastructures cannot be built.

The price that they all agreed to pay to be able to live again

The treaty of Westphalia - a treaty by society with itself

1648 The Principle of The Advantage of the Other

Ratification of the Peace of Münster between Spain and the Dutch Republic in the town hall of Münster, 15 May 1648. Painting by Gerard ter Borch the Younger (1617–1681)

The principle of forgiveness appears to have been understood to some degree in 1648 when the principles for the Peace of Westphalia were developed. A series of meetings had been conducted in various places over several months until a workable platform was erected on which all the nations of Europe could live securely and productively with each other after a hundred years of war, destruction, and ideological clashes in which a third of the populations had perished.

The price that they all agreed to pay for that greater objective, to be able to live again, was largely paid in forgiveness.

They were victorious to free themselves from the swamp

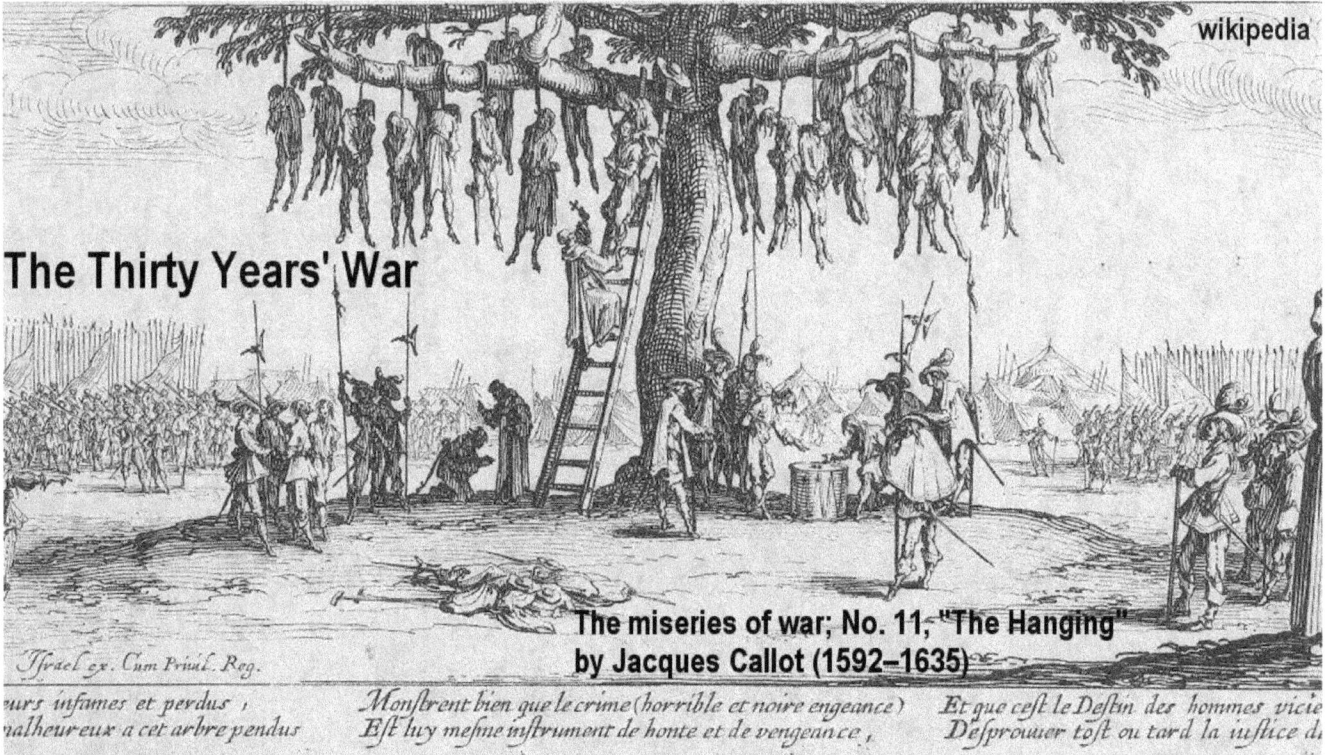

wikipedia

The Thirty Years' War

The miseries of war; No. 11, "The Hanging"
by Jacques Callot (1592–1635)

Ifrael ex. Cum Priuil. Reg.

urs infames et perdus ,   *Monftrent bien que le crime (horrible et noire engeance)*   *Et que ceft le Deftin des hommes vicie*
nalheureux a cet arbre pendus   *Eft luy mefme inftrument de honte et de vengeance ,*   *Defprouuer toft ou tard la iuftice de*

How they managed to succeed is unknown. We only know that they were victorious over their smallness and achieved what they all treasured the most, no matter the cost in forgiveness, in order to free themselves from the swamp they all had became drawn into. And they did live again. They created a great renaissance environment in which such musical geniuses emerged, as Bach, Mozart, Beethoven, Brahms, and so on. Only when the swamp was allowed back, under Napoleon, and claimed their life anew, did the renaissance spirit gave way once more to war.

In our times the swamp is deeper, bigger, with a longer history

Dresden 1945

image by Deutsche Fotothek .
Licensed under CC BY-SA 3.0 de
via Wikimedia Commons

In our times the swamp is deeper, bigger, with a longer history than in 1648, and with more to recover from. The modern 'sons' of the swamp are too numerous to count, ranging from colonial slavery, to today's food burning, looting economics, financial collapse, endless war, and even nuclear war, and all that with evermore terror and destruction in the wings that the destruction of Dresden was but a small example of.

We even have our own 30-Years War to forgive

Mass Murder with Biofuels

El Tres de Mayo, by Francisco de Goya - Wikipedia

We even have our own 30-Years War to forgive that flowed from the lie of Manmade Global Warming that we have sacrificed so much for and still do, from which flows the biofuels food-burning holocaust that consumes agricultural resources in a starving world that would normally nourish 400 million people, in which nearly the whole of society participates at the gas pump. The victims by starvation may add up to 100 million per year.

With forgiveness, as love opens the mind to the truth

 A lot of forgiveness is needed by all of us.

However, the principle for stepping away from the swamp, even from today's giant swamp, remains the same as it always had, historically. The Principle that remains is forgiveness, with which truth comes to the foreground. With forgiveness, as love opens the mind to the truth, society writes itself a ticket to build itself a New World as a foundation for one another to live, and to have a bright future, in spite of the challenges.

Climate is not a factor in the unfolding history of love

Climate is <u>not a factor</u>
in the unfolding history of love

Climate is not a factor in the unfolding history of love

We have experienced the human potential in supporting one-another

Wheat harvest on the Palouse, Idaho, USA

Food for eating!

wikipedia

Ultimately, the climate factor is not the critical driver when love guides the way. We have experienced the human potential in supporting one-another when the global climate was rich to help us along the way, as it still largely is. This history sets up a standard.

The same love has the power to impel us to move forward

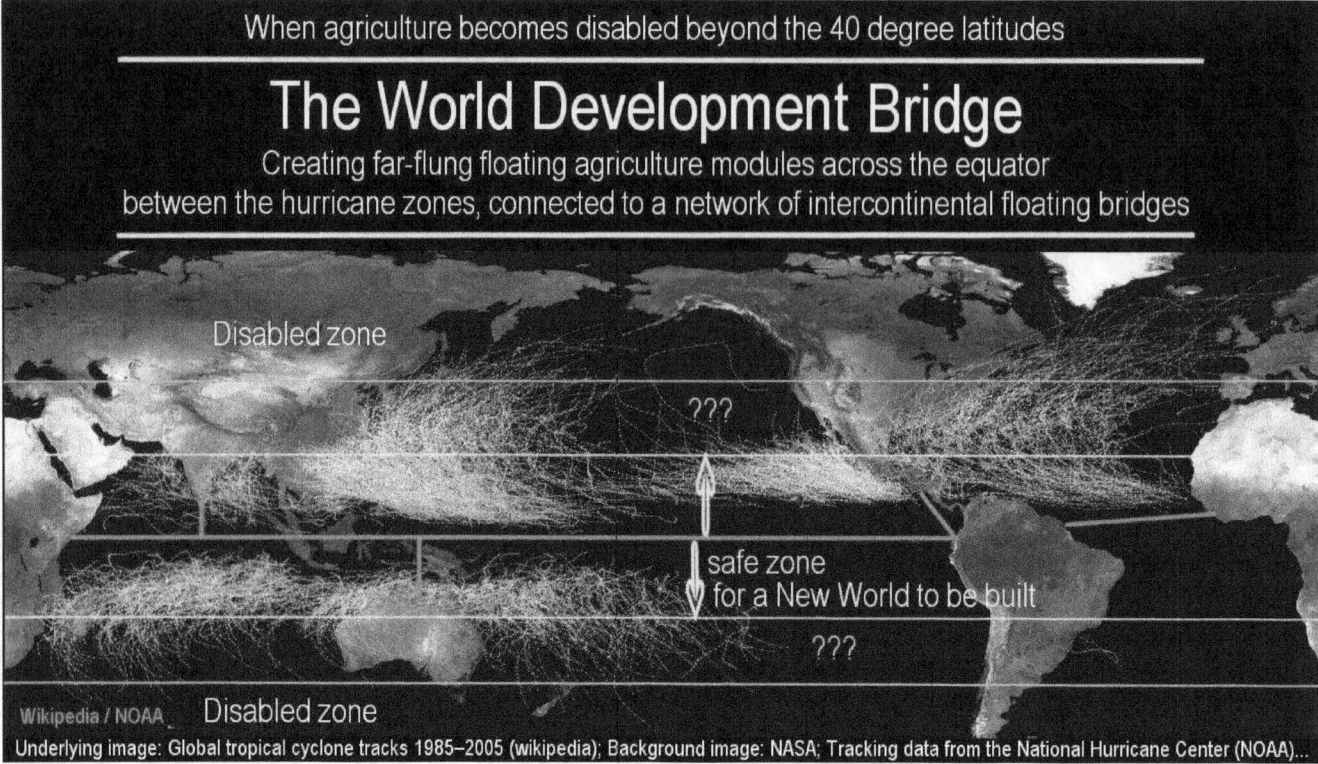

Thus, as the climate is now getting cold, the same love has the power to impel us to move forward, to migrate away from the cold and build us a New World in the tropics with our intelligent inner resources, so that we can continue to live richly, and live richer still than at the present.

Impelled by our love for one-another

Impelled by our love for one-another, we have the potential to become masters over the climate, not to change the climate, but to uplift us above its grasp.

Only in the tragic cases when we foolishly step away from our humanity in self-denial, can climate factors become factors that we need to fear.

But why should we? With love in our heart for our universal humanity, the swamp-like self-denial will fade from the landscape as the unending history of love asserts its claim and impels us onward.

So let us rally around the standard of love and raise it up with scientific spiritual development, for after all, love is our light. Love is the Sun of the human world.

Who Speaks for Humanity? The End of Agriculture is Near!

Who Speaks for Humanity?

Who Speaks for Humanity? The End of Agriculture is Near!

The scene in Goya's painting can be seen in two different ways

Humanity executing humanity in the name of empire

El Tres de Mayo (The Third of May) in 1808, by Francisco José de Goya in 1814
of the shooting on Principe Pio Mountain, part of a larger massacre in the Napoleonic occupation of Spain

Yes, you have read correctly. The end of agriculture is on the agenda. In this context the scene in Goya's painting can be seen in two different ways.

In the present context the target for execution is Truth in Climate Science. The execution is designed to assure that the end of agriculture on Earth will happen. The end of agricultures is assured when science fails to inspire society to build itself a New World with large-scale technological infrastructures strung across the Equatorial seas, with which agriculture can continue and develop further. The executioners are creatures of the swamp.

In 5 to 15 years the scene takes on a different meaning. At this late stage the target of the execution, the man in the white shirt, is society itself. It accepts a fate that at this late stage it cannot avoid. At the present rate of collapse in solar activity, the end of today's agriculture, in nearly all areas of the world will happen, forced by increasing cold, drought, climate extremes, and the lack of freshwater.

In this tragic scene, in both cases, the tragic figure is society, just as society is the tragic figure in Shakespeare's Hamlet.

In the play, Hamlet, a nation is under attack

Craig's design (1908)
for Hamlet 1-2
Moscow Art Theatre

In the play, Hamlet, a nation is under attack from without. Its king is murdered, and the murderer sits on the throne. The rightful successor who should right the wrong is petrified by fear. In the wake of his failing to act, the scene becomes worse. The tragedy here is that no one defends the nation, whereby the nation becomes defeated. But the real tragic figure in the play is society. It suffers a deep tragedy by its failing to assure its future, by its failing to support Hamlet at the critical stage. In the end everyone dies, and society dies with it, which is essentially already dead when the play begins, hidden in the foreground under its blankets of mud from the swamp that encourages inaction.

Who speaks for humanity at today's critical stage?

Humanity executing humanity in the name of empire

El Tres de Mayo (The Third of May) in 1808, by Francisco José de Goya in 1814 of the shooting on Principe Pío Mountain, part of a larger massacre in the Napoleonic occupation of Spain

With this said, I must ask, "who speaks for humanity at today's critical stage?" The climate collapse is in progress. The end of agriculture is on the horizon. Science flinches. It cannot speak the truth nor is society willing to hear it. That's where we stand toady. The truth is plain. The climate principles are understood. The forces have been measured? But who stand up for the truth? If Hamlet isn't encouraged by society to speak for its humanity, who then speaks for it?

Who inspires humanity to build itself a technological New World ?

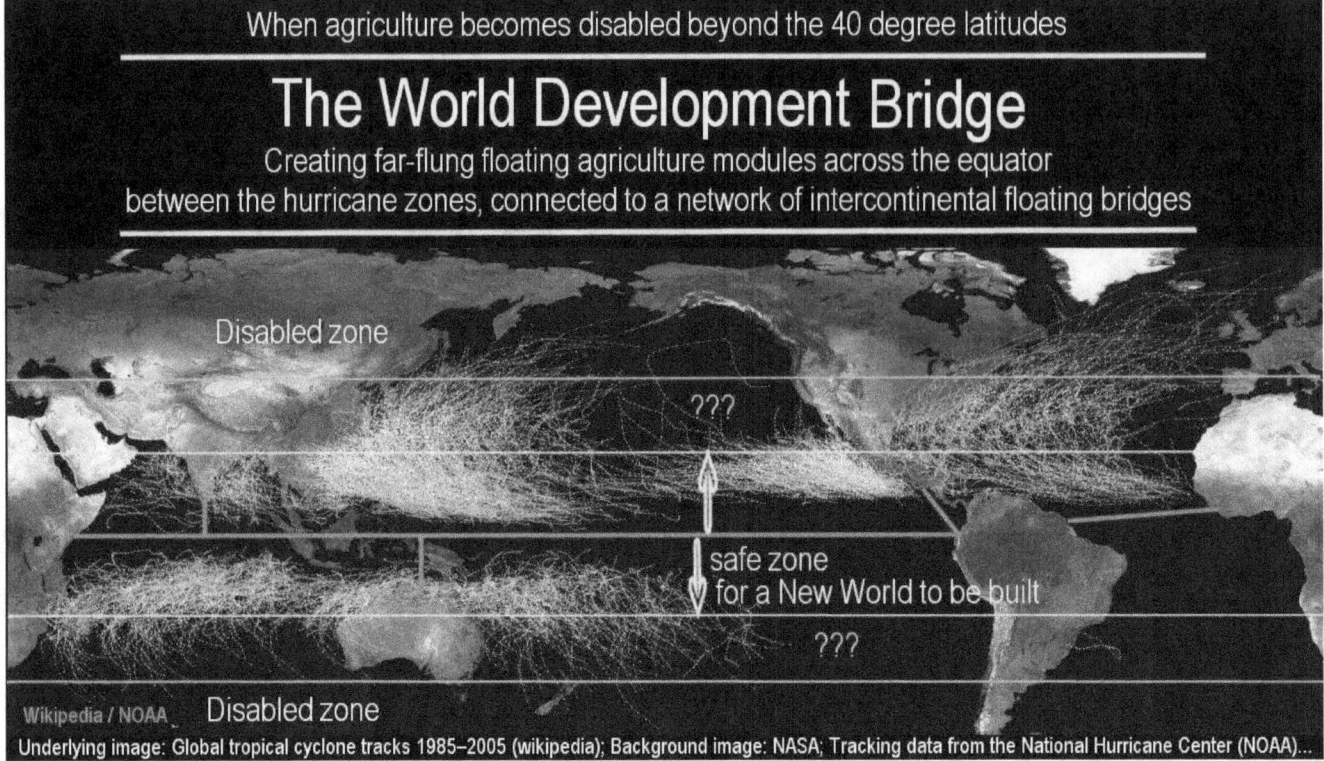

Who speaks the truth and inspires humanity with it to build itself a technological New World in which agriculture can continue, unaffected by Climate Change and by the near Full Ice Age? Who speaks for humanity in the hustings and inspires it to raise its head and act in defense of its future?

In Hamlet, the relationship of society with its humanity fails

Craig's design (1908)
for Hamlet 1-2
Moscow Art Theatre

In the play, Hamlet, the relationship of society with its humanity fails. No heads are raised. Tragedy occurs. Should this be the fate of the world?

If President Trump should succeed to inspire America

If President Trump, against all odds, should succeed to inspire America, and by example the World, to walk away from the swamp and thus uplift the climate scene to the level of real science, backed by volumes of measured evidence, and heed their imperatives, his place in history as the greatest President of all times, would be assured. This much is guaranteed.

Inversely, any failing to act in this manner, whether by the President or by society itself, would guarantee that there won't be any history for anyone to remember, as too few of humanity would remain alive to remember our time.

But why should we fail? Why should we even flinch? The dark age, the age of the swamp, is ending. The recognition of the truth is dawning that we, humanity, are the brightest gem of life on the Earth with infinite value and with an amazing inner substance that promises to power a new renaissance in our time, as we nourish our sublime substance as human beings and let it unfold in the form of a New World for us, along the line of the World-Bridge principle.

Let's hope therefore, and let's work to assure this

Let's hope therefore, and let's work to assure this, that President Trump's proposed Presidential Committee on Climate Science gets started promptly, and gets the ball rolling toward a World Truth Festival.

A World Truth Festival is possible

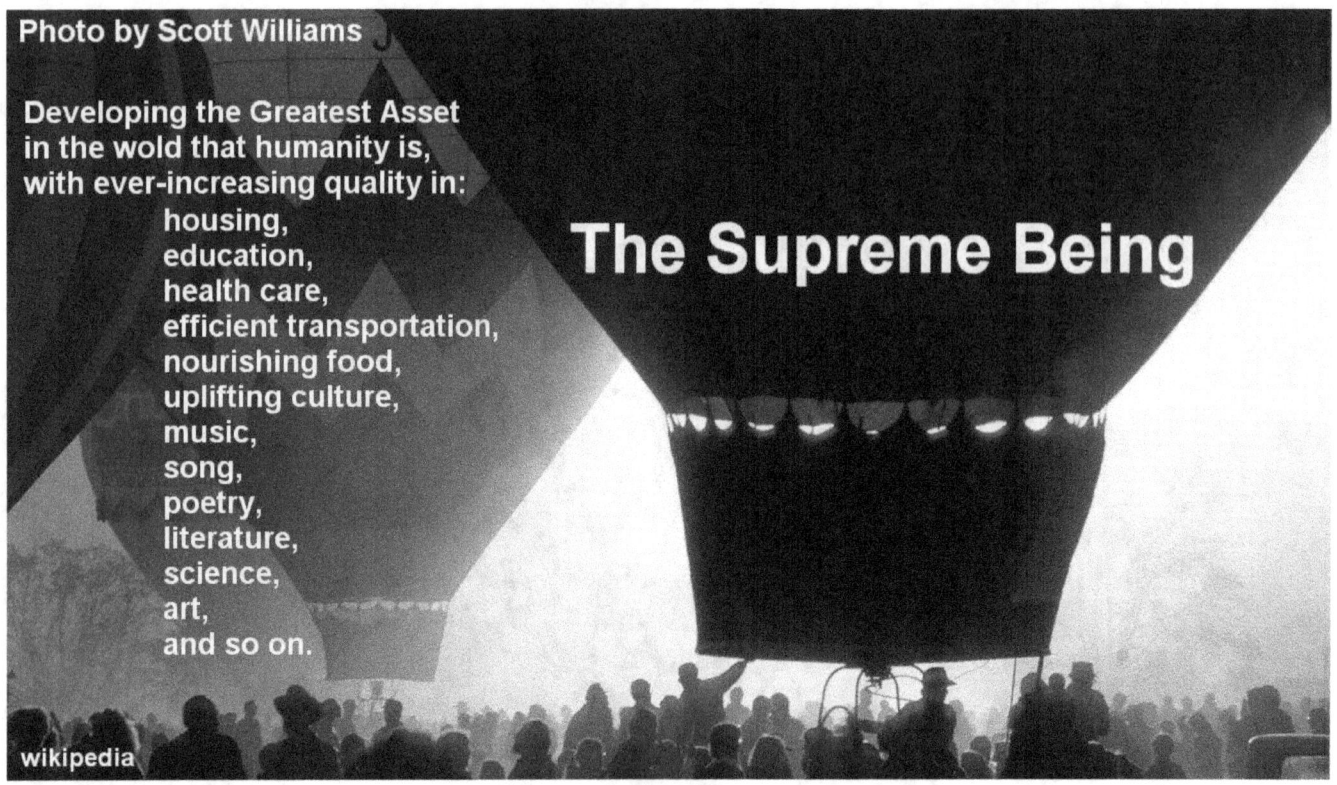

Photo by Scott Williams

Developing the Greatest Asset
in the wold that humanity is,
with ever-increasing quality in:
 housing,
 education,
 health care,
 efficient transportation,
 nourishing food,
 uplifting culture,
 music,
 song,
 poetry,
 literature,
 science,
 art,
 and so on.

The Supreme Being

wikipedia

And why should we fail? A World Truth Festival is possible. Our continued thriving on this planet is possible. We have its realization in our hands. Their grand realization is possible, because we have already achieved amazing victories on this line in the past with great renaissance-type settings unfolding.

Why should a World Truth Festival not be achieved ?

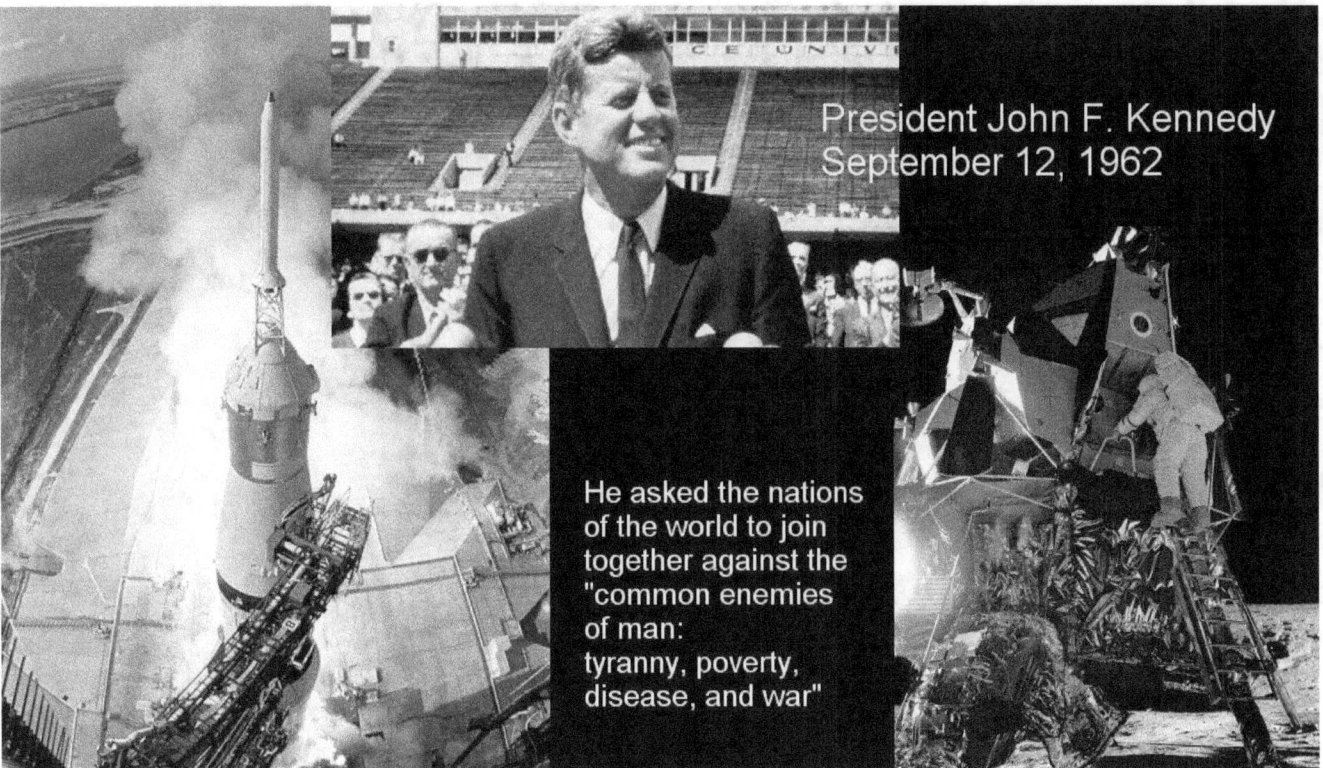

President John F. Kennedy
September 12, 1962

He asked the nations
of the world to join
together against the
"common enemies
of man:
tyranny, poverty,
disease, and war"

Why should a World Truth Festival not be achieved to assure us a future, even of the magnitude that is required, in the manner as President Kennedy had succeeded to make the nation's space-flight project to the moon a reality, and had succeeded with flying colors?

Building of the World-Bridge a mere anticlimax

In considering the vast technological challenges that had to be overcome to accomplish the moon landing objectives, the building of the World-Bridge in our time, to place agriculture and cities onto the equatorial seas for the continued existence of humanity on a renaissance platform, will in comparison, when it happens, be a mere anticlimax. It will be an anticlimax in the light of the great feats that have already been achieved, even while the World-Bridge project promises infinitely greater benefits in return than landing on the moon had wrought us as a renaissance project. We have no cause to fail?

With this in mind, support the President's intended Truth Festival. Share this video. Uplift the world.

Speaking the Truth is Liberating

Speaking the Truth is Liberating

Speaking the Truth is Liberating

We are giants with what we have in our hands today

We are not so small that we should deny ourselves and fail. We are giants with what we have in our hands today, even the power to shape politics. All of this is worth celebrating. This is worth the greatest joy, and also the greatest commitment to make the brightest future yet imagined, that we have in our hands to create, come true.

I am but one man, but I am one of us all

I am but one man,
but I am one of us all,
I believe in us, in humanity,
we are the diamond in the sky,
incomparable, with the power to win,
we give light a new meaning, with a sparkle
in the heart that in its brilliance supersedes the Sun.

I am but one man,

but I am one of us all,

I believe in us, in humanity,

we are the diamond in the sky,

incomparable, with the power to win,

we give light a new meaning, with a sparkle

in the heart that in its brilliance supersedes the Sun.

More Illustrated Science Books by Rolf A. F. Witzsche

Quick Index to My Books
printed books by Rolf A. F. Witzsche

All Books available from Amazon - follow the links

Ice Age Science - Illustrated New 8.5x11 transcripts (books) from my videos	Ice Age Science - Illustrated Early 6x9 transcripts (books) from my videos
My 14 Novels	My Research Books
Winning Without Victory series New	Kaleidoscope series
Sex and Sacrament series	Christian Science Books

Link to *Cool Science for Kids...* (interactive)

Please Donate · *Home Page*